MW01624290

Conversations on Conservatism, Vol. II: Controversies Among Conservatives

Edited by Marcus M. Witcher, Kevin L. Hughes, and Allen Mendenhall

ISBN: 9781630695392

Cover art: Vanessa Mendozzi

Contents

Editor's Note

This edited collection has been almost three years in the making. It began shortly after we completed the first volume of the Philadelphia Society talks. While most reviews of the first volume were positive, some called for us to include the more contentious moments from later in the Society's history. This volume has attempted to chronicle some of those debates, while also presenting reflective talks from a number of the conservative movement's most influential members. The most memorable moment in the Philadelphia Society's history—Stephen Tonsor's evisceration of neoconservatives—is presented in Chapter 1 along with the much more measured remarks of Burton Yale Pines.

Our goal in assembling these talks into a second volume was to preserve some of the most important moments from the Society for the next generation of conservative activists, educators, and intellectuals. We hope that the wisdom contained in this volume will help conservatives in our present moment as debates rage about the future of conservatism. We also hope that this volume will demonstrate that there has never been conformity or unanimity among conservatives. Conservatism contains many different factions and varieties of thought. The Philadelphia Society has always been dedicated to fostering conversation. This volume is published in that spirit.

We'd like to thank Lenore Ealy for her unwavering support for this project and for taking my phone calls and text messages at all times of the day. We'd also like to thank Charissa Reul for assisting with the finer details of this edited collection and for helping make every Philadelphia

Society meeting a success. We are also very appreciative of all those who have served on the Board of the Society for their encouragement and support of this project. This project took an extensive amount of time and effort. We would like to thank Lee Edwards for expanding his wonderful history of the Philadelphia Society and allowing us to publish it as the introduction to this volume. We'd also like to thank Mac Brooks and Daphne Posadas, who spent many painstaking hours on the initial transcriptions. We know that the work wasn't easy, and we very much appreciate it! I'd like to thank my co-editors, Kevin Hughes and Allen Mendenhall, for all their hard work making sure we did the best we possibly could to ensure that the talks in this volume are true to the original recordings.

Finally, we were very lucky to have resources to make this edited collection a reality. To that end, the publication of this book was made possible through the generous support of the John William Pope Foundation through the Future of Freedom Initiative.

MARCUS M. WITCHER
Huntingdon College, 2024

Introduction

A Unique Society: Six Decades of Defending Freedom

By Lee Edwards

In the waning days of 1964, conservatives had little to be happy about. Presidential candidate Barry Goldwater had offered a conservative choice, not a liberal echo, and had been buried in an electoral landslide engineered by President Lyndon B. Johnson. The most defiantly conservative candidate of modern times, Goldwater received just 38.5 percent of the popular vote and won only six states, including his home state of Arizona. Walter Lippmann, the leading columnist of the day, wrote that the "Johnson majority is indisputable proof that the voters are in the center."

No slur about the Goldwater candidacy had been deemed too extreme. Goldwaterism was equated with Stalinism. Goldwater's political bible, said one prominent Democrat, was *Mein Kampf*. His campaign slogan "In your heart, you know he's right" was cruelly converted into "In your guts, you know he's nuts." By association, so were all his supporters.

Things were no better in the non-political world. The American campus leaned sharply left. A poll of Harvard undergraduates revealed that one-seventh supported "full socialization of all industries," more than a fifth favored socialization of the medical profession, nearly a third believed that the federal government should "own and operate all basic industries," and two thirds supported wage and price controls to check inflation. Liberals dominated the professoriate, the journals of opinion, the mass media, and the bestseller lists of the *New York Times.*

And yet, conservatives were more resilient than liberals and perhaps even conservatives themselves realized. They insisted that while a conservative candidate had been rejected, conservative ideas had not been repudiated. Ronald Reagan, a rising star in the West, wrote in *National Review* that "the landslide majority did not vote against the conservative philosophy, they voted against a false image our liberal opponents successfully mounted." The ever-resilient Frank Meyer pointed out that despite the campaign to make conservatism seem "extremist, radical, nihilist, anarchic," two-fifths of the voters still voted for the conservative alternative. "In fact," Meyer insisted, "conservatives stand today nearer to victory than they ever have since Franklin Roosevelt." Conservatives publicly welcomed Meyer's sanguine rhetoric while wondering privately how long a march would be necessary to achieve even a limited victory.

One far-sighted conservative warned against measuring success or failure at the voting booth. The critical thing, ISI president E. Victor Milione wrote to Notre Dame professor Gerhart Niemeyer, was to continue to assert the importance of education, not politics, "in shaping the course of future events." And so when Donald Lipsett, ISI's Midwest director, suggested the formation of an organization that would keep ISI "graduates" involved in the battle of ideas, Milione quickly gave his approval.

In the spring of 1964, Lipsett organized regional meetings of the new organization (already named the Philadelphia Society) in Indianapolis, Philadelphia, and San Francisco for the purpose "of forming a society of conservative scholars patterned after the Mont Pelerin Society." Ninety persons attended the three sessions that featured remarks by such luminaries as Milton Friedman, Russell Kirk, Willmoore Kendall, Stephen Tonsor, Glenn Campbell (who would become the Society's first president), Thomas Molnar, Stefan Possony, and Father Stanley

Parry. An organization committee was formed, and M. Stanton Evans (who else?!) was drafted to compose a statement of purpose for the Society, which began: "Its purpose will be to sponsor the exchange of ideas through discussion and writing in the interest of a deeper comprehension of the American Experience. The Society holds that America is the inheritor of the Western achievement, the leading principle of which is the liberty of the person under the moral law."

Two guidelines emerged from the organizational discussions: "A fundamental purpose of the Society should be a continuing dialogue between the 'traditionalist' and 'libertarian' emphases" of conservatism. And: "The Society should sponsor no resolutions, political statements or corporate programs of action." As to the name, the organizers explained that the Philadelphia Society was selected because it was in Philadelphia that the Founding Fathers produced the essential documents of the American Republic—the Declaration of Independence and the Constitution.

Following the Goldwater debacle and anxious to strengthen the Society, Lipsett proposed a New York City meeting in December of editor-author William F. Buckley Jr., representing the traditionalist wing of the conservative movement, and economist Milton Friedman, representing the libertarians or classical liberals. Also present at the New York meeting were Frank Meyer of *National Review*, Edwin J. Feulner, Jr., then a graduate student at the University of Pennsylvania's Wharton School of Business, and Lipsett. Remarkably, recalled Feulner, "this was the first time that Buckley and Friedman [had] ever met each other."

The two conservative leaders agreed to lend their names to "an American multi-discipline organization patterned after the Mont Pelerin Society," which had been started in 1947 by F. A. Hayek, Friedman, and other free-market advocates when socialism seemed to be sweeping across Western Europe and much of the free world. Buckley put up $100, Feulner said, "so we could open a bank account." Lipsett became Secretary and immediately set about organizing the Society's first national meeting to be held the last weekend of February in the geographically convenient city of Chicago. The theme was "The Future of Freedom: Problems and Prospects."

One hundred and twenty-five conservatives—writers, teachers, economists, historians, philosophers—met, as Guy Davenport wrote in *National Review*, to discuss "the fate of the West, its decline, survival, or metamorphosis." Following remarks at the Friday night dinner by Antony Fisher (who would later spawn a global network of free market think tanks) the first panel met that same evening after dinner and took up the "problem" of philosophy.

Milton Friedman, calling himself a classical liberal, discussed freedom in terms of the free-market economy based on "cooperation." He said that classical liberalism represented a "healthy" breaking away from the authoritarianism and traditionalism of the past. For him individual freedom was the central problem in social organization. Father Stanley Parry of Notre Dame quietly disagreed, stating that man must perceive the metaphysical rather than the economic basis for freedom. This being so, Parry said, conservatives "are the heirs of Western civilization." Fusionist Frank Meyer suggested that American conservatism was a "blending" of traditional values and individual freedom. The raison d'être of the Philadelphia Society, he emphasized, should be to abandon "partisan concepts of truth" and exchange ideas "frankly."

On Saturday, there were three panels—one in the morning and two in the afternoon—that explored the problems of foreign policy, persuasion, and the intellectual task ahead. Robert Strausz-Hupé, director of the University of Pennsylvania's Foreign Policy Research Institute, argued that the Kennedy and Johnson administrations' hope of stopping the proliferation of nuclear power and of cooperation with Communism was hollow and unrealistic. Anticipating the forthright foreign policy of Ronald Reagan, Strausz-Hupé said that "this side of surrender, cooperation with Communism is impossible." L. Brent Bozell, former senior editor of *National Review* and author of a forthcoming critical analysis of the Supreme Court, *The Warren Revolution*, expressed the fear that the West, as a self-conscious embodiment of Christian truth, had forgotten its identity.

In the third conference session, LeBaron R. Foster of the Opinion Research Corporation quoted extensively from polls to show that the American people, Democrats as well as Republicans, were basically conservative in their views. The conservatives' task, he asserted, was clarification and persuasion. Economist Warren Nutter of the University of Virginia asserted that persuasion must happen between and not just during campaigns. He called for "a new Federalist Papers" and greater courage in speaking out by informed conservatives.

The concluding panel comprised three intellectual heavyweights of the American conservative movement—philosopher Eliseo Vivas, historian Russell Kirk, and economist George Stigler of the University of Chicago, with Wabash College's Benjamin Rogge as chairman. All asked for an end to rallying around the flag as "the primal conservative gesture," and a commitment to the hard work of defining and defending conservative ideas. Stigler noted that conservatives were no longer "an entertaining minority" and could be heard when they questioned the Establishment.

The closing talks and the thoughtful responses from the floor (which lasted until 6:00 p.m.) centered on two themes: (1) ideology and fanaticism are always to be feared, and (2) rather than liberal ideology—a reflection of socialist totalitarianism—conservatives must rely on reason. At the very end, there was a standing ovation for Don Lipsett's organizational and programmatic skill and a conviction among the attendees that something important for the conservative movement and the nation had begun.

For the following three decades until his premature death in 1995, Don and his devoted wife Norma kept the books, looked after the membership, developed the programs, and found the young scholars who attended the national and regional meetings. Don Lipsett never gave a speech, longtime friend John Von Kannon noted, preferring to sit at the back of the room puffing on his pipe and taking notes that he incorporated into what he called "A Listing of Important Laws." Here are a couple showing Don's contrarian sense of humor:

> **John Lathrop Ryan's Law of Public Oratory:** "Everybody except me speaks too long."
>
> **William Rusher's Other Law:** "When you find a good thing, run it into the ground."
>
> **The Harris Law of Nugatory Achievement:** "If a thing isn't worth doing, it isn't worth doing well."
>
> **Mike Mooney's Law:** "You can't always count on your friends, but you can always count on your enemies."

Those who drank "from the refreshing waters" of the Philadelphia Society's meetings during the Lipsett years, wrote the *Detroit News*, knew how fortunate they were.

Born in Woodburn, Indiana, in 1930, Don received a B.S. in Business and an M.B.A. from Indiana University. He joined the U.S. Coast Guard attaining the rank of lieutenant JG. His intense interest in naval history led him to the naval war hero, Commodore Stephen Decatur. His friends began calling him "The Commodore." He founded the Stephen Decatur Society, collected memorabilia about the man who defeated the Barbary Pirates, and created the famous stationery for the society that featured an eagle with arrows in both talons.

His commitment to the conservative movement was total. In the 1950s, he worked for the Foundation for Economic Education and *The Freeman*, *National Review*, and ISI as its national field director. He later served as a senior staffer of the American Security Council, executive secretary of the American Conservative Union, and director of the Center for Constructive Alternatives at Hillsdale College.

For eighteen years, he was counselor to the president of the Heritage Foundation.

As the de facto organizer of every meeting of the Philadelphia Society, he included conservatives of all stripes—traditionalists, libertarians, and neoconservatives—on the panels, following faithfully the Society's mission statement that "we shall seek understanding, not conformity." When pressed, he would confess a personal liking for the individualist views of Albert Jay Nock and the iconoclastic writing of H. L. Mencken.

In his moving tribute to Don Lipsett, his able successor William F. Campbell said that just as the Jews leave a place at the table for the prophet Elijah, "so too shall we leave a place for Don at the meetings of the Philadelphia Society, the rooms of the Intercollegiate Studies Institute, and the Corridors of the Heritage Foundation...He is [always] with us in spirit."

Writing about the second national meeting—from the Golliwog Lounge of the Chicago Sheraton Hotel—columnist James J. Kilpatrick acknowledged the thoughtful formal presentations on the theme of "Civil Rights and Individual Responsibilities" but argued that as great value lay in the informal encounters, "the gossip of old combats, the family jokes." Within the conventional frame of the American convention, Kilpatrick wrote, conservatives "met, and touched hands, and broke lances, and tested improbable schemes." And so it has been for 60 years.

In the late 1960s and early 1970s, when the American campus was riddled with protests, demonstrations, and even the bombing of buildings, the Philadelphia Society took the long view as when Walter F. Berns of Colgate—at the 1970 national meeting—scolded his former colleagues at Cornell for wavering in the face of threatened student violence. At the same conference, youthful scholars David Friedman, John Marlin, Gary North, and Danny Boggs handled such weighty issues as the transfer of government functions into private hands and the theoretical tensions between the traditionalists and the libertarians with impressive aplomb. Although it did not have the funds to print the serious papers read at the meetings, the Society was confident that the ideas expressed would linger long in the minds of the listeners. Today, there is the Internet, ready, willing, and able to disseminate anything, including the Society's proceedings.

On the occasion of the Society's 10th national meeting in the spring of 1974 (there had been at least one and often two regional gatherings every year), Ben Rogge offered a tongue-in-cheek history of the first decade that began by explaining why the organization was called the Philadelphia Society—"because its annual meetings are always held in Chicago." Its activities were "the result of human action, but not the execution of any human design." As to membership, it was not required, as rumored by some, that you had to be a disciple of Milton Friedman. Indeed, nine of the original 12 members of the organization committee were traditionalists, not libertarians.

Rogge dismissed the story that Vic Milione and Don Lipsett had received instructions to form the Society from "a voice speaking from a burning bush," pointing out that neither Milione nor Lipsett "has ever listened to any voice from any source whatsoever." Apologizing for not being a more "rigorous" historian, Rogge revealed he had discovered several important "firsts" that could be laid at the door of the Philadelphia Society.

It was at a Society meeting that Russell Kirk formally presented to the conservative world his "beauteous" wife, Annette, who had missed so many meetings because she was invariably pregnant in the spring. And it was at a Society meeting that former Trotskyite Irving Kristol first gave public notice that "he was no longer one of them, but one of us." Long may the Society and its operations endure, Rogge proclaimed, reassuring its members at least once a year that "there are a number of people of first quality who do indeed stand for the open society and are capable of defending it with vigor, warmth, and eloquence."

One of those defenders was the new Nobel laureate Friedrich A.

Hayek, who said at the 1975 national meeting that interventionism was so built into government that it would be difficult for even a majority of freedom-minded citizens to make the state resist the temptation to meddle. Statism had become so pervasive, Hayek said, that we now spoke "not of preserving but of returning to the free society." Another defender of the free society was publisher Henry Regnery (one of a long line of distinguished Society presidents), who quoted an Ezra Pound translation of Confucius: "The men of old…wanting good government in their states…first established order in their own families."

A long-standing topic of the Society—the similarities and differences of (traditional) conservatives and libertarians—was the theme of the 1979 annual meeting, led off by sociologist Robert Nisbet, who said the two groups shared several prejudices: resentment of government intrusions, fondness for economic freedom, distaste for mass democracy. But they did not share a common intellectual framework. Nisbet, wrote Richard Brookhiser in *National Review*, traced modern conservatism to Edmund Burke's stand against the French Revolution and its crusade against traditional institutions while libertarians appealed instead to John Stuart Mill and the sanctity of the individual. Conservatives such as Walter Berns and libertarians such as Murray Rothbard briskly and sometimes forcefully debated the topic. In a burst of triumphalism, the Cato Institute's David Theroux referred to "the amazing growth of libertarianism," which offered, he said, "the only guide" for the future of humanity. The debate demonstrated, once again, the Society's willingness to explore publicly the most fundamental issues from different perspectives.

In days past, the Society did not talk publicly about how its president was chosen—it was a process as mysterious and Byzantine as the election of the pope. Indeed, when Russell Kirk was installed as president at the 19th annual meeting, he compared his accession to that of Pope Sixtus V in 1585. Three powerful cardinals were deadlocked for the papacy when the assembly turned to the man who would become Sixtus. He was thought to be over ninety, in bad health, perhaps even an idiot; he had lived for years in monastic obscurity. Surely his reign would be brief and uneventful. But once installed Sixtus turned out to be vigorous, twenty years younger than anyone thought, intelligent, and a reformer. "What have we done?" gasped Ed Feulner, the outgoing Society president. There was little cause for alarm: the redoubtable Kirk was all of the above but the very last and supported no reform save beginning the cocktail reception a half hour later.

In addition to Kirk, the Society's presidents have included such luminous conservatives as the bestselling publisher Henry Regnery, Constitutional historian Forrest McDonald, Hoover Institution director Glenn Campbell, former attorney general Ed Meese, Heritage Foundation president Ed Feulner, Catholic libertarian Leonard Liggio, author-journalist-raconteur Stan Evans ("Liberals don't care what people do, as long as it's compulsory"), liberal-neoconservative-conservative author Midge Decter, Rockford College president John Howard, polymath professor Ernest van den Haag, long-time ISI president T. Kenneth Cribb Jr., Southern partisan M. E. Bradford, Voegelin Institute founder Ellis Sandoz, and author-historian-Hoover biographer George H. Nash. Today, a nominating committee presents a slate of officers to the board of trustees, which elects the officers for one-year terms. The president is succeeded by the first vice president, who is followed by the second vice president. The nominating committee also names annually a slate of five to six new trustees who are elected by Society members.

Prior to Jimmy Carter's presidential victory in 1976, President Henry Regnery compared the role of the Society to that of the *samizdat* people in Soviet Russia. "While we don't run the risk of exile or imprisonment in Siberia," he said, "our position is very much against the stream and is certainly not viewed with favor by the ruling liberal establishment. It is exactly this circumstance, however, that makes such an organization as the Philadelphia Society all the more important and a privilege to be associated with."

When the Philadelphia Society turned twenty in 1984, it was discovered to have a membership of 321 and a deficit of about the same dollar figure. Whereas the first meetings were often devoted to knitting together the disparate strands of the movement—traditionalist, libertarian, and anti-communist—more recent meetings discussed broader matters such as "Do Conservative Ideas Necessarily Have Conservative Consequences?" and "Intellectual Resistance to the Wave of the Future." But at its core, wrote Timothy J. Wheeler in *National Review*, the Society was little changed, remaining "a society of the like-minded, who convene to cross-pollinate each other's efforts to restore the moral foundations of liberty."

At the 20th national meeting's Saturday lunch, Forrest McDonald related his pilgrimage to Elvis's birthplace in Tupelo, Mississippi, to obtain a suitable gift for the Society's first vice president, Stan Evans. One was found: a handsome 1-ELVIS license plate. After his acceptance, Evans responded with a few late-breaking news stories that members, cooped up in a hotel, might have missed. It seemed that there had been a startling turnaround by the Rev. Jerry Falwell and New Right guru Paul Weyrich, who now endorsed sex education in the schools—on the grounds that if the schools taught sex the way they taught everything else, soon nobody would know anything about it. And it appeared that the National Council of Churches had denounced Falwell for mixing religion and politics—a charge from which the NCC itself was immune, as it never had anything to do with religion.

The formal luncheon address, traditionally given by the Society's outgoing president, was delivered by Russell Kirk, who argued that because men are moved by visions, not sterile self-interest, the true battle of the age was not for any particular political or economic system but for the imagination. Kirk was not referring to the "diabolic imagination" that ruled the world but to a moral and beneficent imagination. Only "the changing of our visions," he said, "can achieve large political changes."

A long smoldering dispute between conservatives and neoconservatives burst into flame at the 1986 national meeting. The "Big C" conservatives had provided a preview of their case against Irving

Kristol, Norman Podhoretz, and others in the spring issue of ISI's *The Individualist Review*, charging that neoconservatives were not religious enough, were thinly disguised "welfare state Democrats," did not share formative experiences with real conservatives such as in the Goldwater movement, and had been alarmingly successful in getting jobs and establishing priorities within the Reagan administration to the exclusion of conservatives.

In the first panel of the Chicago meeting, historian Stephen Tonsor, a former Philadelphia Society president, explained why he was not a neoconservative and offered one of the more memorable quotations in Society history: "It has always struck me as odd, even perverse, that former Marxists have been permitted, yes invited, to play such a leading role in the Conservative movement of the twentieth century. It is splendid when the town whore gets religion and joins the church. Now and then she makes a good choir director, but when she begins to tell the minister what he ought to say in his Sunday sermons, matters have been carried too far."

While traditionalists applauded loudly, neoconservatives protested just as loudly, unappeased by Tonsor's qualification that he and other conservatives welcomed "the assistance of neoconservatives…in the work of dismantling the failed political structures erected by modernity." During the question period, Arnold Beichman of the Hoover Institution inquired whether Tonsor was rejecting James Burnham, Whittaker Chambers, Frank Meyer, George Orwell, Arthur Koestler, and Paul Johnson. Tonsor riposted, "Would you accept an ex-Nazi?" Beichman later wrote in his newspaper column, "Are the early sins of the Burnham-[Will] Herberg-et al. generation no more to be forgiven than the sins of the younger Kristol-Podhoretz generation?"

In the absence of master fusionist Frank Meyer, it remained for Leslie Lenkowsky of the Institute for Educational Affairs to point out that neoconservatives such as Charles Murray and James Q. Wilson had done much serious analysis of welfare and crime. Stan Evans shifted the discussion from personalities to principles, suggesting that conservatives should welcome the help of the neoconservatives—essentially Aristotelian in their philosophy—on the "proper affirmative uses of the state" such as internal order, criminal justice, and foreign policy. In his luncheon talk, Society president M. E. Bradford, as staunch a traditionalist as could be found, called for a rhetoric of the Common Good that asserted the larger over lesser goods.

It was one of the most disputatious meetings in the Society's history, caused in large part by the fact that just twenty years after the Goldwater debacle, conservatism was no longer on the periphery but at the center of national politics because of the Reagan administration. Was this the time, wondered some members, to engage in recriminations or to count blessings? Eugene Meyer, the executive director of the Federalist Society and the younger son of Frank Meyer, suggested that conservatives, while reserving the right to take issue in specific cases, should "welcome the contribution, both prudential and intellectual, of neoconservatives to the defense of Western civilization." By coincidence, or perhaps not, the next annual meeting was held for the very first time in Philadelphia, the City of Brotherly Love.

And indeed, philosophical disputes were set aside for a sober discussion of Constitutional government on the occasion of the 200th anniversary of the U.S. Constitution. Judge Robert Bork (before his failed nomination to the Supreme Court) led off with a brilliant analysis that explained the present lamentable state of constitutional law. After World War II, said Bork, "the courts addressed what they regarded as social problems...and often did so without regard to any recognizable theory of constitutional interpretation." A tradition of looking to original intention was shattered. Academics began constructing theories to justify what was happening—and "so was non-originalism born." That legal wave has become a tsunami, but "a second wave," composed of those who believe in first principles, "is rising." Judge Bork predicted that it might take ten or twenty years "for the second wave to crest, but crest it will" and sweep the "toxic detritus of non-originalism out to sea."

Bork's optimism was sparked by the public campaign of Attorney General Edwin Meese III (a future Society president), who declared that the current judicial activism, "which anchors the Constitution only in the consciences of jurists," was "a chameleon jurisprudence, changing color and form in each era." Meese's call for a return to Constitutional "originalism" produced howls of protest from the proponents of a "living constitution," but it precipitated a sea change in American jurisprudence, underscoring the difference that a few good men with the right ideas can make.

By the time of the 30th national meeting in April 1994, the Society had witnessed the fall of the Berlin Wall and the collapse of Soviet communism as well as the acceptance by nearly everyone—except the tenured faculty at Harvard—that capitalism rather than socialism was "the way to go," as Milton Friedman put it in his telephoned remarks to the Friday dinner session. Friedman quoted from his talk at a 1964 founding meeting in Indianapolis: "There is a tendency to underestimate the power of ideas because of the length of time it takes for them to work."

In the realm of ideas, insisted the Nobel laureate, "we have won the battle," but in the realm of practice "we have lost." America, he said, had gone from a society that was approximately one-third socialist to a society "that is more than half socialist today." And yet Friedman remained optimistic because "we just simply haven't waited long enough." He still believed that the "American people are not going to stand for a conversion of our society into a wholly centralized, socialized, collectivist society."

Critical to the dissemination of the right ideas, Friedman said, was "some organization of principle that can serve the function that the Socialist party served in the 1920s." "The Philadelphia Society," he said, "has done a great deal in playing that role and as a result has had a great deal of influence on the climate of ideas. But we have to keep pecking away," he added, "to make sure that that change in the intellectual climate is converted into a change in practice."

Thirty years later, Friedman's optimism can be challenged, given millennials' reported fascination with socialism and the general public's passive acceptance of a federal government bearing entitlements. That makes the role of the Philadelphia Society all the more important.

Fortunate was the Society in 1995 to find a worthy successor to the redoubtable Don Lipsett in Dr. William F. Campbell, Jr., professor of economics for three decades at Louisiana State University and a charter member of the Society. For the next nineteen years, until 2014 and the occasion of the 50th anniversary, Bill and his wife Helen and the omnicompetent Julie Flick helped the Society attain new levels of membership and financial stability. Particularly impressive was the outreach to those members of the rising generation who are eager to spend a weekend with some of the best minds of the West. Essential to this outreach was the generous financial support of Earhart Foundation and other grant-making institutions. Their assistance reflected the wisdom of the great Jewish philosopher Maimonides, who said that the highest form of philanthropy is to help one's fellow man stand on his own.

Born in Indianapolis, Indiana, Bill Campbell was raised a Hoosier, a Methodist, and an admirer of free markets. His high school graduation present from Pierre Goodrich, the founder of the Liberty Fund and a good friend of his father, was a copy of Ludwig von Mises' *Human Action*. An important book in the family library was a first edition of Russell Kirk's *The Conservative Mind.* Voila, a fusionist in the making.

After majoring in philosophy at DePauw University, Bill did graduate work at the University of Minnesota, studied under the classical liberal Bruno Leoni at the University of Pavia, and finally settled down to earn his Ph.D. in economics at the University of Virginia. Learning of an opening in the economics department of Louisiana State University, Bill left blizzard conditions in Virginia to interview at LSU in February 1966. "The flowers were in full bloom," he later recalled, "the weather was balmy, and the people were pleasant. I accepted a full-time teaching position that lasted for 32 years."

A lover of fine food and the Great American Songbook, Bill Campbell is devoutly committed to the mission of the Philadelphia Society—to encourage a dialogue between the traditionalist and libertarian emphases of conservatism to bring about a deeper understanding of the American Experience. He is a conservative because of his free market Christian father, his classical education, his deep reading in the conservative canon, and his friends in his personal and professional life. "The conservative," he wrote, "is not found in any arid philosophical abstraction or (worse) dogmatic ideology but in particular families, particular communities, particular churches and particular locales."

The privilege of working with a wide variety of presidents of the Philadelphia Society, he says, looking back on his nearly two decades as Secretary, "has been something that I would not change for a minute."

Through the 1990s and into the 2000s, the Society continued to chip away at the twin pillars of collectivism and cultural nihilism that tower over much of American society. At national meetings, it has probed the welfare state, the religious roots of liberty, the survival of Western civilization, and American foreign policy. It provided a platform for such distinguished conservatives as Michael Novak, Erik Ritter von Kuehnelt-Leddhin, Alan Charles Kors, Robert Conquest, Eugene D. Genovese, and Harry V. Jaffa. It mourned the loss of such colleagues, friends, and mentors as Russell Kirk, Mel Bradford, Gerhart Niemeyer, Henry Regnery, Manuel Ayau, and Milton Friedman. It pursued an aggressive recruiting program to bring members of the Fourth Generation of conservatives to its meetings and into membership. For the first time in its history the Society urged members to consider mentioning the organization in their wills. The response was modest but encouraging.

From the dark Goldwater days through the upbeat years of Ronald Reagan to the terrorist attacks of 9/11 and America's aggressive response led by President George W. Bush down to Barack Obama's Machiavellian maneuverings, conservatives were able to draw lessons in ordered liberty and a lifting of the spirit from the 100 meetings, spring and fall, of the Philadelphia Society.

To mark its 40th anniversary in 2004, the Society returned to its birth city of Chicago and assembled an "awesome" roster of conservatives—including Milton Friedman, George Nash, George Gilder, Forrest McDonald, Midge Decter, Roger Scruton, and Leonard Liggio—to discuss the achievements and prospects of the conservative movement. The keynote address was delivered by the renaissance conservative, William F. Buckley Jr., who began by offering a eulogy to Don Lipsett. Don never asked too much, Buckley said, "which is why when he did ask for something, it was granted as the only alternative to lifelong self-hatred." He noted that the commodore did not tell his friends that leukemia had been detected. "No one had any advance notice when the news came that he was gone, the most attractive and selfless American to figure prominently in the revival of the conservative spirit."

Having elicited tears in more than a few Society members, Buckley quickly turned to policy and politics. After admitting his fondness for the arch libertarian Albert Jay Nock, he cautioned against talk of "eliminating" the state for that would end in "ugly anarchy." Exercises in the limitation of the state, he said, "have to be done on finer canvases than some, even some members of this Society, have enjoyed drawing on for substitute constitutional blueprints."

He suggested that the scant popular reaction to taxation and regulation is simply that "people get used to things." Also, an affluent society like America "can afford extravagances ill-suited to poorer nations." Nevertheless, he said, conservatives have a duty to be cheerful "because we have no right to be disappointed by failures, knowing as we do the limitations of the state and the weaknesses of human beings." Such realism, Buckley added, "shone always through the face and the attitude toward life of Don Lipsett." Manifestly, he insisted, there has been a slowing down of statist impositions, "even if not on the scale the Philadelphia Society seeks." The work of the Society has made a substantial difference as proven by "our meetings here with one another. My investment of $100 in our society...has surely yielded a historic harvest. I am in your debt, and so is the Republic."

In the decade leading up to the 50th anniversary, the Society examined "Black History and Conservative Principles," led by Shelby Steele of the Hoover Institution and assisted by black scholars William B. Allen and Walter Williams and black activists Jay Parker and Lee H. Walker. It asked "What Is an American?" and called on Hoover scholar Victor Davis Hanson to lead the discussion. It considered how much liberty and limited government in America were endangered, and received a sober assessment from Boston University professor Angelo Codevilla. It addressed the place of ethics in a digital age and pondered the remarks of James Ceaser of the University of Virginia, George Gilder of the Discovery Institute, AEI's Stephen Hayward, and Carnes Lord of the U.S. Naval War College. It took up the clear and present danger of progressivism in America as outlined by author Jonah Goldberg, Heritage scholar Matthew Spalding, ISI's Mark Henrie, and *Claremont Review of Books* editor Charles Kesler.

For the 2000 fall regional meeting in Grand Rapids, the Society went out on a cultural limb and commissioned a musical setting of Psalm 56 for the invocation at the Friday night dinner. The young composer was Monroe; the singers comprised the Hillsdale College Chamber Choir. It was the first time that the Philadelphia Society had sponsored a new musical piece, and the cultural experiment was warmly received.

All the while, far-sighted members of the Society were taking a hard look at the organization. Fifty is not old for an individual, but it is at least the beginning of old age for a non-profit organization. Had the Philadelphia Society fallen into an intellectual rut of considering the same topics year after year? Was the average age of its members rising faster than unemployment? Was the Society still loyal to its mission of free and open debate between all strains of conservatism? Was the Society doing all it could to reach out to young conservatives as speakers and members? Notwithstanding Bill Buckley's flattering remarks at the 40th anniversary meeting, did the Philadelphia Society still make a difference in the conservative movement and beyond? The Society went looking for answers.

In 2009 and 2010, Presidents Roger Ream and Steven Hayward challenged members to up their financial contributions to the Society, with Hayward memorably pulling out his checkbook to make a lead gift at the annual membership breakfast.

In 2011, President Peter Schramm interviewed twenty-eight members of the Society *in extenso*, most, although not all, "PhillySoc" veterans. In his report, he offered several general observations: "The great vice to which our Society is inclined is splintering or factionalism." However, the bad effects of splintering and faction can be ameliorated. "A kind of trust has to be re-established between the factions" or, he warned, "our Society will die a natural and well-deserved death." Our members are interested in a conversation about a free society that takes place nowhere else—not in universities, think tanks, places of commerce, or the public square. "It would be a shame to see the opportunity for that kind of conversation slip away." "The political and moral axiom upon which our conversations build is freedom and its conditions." We should talk to each other, Schramm said, "not only with the civility necessary to any community but with charity to those with whom we may disagree."

Based on the interviews, Schramm suggested what could be done to encourage the right kind of conversation:

- A massive effort should be undertaken and soon to recruit new and younger members, particularly young academics.
- The Society should refrain from drifting too far into policy issues.
- The panels should be less structured and there ought to be fewer of them. More time should be devoted to conversation.

In conclusion, Schramm repeated the opinion of almost everyone he talked with: The Philadelphia Society is a society of friends, not a professional organization. "It is good to get together once a year for stimulating and enlightening conversations among friends."

President Philip Hughes took up immediately the issue of membership, initiating an aggressive campaign—with tremendous legwork provided by trustee Jackee Schafer and business manager Julie Flick—that netted fifty-three new members, a 20 percent increase in the Society. "A few more," he reported, "are waiting in the wings." It was decided not to cut back to one meeting a year on the grounds that it would limit the Society's visibility, impact, and fund-raising potential. Nor did the board of trustees adopt a "paid speakers" policy, because it was "incompatible" with the Society's current—and likely future—finances. Among Hughes's conclusions after his presidential year: The "Society cannot be run on an all-volunteer basis," and thinking otherwise would be a "fatal delusion."

Following a successful fall meeting in Memphis on "The Restoration of Federalism"—during which the organizers were careful not to schedule any event that conflicted with the twice-daily Parade of the Ducks through the lobby of the Peabody Hotel—President Lenore Ealy led the first-ever planning retreat of the Society. Held in Annapolis, Maryland, on the first weekend of February 2013, the twenty-five participants, including many former presidents and trustees, set to work to think about Society governance, membership, programs, and resources. At the end of some 36 hours of intense discussion and debate, the group arrived at certain conclusions: The mission of the Philadelphia Society is still relevant and needed. The Society should continue to strengthen "the intellectual undergirding of the Conservative Movement." Neither politics nor policy is our primary business. Our business is "to refine and spread ideas, so that conservatism will not disappear." To do this, it was agreed, a return to the fusionist roots of the Society is essential.

It was also agreed that the Society must intentionally focus on the younger generation. We must reclaim the energetic "insurgency" of our founders who were not members of the establishment. Our role, in the very evocative words of Stan Evans, is to "surf the zeitgeist," to identify and elaborate the principles that should guide politics, but not to get mired in it.

The Philadelphia Society, concluded the retreatants, should be the center of the conservative intellectual discussion, meaning we should continue not only to promote scholarly production but also to inform and educate the leaders of the ever-growing number of conservative think tanks and research centers that were not in the organizational landscape when the Society was born. There were specific recommendations, close to one hundred of them, such as (a) replacing the secretary's position with an executive director, ideally in a half-time role; (b) implementing a new governance and committee structure to give more program responsibility to the board of trustees; (c) establishing a task force to plan and oversee a redesign of the Society's website; (d) continuing to hold two meetings a year but replacing the names "national" and "regional" with "spring" and "fall"; (e) changing the traditional seating of the panelists and the audience to allow "more relaxed conversations"; (f) creating a special level of membership for younger members; and (g) developing a new brochure for membership and fundraising.

Confronting the long litany of reformist recommendations, some members recoiled and cited Edmund Burke's reflections on the French Revolution. But far more members recognized that now was the time for prudent change, lest the Society fade away. The process began with the selection of Lenore Ealy as the new executive director, effective with Bill Campbell stepping down as secretary after the 50th Anniversary Meeting in Chicago in April 2014.

In a society of esteemed intellectuals, Ealy easily holds her own with a Ph.D. in the history of moral, political, and religious thought from Johns Hopkins University, an M.A. in history from University of Alabama (where she studied with Forrest McDonald, who sponsored her first attendance at a Philadelphia Society meeting), and a B.S. with highest honors from Auburn University. She has edited three books, published and presented over twenty papers, and has led or participated in some seventy conferences, seminars, and colloquia, many of the latter under the sponsorship of the Liberty Fund.

She knows the conservative movement well, having worked in different administrative capacities for the Milton and Rose. D. Friedman Foundation, ISI, and the Heritage Foundation. As president of The Philanthropic Enterprise—which she co-founded with Dick Cornuelle (a speaker at the first national meeting of the Philadelphia Society in 1965)—and editor of the annual journal *Conversations on Philanthropy*, Ealy has become a nationally recognized expert on the role of philanthropy and voluntary action in a free society.

Her professional interests are wide and deep, beginning with helping the Philadelphia Society remain the premier conservative intellectual organization in America. "I was not yet two years old when the Society was founded in 1964," she said in her President's Report in 2013. "I hope and I expect that there is a toddler today who will have the privilege in 50 years of standing where I now stand and who will address a new generation inspired by our conversations to dedicate themselves to keeping and passing on the tablets."

At about the same time as the Annapolis retreat, the Society conducted a membership survey, receiving nearly one hundred replies, more than one-fourth of the members, an impressive response. Among the things learned: Philadelphia Society members are not as old as they look, with a large plurality of 46 percent between the ages of thirty-sex and sixty-five. They are predominantly male—89 percent. They are highly educated, with 41 percent holding Ph.D. degrees. They are members for reasons of prestige and heritage, and most come to meetings to meet leading conservatives. Among the issues they believe the Society must explore in coming years are the meaning of conservatism, the role of religion in America, Islam, fusionism, and whether there still is a conservative movement. They also hope to see the Society invite more young scholars, not shy away from controversial debates, and balance attention to the traditional and the current. In other words, they want to preserve the status quo of the Philadelphia Society as a gathering place where ideas are taken seriously and debated with vigor, but where laughter and intimate conversations among friends can also be found in the halls and hospitality suites.

Reflecting on her year as president and facilitator at the Annapolis retreat and looking forward to her duties as executive director, Ealy was optimistic: she believed that the Society could transcend factionalism and create a place where "conservatives of all stripes can engage in the lively, fresh, and important conversations" we all desire. Setting a splendid example of fusionism, Ealy quoted Hayek and Kirk. When F. A. Hayek warned us about the dangers of the road to serfdom, he was "cautioning us about the dangers of desiring too much security." To choose liberty, in the words of Russell Kirk, is "to embark on a never-ending quest against `Chaos and old Night.'"

Which brings to mind what T. S. Eliot said: "If we take the widest and wisest view of a Cause, there is no such thing as a Lost Cause, because there is no such thing as a Gained Cause. We fight for lost causes because we know that our defeat and dismay may be the preface to our successors' victory."

As the year 2020 drew to a close, wrote Philadelphia Society member Marcus Witcher, the conservative movement again stood at a crossroads. It had been there after Barry Goldwater's crushing defeat in 1964, during the height of the Vietnam War, at the victorious end of the Cold War, in the historic 1994 congressional elections, in opposition to "compassionate conservatism" and Big Government in 2010, and in the wake of Donald Trump's turbulent reelection defeat in 2020. What should the conservative movement look like moving forward? Conservatives inside and outside the Society spoke up.

National Conservatism has attracted a number of seasoned conservatives including Christopher DeMuth, the former head of the American Enterprise Institute, and Philadelphia Society members like Hillsdale College president Larry Arnn and *Modern Age* editor Daniel McCarthy. In a statement of principles, DeMuth and his colleagues expressed alarm at how traditional beliefs and institutions had been "undermined and overthrown." They declared their support for a world of independent nations, rejection of globalism, a strong but limited state, the

Bible as "the first among the sources of a shared Western civilization," respect for the rule of law in accordance with the Constitution of 1787, an economy based on private property and free enterprise although not an "absolute" free market, the traditional family as the source of society's virtues, a rejection of an "unconstrained individualism, and condemnation of state and private institutions that "discriminate and divide us on the basis of race."

National Conservatives sound like traditional conservatives when they say that "we revere the American founding," but they are more willing than Goldwater/Reagan/Buckley conservatives to use the formidable power of the state to counter the cultural institutions taken over by the progressive Left. Some National Conservatives have gone so far as to support a national industrial policy that would be anathema to libertarians and at odds with Fusionism. Nevertheless, as much as one may disagree with National Conservatism, writes conservative historian Matthew Continetti, "one cannot dismiss its significance." According to Continetti, Republican candidates Donald Trump, Ron DeSantis, and Vivek Ramaswamy all reflect National Conservative views. Much of National Conservatism's energy, he says, comes from young people who see "no compelling alternative."

Proof of the deepening debate among conservatives about the future is the entry of "Freedom Conservatism: A Statement of Principles," endorsed by more than one hundred policy wonks and political activists including social conservative Jay Richards and Kim Holmes, former executive vice president of the Heritage Foundation. Freecon principles range from the centrality of individual liberty and free enterprise to "a rational immigration policy" and opposition to "racial discrimination in all its forms." However, *Law & Liberty* editor John Grove has pointed out, immigration is a political question, not a philosophical principle. "The shining city on a hill" is a slogan, not a foreign policy strategy. Freedom Conservatism uses the language of fundamentals, Grove admits, but does not suggest "how or why we learn from our past" and offers little about "the need to rely on prescription." Still, for Matthew Continetti, Freedom Conservatism "opened a new front in the war for American conservatism.

National Conservatives and Freedom Conservatives will have to find room for National Affairs editor Yuval Levin, who seeks to transform American government into a "government that works to sustain and expand the space between the individual and the state and strengthen the family, civil society, and the market economy." The "space" he refers to are the "little platoons" of Edmund Burke and the "mediating institutions" of Alexis de Tocqueville. Another voice deserving of attention is Hoover fellow Peter Berkowitz, author of "Constitutional Conservatism," who argues that the political priority for all conservatives is to rally around the principles of liberty embodied in the Constitution with its adherence to political moderation. Cultural conservative Elizabeth Corey, a Philadelphia Society member, says that many young people are searching for traditional ideas like imperfection and mortality. Libertarian author Charles Murray, a Philadelphia Society speaker, calls on the upper class (the natural aristocracy of Thomas Jefferson and Russell Kirk) to preach and practice "American exceptionalism" based on such traits as industriousness, neighborliness, and optimism.

ISI editor Daniel McCarthy promotes what he calls "virtue libertarianism" that harkens back to a classical liberalism fathered by faith. The late Angelo Codevilla, a frequent contributor to *The Claremont Review of Books* edited by Philadelphia Society member Chares Kesler, argued for a revitalized federalism that allows states to go their way on controversial issues like abortion until "a consensus of the common good takes hold." Stephanie Slade, managing editor of the libertarian *Reason* magazine, has offered qualified praise for Frank Meyer and Fusionism, saying that "Meyer's writings show us that virtue and liberty can both be pre-eminent, so long as each is situated in its proper domain"—the political and the societal. Slade quoted "PhillySoc" founder Meyer: "Freedom is not the end of man's existence. It is a condition, a decisive and integral condition, but still only a condition of that end, which is virtue."

To help traverse the right road, the Society surveyed its past presidents. The purpose of the Society, responded Hillsdale president Arnn, is "to think and talk," and the Society is full of people interested in the questions that arise in dangerous times. "I expect," says Arnn, "they will think and talk more urgently and get closer to the truth" because of the fundamental adjustments underway in the nation, the world, and our government. Arnn is most concerned about the current trend to control speech, declaring that "the Philadelphia Society must resist that … and keep talking."

Long associated with the Liberty Fund, William Dennis took time to listen to the recordings of past "PhillySoc" meetings and was impressed by the presentations of the various strains of what Frank Meyer called "the Conservative-Libertarian Academic Community." The Society turned again and again to the same themes—"the nature of a free society and its enemies foreign and domestic." Now retired and obliged to pay his own way to meetings, Dennis told Lenore Ealy he would rather contribute an equivalent amount to the Society's treasury than get on another plane. Ealy emphatically disagreed. "No!"she said, "the Society only works if members attend regularly again and again to see old friends and make new ones." Upon reflection Dennis agreed: "Younger members need the opportunity to meet and hear their more senior colleagues …and seniors need to learn from the younger."

Argentina-born Alejandro Chafuen has expanded the membership of the Society to include influential policymakers from Latin America, such as Antonio Cabrera, the youngest cabinet minister in Brazil. Since leaving public office, Cabrera has founded a think tank, Faith and Work, which already has over 200,000 followers. Its mission is to reduce Brazil's onerous tax system and highlight family and pro-life issues. Chafuen also introduced Spain's Daniel Lacalle, a leading European economist, to U.S. audiences. He wrote the introduction to Lacalle's well-received book, *Freedom or Equality: The Key to Prosperity and Social Capitalism*. In keeping with the Society's fusionist philosophy, Chafuen arranged for banker John Allison, a champion of Objectivism, and Father. Robert Sirico of the faith-based Acton Institute to deliver keynote addresses. As president and since, Chafuen has stressed the importance of attracting young scholars and introducing them, perhaps for the first time, to the religious side of man. Too many young scholars are taught that a human being is "just a collection of cells." Such a "belief," says Chafuen, is only possible "if you negate spiritual reality." Neither Friedrich Hayek nor Russell Kirk counseled that.

"The Philadelphia Society is one of the last organizations to preserve the old fusionism, providing a forum for disparate voices." So replied Troy University dean Allen Mendenhall to the Society survey. "My hope," he said, "is that [it] can hold together the different strands that made up the conservative movement over the last 50 years or more." He is more cautiously optimistic than some past presidents, saying that "some of the best and brightest young minds now seek to attend our meetings." The ultimate goal is "a society that's good and virtuous with a shared sense of morality." Such a society can undertake voluntary governance and doesn't need overwhelming state intervention to guide its affairs. "That's why conservatives and libertarians need each other." To the question of how important is the Philadelphia Society, Mendenhall answers: "A movement without intellectual substance cannot last."

Consistent with the virtue of prudence, historian George Nash advocates not Fusionism per se but "a more fusionist sensibility" among conservatives. "An ecumenical disposition," he suggests, would lead the different actors of the conservative coalition to admit that each has something to offer. Each would accept what the veteran fusionist Donald Devine calls an "enduring tension." Borrowing from James Madison and his theory of competing factions, each side would act as a constraint on the excesses of the other. Each, says Nash, contributes something "to our understanding of the foundations of a free and ordered society." Nash calls his proposal "Common Sense Conservatism." He urges conservatives to avoid ideological thinking and in particular "soundbite sloganeering." In the midst of the debate, he says, the Philadelphia Society has a key role to play—not to issue its own manifesto but to provide an open forum for conservatives of all kinds to make their case.

In remarks at the Fall 2023 meeting, "PhillySoc" President Bridgett Wagner previewed topics from past Society meetings that could be explored at the spring 2024 meeting. The theme of the sixties was "A Free Society in Ferment," an appropriate title for the present decade as well. In the seventies, the Society regularly examined the crisis in our institutions, a number of which clearly lost ground in approval and influence. In the eighties, notwithstanding the electoral success of Ronald Reagan, we asked, "Do Conservative Ideas Lead to Conservative Outcomes?" In the nineties, the Society debated whether it was possible to limit the ever-expanding federal government. In the 2000s, we discussed America's role in the world, leaning toward a more activist role than that shared by many conservatives, particularly when America seems unable to secure its own borders.

Polls report that a large majority of Americans believe that the country is headed in the wrong direction and are pessimistic about their future and that of their children. "The Philadelphia Society was really made for moments like this," Bridgett Wagner declared, "to bring together the various strains of the conservative movement." The purpose is not to forge a political agenda, she said, but to build the understanding of the Left's radical actions and "the principles and traditions that are necessary to maintain a free and virtuous society."

The Philadelphia Society has ever sought to facilitate the frank and open exchange of views on the great issues of the day and to contribute to the preservation of the free society. In furtherance of these goals, the Philadelphia Society has looked to many for guidance, including the late Forrest McDonald, a former Society president and distinguished member, an award-winning historian and teacher at the University of Alabama, who in his final university lecture in 2002 suggested the following survival kit for his students preparing to enter the "real" world:

1. Open your mind and keep it open. We need to distinguish, McDonald said, between what is "absolute"—God alone—and what is "relative."
2. Strive to resurrect the English language, "now virtually defunct."
3. Learn anew to think non-scientifically when dealing with non-scientific things. "We must abandon," McDonald said, "our fragmented problem-solving approach to knowledge and take up a holistic view of human affairs."
4. Be grateful and take joy in the "very fact of one's existence" and in the existence of one's fellow human beings.

That is good advice for people of all ages.

CHAPTER 1

The Neoconservatives: The Species and Their Origins

April 18-20, 1986
Chicago, Illinois

Saturday, April 19
10:00-11:30

The Neoconservatives: The Species and Their Origins

John L. Ryan, Chairman

Edward Shapiro

Paul Gottfried

Burton Yale Pines

Stephen J. Tonsor

The Neoconservatives: The Species and Their Origins

By Ed Shapiro

A specter is haunting America, the specter of conservatism. All the powers of the old America have entered into a holy alliance to exercise this specter. Liberals and progressives, old leftists and New Leftists, radicals and populists. Of course, this is a paraphrase of *The Communist Manifesto*.

This of course was not supposed to happen. According to the dominant school of American historiography, the school embodied in Louis Hartz, Arthur Schlesinger Jr., and Allen Guttmann, liberalism was supposedly the only legitimate American intellectual tradition since America lacked the feudal class-ridden society necessary for conservatism to take root.[1] For American liberals, the paradox of American conservatism was that the only thing conservatives have had to conserve was the liberal tradition. The belief that conservative ideas had a place in American life was viewed as bizarre, while a conservative American intellectual was by definition an oxymoron. From this perspective, conservatism was an un-American activity. Ralph Waldo Emerson's 1841 essay entitled "The Conservative" was seemingly the last word on the nature of American conservatism. For Emerson, there was "always a certain meanness in the argument of conservatism…It makes no poetry, breathes no prayer, has no invention;

1 For reference see Louis Hartz's classic *The Liberal Tradition in America* (New York: Harcourt, Brace, and World Inc., 1955).

it is all memory…It degrades whatever it touches."[2] The extent to which Americanism and liberalism have been fused was illustrated by the refusal of even Robert A. Taft to identify himself as a conservative, preferring to call himself a liberal. Admittedly, there were conservatives, but these were simply defenders of big business and white supremacy and did not have to be taken intellectually seriously.

Undoubtedly, the most famous recent explication of the role of conservative ideas in American culture was Lionel Trilling's introduction to his 1958 collection of essays appropriately entitled *The Liberal Imagination.*[3] Trilling, who two decades later would be recognized as a formative figure in the emergence of neoconservatism, said the following: "In the United States at this time liberalism is not only the dominant but even the sole intellectual tradition. For it is the plain fact that nowadays there are no conservative or reactionary ideas in general circulation. This does not mean that there is no impulse to conservatism or to reaction. Such impulses are certainly very strong, perhaps even stronger than most of us know. But the conservative impulse and the reactionary impulse do not, with some isolated and some ecclesiastical exceptions, express themselves in ideas but only in action or in irritable mental gestures which seek to resemble ideas."

These words were written five years after the publication of Friedrich Hayek's *The Road to Serfdom*,[4] one year after Richard Weaver's *Ideas Have Consequences*,[5] the same year as Peter Viereck's *Conservatism Revisited*[6] and T.S. Elliot's *Notes Towards the Definition of Culture*,[7]

2 Ralph Waldo Emerson, "The Conservative." A lecture delivered in Boston at the Masonic Temple, December 9, 1841.

3 Lionel Trilling, *The Liberal Imagination: Essays on Literature and Society*, (New York: Viking, 1950).

4 F.A. Hayek, *The Road to Serfdom* (1944).

5 Richard Weaver, *Ideas Have Consequences* (Chicago: University of Chicago Press, 1948).

6 Shapiro probably meant Peter Viereck, *Conservatism* (New York: Van Nostrand, 1956).

7 T.S. Elliot, *Notes Toward the Definition of Culture* (1948).

one year before Leo Strauss' *Natural Right and History*,[8] two years before Francis G. Wilson's *The Case for Conservatism*,[9] and Hannah Arendt's *Origins of Totalitarianism*,[10] three years before Bernard Iddings Ball's *Crowd Culture*[11] and Eric Voegelin's *The New Science of Politics*,[12] four years before Russell Kirk's *The Conservative Mind*[13] and Robert A. Nisbet's *The Quest for Community*,[14] five years before John Hallowell's *The Moral Foundation of Democracy*,[15] and six years before Walter Lippmann's *The Public Philosophy*.[16]

It was symptomatic that even as perceptive an observer as Trilling, writing in the very midst of the postwar revival of conservative ideas, believed the only meaningful debate among American intellectuals must take place within the American left. By the time of his death in the early 1970s, Trilling would not and could not have argued in this way. Ironic indeed that John Stuart Mill's description of conservatives as the "stupid party" appeared in the 1970s–a decade in which conservative ideas were in the saddle and conservative intellectuals had established the agenda of public discourse. A growing national consensus emerged on the need to cut back taxes and the growth of government, to rethink the social policies of the 1960s, to lift the burdensome restrictions on property and enterprise, and to revise the liberal conventional wisdom on such matters as education and welfare.

---

8 Leo Strauss, *Natural Rights and History* (Chicago: University of Chicago Press, 1953).

9 Francis G. Wilson, *The Case for Conservatism* (Seattle: The University of Washington Press, 1951).

10 Hannah Arendt, *Origins of Totalitarianism* (New York: Harcourt, 1951).

11 Bernard Iddings Ball, *Crowd Culture* (1952).

12 Eric Voegelin, *The New Science of Politics* (Chicago: Chicago University Press, 1952).

13 Russell Kirk, *The Conservative Mind* (1953).

14 Robert A. Nisbet, *The Quest for Community* (1953).

15 John Hallowell, *The Moral Foundation of Democracy* (Chicago: Chicago University Press, 1954).

16 Walter Lippmann, *The Public Philosophy* (1955).

Such was the power of conservative ideas that even charter members of the American liberal establishment were reluctant to be identified as liberals. Both George McGovern and Walter Mondale preferred to be called progressives. And in McGovern's case, there was a certain justice in this because of his involvement in the Henry Wallace movement of 1948. These temporary disguises did not prevent these erstwhile liberals from suffering two of the most humiliating defeats in American presidential history.

The ultimate tribute to the power of conservative ideas was of course the 1980 election, one of the most ideological in recent memory. The election of a president who identified closely with conservative ideas could not have occurred without the emergence of a conservative ideological opposition. This included the founding of such conservative magazines as *Modern Age*, *National Review*, and the *American Spectator*. The change in orientation of *Commentary* and *Encounter* and other journals, the establishment of the Heritage Foundation, the American Enterprise Institute, and other conservative think tanks, the founding of the Conservative Book Club, the creation of such organizations as the Philadelphia Society, the work of the Intercollegiate Studies Institute, and the enlargement of the editorial page of the *Wall Street Journal*. In this case, at least, Richard Weaver was certainly correct in arguing that ideas certainly do have consequences.

The other side of the coin was the eclipse of radicalism and liberalism as viable intellectual alternatives. As Daniel Bell, the self-proclaimed socialist, noted recently, in fact last year, "The death of socialism is the most tragic political fact of the 20th century and those who still mount phrases about strategies for revolutionary change rarely if ever match that utopian ideal with the brutal consequences that have followed everywhere in its wake." The left has been reduced to defending its redoubts, unable to advance and conquer new ground, or to do other than to respond to conservative intellectual initiatives. Former leftist intellectuals and politicians now vie with one another in preempting conservative ideas. Thus, we see liberal politicians sponsoring tax reduction measures, the *New Republic* warning us of the Soviet threat, and Ted Kennedy leading the campaign to liberate important sectors of the economy from government regulation.

Ironically, at a time when conservative ideas are seemingly in the ascendency, conservative intellectuals are engulfed by self-doubt, pessimism, and discord. A recent symposium in the *Intercollegiate Review* on the "State of Conservatism" drew attention to the state of malaise and a sense of demoralization and discouragement among conservative intellectuals. What particularly distressed the contributors to the symposium–Gregory Wolf, Clyde Wilson, George Carey, Melvin Bradford, Paul Gottfried, George Panichas–was their belief that in the eyes of the general public, and even of many conservatives, a group of former liberals now known as neoconservatives had supplanted traditional conservatives as the voice of authentic conservatism. As Clyde Wilson contended, "These refugees now speak in our name, but the language they speak is the same they have always spoke. We have grown familiar with it, we learn to tolerate it, but it is tolerable only by contrast to the harsh syllables of the barbarians over the border. It contains no words for the things that we value. Our estate has been taken over by an impostor just as we were about to inherit. Conservatives must be determined not to be taken in by any interloper, no matter how plausible, finely turned out, and full of seductive promises." Mel Bradford agreed "Our first priority is to refuse firmly and vigorously to surrender our hard-won identity to those who would use it as a cloak for policies contrary to what we intend. Lines of demarcation must be drawn, and swiftly." Panichas protested against what he called a sham conservatism which merely temporalizes and trivializes and dissimulates spiritual laws and truths. Such a conservatism belongs almost exclusively to the world and is impervious to the primacy of God as the measure of the soul. Panichas called for "an unconditional conservatism, lean, ascetical, disciplined, prophetic, unswerving in its (indiscernible) task, strenuous in its mission, strong in its faith, faithful in its dogma, pure in its metaphysics." Those are his words, not mine.

These disaffected conservatives seem oblivious to the fact that diversity is a sign of vitality for any movement. Thus Christianity spawned heresies during its periods of greatest strength. Uniformity, on the other hand, indicates that a movement is no longer able to evoke passionate responses. Furthermore, observers of contemporary conservatism should not take literally the laments of conservatives regarding its future. Sociological studies of the American military during World War II noted that there usually was a correlation between the morale of a military unit and how much bitching it exhibited.

Not all prominent conservative intellectuals favor purging all those except true believers. As Robert A. Nisbet recently noted, "There are no guillotines in sight of the Mall, but no Jacobin ever hissed hypocrite more malevolently than so-called hard-liners have at suspected pragmatists these last few years." Nisbet's warnings appropriately appeared in the *Public Interest*, the house organ of neoconservatism. Similarly, Russell Kirk cautioned against heresy hunting within conservatism. He noted, "The existence of various factions within the conservative movement ought not to alarm us overmuch. Various emphases upon this or that aspect of public policy will remain among the several conservative groupings, but enough common ground can be cultivated to maintain a useful unity on certain large questions, supposing we abjure narrow ideology and condescend to think." What conservatism certainly didn't need was something similar to the continual sectarian quarrels which has marked the American Left. Kirk's advice concluded the Intercollegiate Review Symposium.

Now, the emergence of neoconservatism had been predicted by Jeffrey Hart in his 1966 book, *The American Dissent*.[17] Writing during the social and intellectual disillusions stemming from the Vietnam War and the rise of the New Left, Hart foresaw that under the pressure of the world revolution, as contradictions and evasions are exposed to

---

17 Jeffrey Hart, *The American Dissent: A Decade of Modern Conservatism* (New York: Doubleday, 1966).

an ever-greater extent, liberalism will certainly undergo fragmentation. Many liberals will move to the left, jettisoning their remaining Western cultural attachments. Others just as inevitably will move to the right, becoming more conservative. The process anticipated by Hart had already begun. The first issue of the *Public Interest*, edited by Daniel Bell and Irving Kristol, had appeared in 1965. The *Public Interest*'s healthy skepticism towards social reform and its distrust of political bureaucracy struck a discordant note in the mid-1960s, coming as it did at the zenith of the Great Society. Also within a short time, *Commentary* was to undergo that metamorphosis which transformed it into perhaps America's leading and most eloquent opponent of what Trilling had termed the "adversary culture." The neoconservatives were, and Norman Podhoretz recounted, united in opposition to the "armies of the alienated."

Despite the widespread use of the term neoconservative, very few of the supposed neoconservatives, including Podhoretz, identified themselves as such. And the word itself was coined as a mark of opprobrium by the socialist, Michael Harrington. Irving Kristol was one of the few who openly admitted to being a neoconservative and almost by default became the movement's guru. His 1983 volume, *Reflections of a Neoconservative*, is the nearest thing to an apologetic that we have.[18] It also reveals why some conservative devotees have reacted so negatively to neoconservatism. Neoconservatism, Kristol maintained, was a syncretic, intellectual movement combining elements of classical economics and precapitalist moral and philosophical traditions. It simultaneously supported the free market and government intervention on behalf of manners and morals–both a desire for liberty and the need for community. But neoconservatism, according to Kristol, aims at more than syncretism, it seeks a new synthesis. It has its own distinctive inclinations. One of these was an acceptance of the welfare state, which,

18 Irving Kristol, *Reflections of a Neoconservative: Looking Back, Looking Ahead* (New York: Basic Books, 1986).

suitably purged of paternalism and statism, could bolster what Kristol called the conservative predispositions of the people. For Kristol, the essence of neoconservatism was its effort to intellectually and morally reinvigorate the heritage of 19th-century liberal capitalism–to return to the original sources of liberal vision and liberal energy so as to correct the warped version of liberalism that is today's orthodoxy. Neoconservatism represented the spirit of "bourgeois populism," those are his words, while the task of neoconservative intellectuals was to explain to the people why they were right and their liberal intellectual detractors were wrong.

Neoconservatism's freedom from nostalgia, its willingness to play fast and loose with some of conservatism's sacred pieties–including opposition to the welfare state–its advocacy by former liberals and even Marxists, and its acceptance of the basic outlines of American political and economic development since the New Deal and prior of the Great Society were enough to discredit it in the eyes of some conservatives. But there is more. Neoconservatism's roots are essentially in the social sciences, especially sociology and economics, while traditional conservatism's roots are in the humanities: political philosophy, theology, history, and literature. Neoconservatives seek to make government more cost-effective; traditional conservatives are concerned with the nature of government and the meaning of a constitution. The writings of the neoconservatives are heavily factual, dependent on the latest findings in social sciences and concerned with what can be. Irving Kristol's famous statement is apt: "A neoconservative is a liberal who has been mugged by reality."

Being of recent vintage, neoconservatism lacks the rich philosophical and historical background of conservatism and its unique view of human nature. Being more concerned with what ought to be than what can be, the conservatives are more philosophical and dogmatic. First principles are to be asserted, not measured. Conservatism, Mel Bradford declared, amounts to "more than opportunism, pop sociology, and a series of position papers." George Panichas agreed: "Endless policy reviews and policy studies lack basic apprehension of the permanent things and are responsive to the empirical ambitions that reflect the taste and power drives of a technological Benthamite world. The theology of conservatism has been sacrificed to the new gods and the new morality of modernity." Thus, while neoconservatives and conservatives alike reject much of contemporary liberalism, neoconservatives do so because it is unworkable and counterproductive, while conservatives do so because it runs counter to what they perceive to be human nature.

The contrast between neoconservatism and traditional conservatism is clearly revealed in their different attitudes toward religion. For neoconservatives, religion is necessary for social stability while traditional conservatives are concerned with man's relationship to God. Neoconservatives are extremely sympathetic toward religion as an institution, but in contrast to traditional conservatives, they generally do not concern themselves with the truths of religion and are not known generally for being religious themselves. Much of the discontent of the Old Right regarding the status of conservatism involves its supposed secularization under the impact of neoconservatism. "We cannot escape the fact," Panichas contended, "that during the past ten years or so, conservatism has experienced a spiritual decline even as it has made considerable political gains."

And yet despite the differences between the neoconservatives and traditional conservatives, they have much in common. Both distrust social engineering and deracinated intellectuals. Both support the widespread distribution of private property and free enterprise, both accept traditional morality, and both strongly identify with the West in general and the United States in particular. Their most important point of agreement concerns the encroachment of the state on the private sector. The origins of conservatism are to be found in the protest of Edmund Burke and the French opponents of the revolution against the aggrandizement of public power at the expense of the private sector. In defending Burke's little platoons and the prerogatives of church, family, and profession, conservatives saw as their task the protection of private social authority against the assault of public political authority. Today, neoconservatives are skeptical as to the benefits of centralized economic planning, while traditional conservatives dread the encroaching state. The neoconservative view of the state was shaped by the events of the 1960s while that of the conservatives was a product of a philosophical, historical, and literary tradition which emphasized the need for roots in community. Southern conservatives have of course an additional reason for fearing centralized power.

But what is important is not that the fears of neoconservatives and conservatives regarding centralized government are derived from different sources, but rather that they lead to similar conclusions, namely the danger of the state. The major issue facing the contemporary Right is the same one which faced Burke: the threat posed to the family, local social institutions, and private economic organizations from the aggrandizement of political authority. Conservative purists can debate the question whether the government should have become involved in education, housing, and public welfare, but in view of the strength of statism, it is certainly counterproductive to spurn support for neoconservatives. No one is without sin or beyond redemption, particularly anticollectivists.

The greatest student of America also wrote the greatest conservative commentary on American life–and I refer, of course, to Alexis de Tocqueville and his great book *Democracy in America*.[19] Tocqueville both feared and admired American democracy. His fears stemmed from the recognition that democracy was a trans-national phenomenon and that in certain respects America resembled post-revolutionary France. In both countries, standardization, egalitarianism, and materialism held sway. "In democracies, the passion for equality," he wrote, "is ardent, insatiable, eternal, and invincible. Democracies will put up with poverty, servitude, and barbarism, but they will not endure

---

19 Alexis de Tocqueville, *Democracy in America*. Volume 1 (1835), Volume 2 (1840).

aristocracy." Tocqueville's admiration for America stemmed from the realization that American society was free of some of the more unfortunate aspects of mass democracy exhibited in France, particularly the political centralization which he underscored in his other great book, *The Old Regime and the French Revolution*.[20] He emphasized the decentralized character of America, her numerous churches, powerful local governmental bodies, vigorous private economic life, influential legal establishment–he called, by the way, the American bar the only counterbalance to democracy in America–and above all the private organizations he called associations. The essence of modern liberalism is the defense of the Leviathan state, while in contrast, Tocqueville's fears of centralized political authority resonate among conservatives of every variety. Whether opposition to the liberal state is derived from philosophical, historical sources or from the social sciences is less important than the opposition itself. As heirs of Tocqueville's intellectual legacy, conservatives and neoconservatives are natural allies and not foes.

---

20 Alexis de Tocqueville, *The Old Regime and the French Revolution* (1856).

The Neoconservatives: The Species and Their Origins

By Paul Gottfried

I intend to be contentious in my remarks, and perhaps even more contentious than I am by nature. I hope I give no offense, but I would like to present what I consider to be substantial differences between the conservative and neoconservative camps and perhaps speak again as somebody who has contributed to what I hope becomes a meaningful discussion between the two sides.

Might and power, as Machiavelli reminded us, do shape human affairs. Both are also relevant to the theme about to be discussed: the rise of neoconservatism as a force on the American Right. Those identified as neoconservatives enjoy demonstrable respect in conservative circles. Conservative foundations fund their enterprises generously, in some cases almost exclusively. Conservative think tanks court neoconservative celebrities. *National Review* solicits their contributions, *American Spectator* and *Policy Review* feature them with predictable regularity, and the neoconservative publications, *Commentary* and *Public Interest*, are often described as the preferred journals of conservative intellectuals. Peter Steinfels' *The Neoconservatives*,[21] whatever its defects, and, more recently, Gillian Peele's *Revival and Reaction*[22] detail the signs of favor that the American Right has bestowed on the

21 Peter Steinfels, *The Neoconservatives: The Men Who Are Changing America's Politics* (New York: Simon & Schuster, 1979).

22 Gillian Peele, *Revival and Reaction: The Right in Contemporary America* (Oxford: Oxford University Press, 1985).

neoconservatives. The hostility to southerners and many traditionalists, indeed people to the right that surface in their publications, usually fails to catch the attention of their conservative admirers. Even traditionalists like to believe that neoconservatives have come a long way or that in any case they're still growing.

Such assertions need to be reexamined. Senator Daniel Patrick Moynihan, who contributes to neoconservative journals and used to be on the masthead of *Public Interest*, was an anti-Soviet, pro-Israeli liberal Democrat in the 1960s and he remains one today. Carl Gershman, Sidney Hook, Daniel Bell, all of whom appear frequently in neoconservative periodicals, have been self-labeled social democrats most of their lives. The same is true for Jeane Kirkpatrick, however savagely she may denounce Communist tyranny. Norman Podhoretz, Nathan Glazer, Walter Burns have usually characterized themselves as Truman Democrats.

The neoconservatives' relationship to the welfare state puts their political allegiances into context. They support the economic redistribution and social reforms of the New Deal Democratic Party up to the point at which that party succumbed to what the neoconservatives call contemptuously the McGovernites. Although George McGovern, the late Hubert Humphrey had almost identical senatorial voting records in the early and mid-seventies, *Commentary* praises Humphrey while excoriating McGovern. The difference is largely symbolic. Humphrey, like Truman, is a neoconservative synecdoche for the old left center. McGovern represents a radicalized Democratic Party which is weak on Israel, soft on the Soviets, and which the neoconservatives abandoned with fanfare in 1972 and again in 1980.

Despite their leftist point of departure, neoconservatives sometimes adopt conservative-sounding rhetoric as part of their mission to the right. Michael Novak, for example, calls Pope John Paul II a neoconservative: "A person of the left who has learned to be critical of the left." In order to fight liberationists and progressive theologians, according to Novak, John Paul has taken the most effective stance possible: "The Pope is not a traditionalist, neither is he a progressive; he is a neoconservative." Is it permissible to ask whether God too is a neoconservative?

Irving Kristol has been even more diligent in distinguishing neoconservatism from the Left. Kristol has described the death of socialism as the process whereby the conservative welfare state has proved itself the best means of combining social responsibility and market incentive. George Will has found a venerable pedigree for the welfare state which he traces through Disraeli, Bismarck, and Burke, all the way back to Aristotle. Most of this rhetoric is mere packaging, as its users must well know. I believe that Will and Kristol are too intelligent to think that they have found precedence for a modern managerial state in either Bismarck's attempt to preserve a military monarchy by creating social pensions for German workers or in Disraeli's search for a popular base for a stratified English society and monarchy. Discovering pre-modern antecedents for a postmodern welfare state requires a leap of faith. Without such faith, it is hard to believe that those bureaucrats who impose minority quotas or who bungle our Social Security are in point of fact a counter-revolutionary vanguard.

Neoconservatives usually follow Ben Wattenberg in viewing history as the battle of times. The closest they come to evoking a past golden age is in depicting student life at City College of New York around 1935. Neoconservatives reminisce about interpreting Marx in the alcoves of the college cafeteria that turned out to be weigh stations on the road to *Commentary*. For most neoconservatives, the happy days are in the present, which they seek to preserve with only minor alterations. This was the point of a series of TV lectures by Ben Wattenberg a few years back. It is also the theme of a recently-published book of his which ascribes high divorce rates and other apparent signs of social decay to newly-won freedoms.[23]

---

23 Ben Wattenberg, *The Good News Is the Bad News Is Wrong* (New York: Simon & Schuster, 1984).

In the November 1985 issue of *Commentary*, other Neoconservatives provide even more exhilarating pictures of contemporary American life in a 40-year perspective. Peter L. Berger for example extols, "The gigantic political efforts to ensure that no group within America is excluded from the cornucopia of industrial capitalism." He marvels that all racial discrimination was abolished in a few years. Looking toward the future for even further progress, Berger calls "for a specifically American version of the welfare state" without the bureaucratic obstacles that has accompanied similar projects in Europe. The Neoconservative literary critic Joseph Epstein sums up his own sense of progress thus: "The southern part of the U.S. has seen and shaken off its medieval torpor, and if you happen to be black, cruelty." In a speech published last summer in *Encounter*, Podhoretz expressed wonder that progressive intellectuals criticize America even though its democratic institutions are perfecting themselves. A French hero of the Neoconservatives, Jean-François Revel, makes the same point even more emphatically in *How Democracies Perish*.[24] According to Revel, the Communist threats to the West has come precisely at a time when Western democracy is internally and most secure. Revel poo-poos Tocqueville's warnings about an overreaching state developing in a democratic culture. Quite the opposite, Revel says, has happened in America, where a socially responsible, but not an intrusive, regime coexists with diversity of opinion.

Neoconservatives do not always write as Pollyanna optimists, but they do so often enough to make me wonder about their reputation as social critics. Looking at the November 1985 issue of *Commentary*, one could distinguish the neoconservative contributors from the more conservative ones by the emphasis on social progress. Most neoconservatives interpret the last forty years as a slightly rocky march toward the New Jerusalem, the conservative contributors do not. This presentist

---

24 Jean-François Revel, *How Democracies Perish* (New York, Harper Perennial, 1983). The original title was *Comment les démocraties finissent.*

view of Western society is intimately related to the neoconservatives' advocacy of a global democratic revolution. Whether one reads Berger or Michael Ledeen in *Commentary* or the statements of the National Endowment for Democracy, which blend neoconservative shibboleths in the interest of organized labor, there are constant themes associated with the revolution desired. It is to lead to a worldwide secular politically egalitarian society with a mixed economy. In the short run, non-Western governments are to be encouraged to hold democratic elections and to undertake land reform, unionization, and capital formation. The entire world, that is to say, is to be reconstructed as a mirror copy of the present-day America celebrated by Neoconservative publicists.

Understandably, those who scorn this vision of progress and who glorify the past have not enjoyed the neoconservatives' esteem. Susan Garman's writing in the *Wall Street Journal* on October 13th, 1985 notes how *National Review* had to struggle to overcome its beginnings: "Today's American Conservatism does indeed have part of its roots in a seedbed infested with racism, chauvinism, and paranoid looniests. When *National Review* was founded in the mid-1950s, the Right's presence on the U.S. political stage was small and fading. Conservatism seemed fatally tied to this pernicious kookiness. From time to time in *National Review*, you can still hear an echo of the Right's distasteful origins. The sound fades as time passes because over the years Mr. Buckley, and his associates, with *National Review* as a rallying point pried conservatism from the fingers of its demented follower."

This battle against paranoid looniness was apparently still raging in the late seventies when Norman Podhoretz and his friends declared for Pat Moynihan in the New York senatorial race. In breaking ranks, Podhoretz depicts himself as supporting the moderate progressive Moynihan against the left-wing extremist Bella Abzug, then equally extremist incumbent Senator Jim Buckley. Podhoretz here was striking a characteristically neoconservative pose as the moderate wedged in between the Right and the Left.

Diane Ravitch, whose writings on educational problems appear often in neoconservative publications, has claimed to occupy the same middle ground. Writing for *American Educator* in Fall 1982, Ms. Ravitch addresses the urgent matter of saving public education from the new rightist danger: "It is not clear that there is much difference between the Old Right and the new Right. The Old Right concentrated on political issues and spied communists behind every idea or book they didn't like. The New Right concentrates on moral issues and blames secular humanists for undermining the morals of children. Both yearn for ideological and moral purity." There is in fact a ruse concealed in this attack on the Old and New Rights. Whereas Ravitch castigates the Right for being insensitive to professional education, she weighs in against the Left for its far-out ideologies of sexual liberation. It is worthy of note that Ms. Ravitch feels obliged to sound like Norman Lear before she allows herself to make the useful point that sex education programs harm the young. She also decries the creationist progressive educators and sex educationists as adversaries of American learning. But as Ms. Ravitch surely knows, not all these groups have aimed at or produced equally far-reaching changes. Creationists have not brought about our deteriorating SAT scores, nor the breakdown of discipline in classes. They have done nothing to encourage sexual promiscuity or contempt for established social institutions. The Religious Right has not even been effective in keeping evolution out of our high schools when putting the deity back into them. Ms. Ravitch's argument shows rigid dependence on a stylistic paradigm which the neoconservatives aren't willing to forsake. It puts them at the vital center of the political spectrum flanked by crazies on both sides. My own sense of things is that the neoconservatives' stress on the middle ground is largely formalistic. Their hearts in most cases are with the Left even though their expense accounts come from the Right.

I make this statement as a qualified generalization in full awareness that one can find genuinely conservative sentiments in the writings of Irving Kristol, Midge Decter, and other self-described neoconservatives.

Indeed, neoconservatives have been tireless in denouncing the Soviet danger, and I think probably much more so than the Old Right, and in warning against the menace of international terrorism. Yet these facts by themselves do not negate the view that the neoconservatives —(Break in audio)— trace the origins of neoconservatism to quarrels among American liberals that were exacerbated by ethnic tensions. Particularly critical, according to Steinfels, was the rift in New York in the early seventies between black civil rights leaders and Jewish educators and other Jewish and mostly white municipal employees. The neoconservatives' disagreement with the intellectual Left has been characterized by painful disappointment. In reading contentions and analysis of news commentary edited by Midge Decter, I am struck by the fact that the contributors spend so much time minutely refuting liberal columnists from New York newspapers. Surely not all the opinion being criticized is apt to have impact. Indeed, much of it hardly gets read beyond the Murray Hill and Greenwich Village districts of Manhattan. But this is the culture, these are the notables whom the neoconservatives take seriously, and an intimate though strange relationship can be shown to exist between them.

Indeed, I would argue neoconservatives seek to justify themselves in the eyes of their liberal opponents. Such is not the case in their relationship with the Right. It should be noted that conservatives, not neoconservatives, misrepresented the movement in question. Neoconservatives are being honest when they state that others started calling them conservative against their will. They have never made a secret of their fear and loathing for that part of the Right which they cannot reshape or convert to their views. Why then do conservatives pursue them with favor? Certainly, it is not because they are the only anti-communists around or the only people who express reservations about minority quotas. The truth of the matter is that conservatives are largely ignorant of their postwar history. So much so that they have embraced a neoconservative interpretation of it. The conservative movement as seen by many conservatives themselves had no brain power, or to use the operative term, academic prestige, before the neoconservatives arrived on the scene. I have heard pre–New Deal Republicans praise the neoconservatives for defending capitalism in difficult times. Since America is not likely to return to a pre-welfare -state economy, so the argument goes, the neoconservatives have taken the realistic position that half a cup of capitalism is better than none at all. The neoconservatives are supposedly protecting that half a cup when they advocate an efficiently-run welfare state that ultimately provides greater revenues for itself by granting tax reductions. This last defense of the neoconservatives is easily refuted. George Gilder has made the excellent point that neoconservatives are principled, not reluctant supporters of a welfare state and planned economy. Their view of the government's role in economic matters differs fundamentally from that of their conservative benefactors and it is foolish to believe that they would seriously work against the social development which, on balance, they applaud.

The intellectual Right, moreover, did not lack for gifted journalists and thinkers before the neoconservatives came along, nor is there reason to assume that the American Right will shrivel intellectually if the neoconservatives become reintegrated into the Left. Have they produced more penetrating social thinkers than Richard Weaver, Robert Nisbet, James Burnham, all self-identified conservatives before the neoconservatives had their falling out with the Left? Was Will Herberg, the religious editor of *National Review* at a time when, according to Susan Garman and Joseph Epstein, the journal was still a rallying point for antisemitic cranks, any less of a sociologist of religion than Peter Berger? Does the *New Criterion* feature more perceptive estheticians than Eliseo Vivas, Russell Kirk, and George Panichas–all long-time editors of *Modern Age*? Are M.E. Bradford and Andrew Lytle, both southern conservatives, and Peter Stanlis less able literary critics than their neoconservative counterparts? Are the contributors to *Modern Age* less learned or less eloquent than those who write for *Commentary*? In my own field history, I cannot think of a certified neoconservative, other than Richard Pipes, who has left any scholarly mark. I exclude Gertrude Himmelfarb, a superb intellectual historian who was a traditional conservative long before she became, I assume for family reasons, a neoconservative.

I offer these comparisons not to disparage those who have benefitted from the neoconservative ascendency. I am only challenging the tendentious view of the Old Right taken by the neoconservatives and those influenced by them. This view of an intellectually-sterile, bigoted Right redeemed by the neoconservatives is in fact related to a second historiographic myth that the neoconservatives' current prominence was already apparent in the 1950s. The devotees of this myth assign excessive importance to journals of progressive but anti-Soviet opinions centered in Midtown Manhattan as molders of the postwar political environment. In *The Liberal Mind in a Conservative Age*, for example, Richard H. Pells, a famous historian of the Left, discusses what may be styled incipient neoconservatism.[25] Although Pells puts into focus the growing gulf between Cold War liberals like Irving Kristol and forerunners of the New Left like Philip Rahv, he also and happily produces a typically neoconservative interpretation of the fifties. His survey of its intellectual life, as John Lukacs has observed, rarely moves beyond two or three blocks in midtown Manhattan. Pells identifies James Burnham with *Partisan Review* and *Dissent*, totally ignoring Burnham's more substantial contributions to *National Review*. He refers anachronistically, from the perspective of the fifties, to anti-Communist liberals as conservatives. Pell shows no awareness of the critical difference between Sidney Hook and James Burnham–that is between an anti-Soviet socialist and a key architect of the Old Right. His world of ideas is that of social democratic sectarianism, as it expressed itself among contributors to several New York–based journals all with local readerships.

25 Richard K. Pells, *The Liberal Mind in a Conservative Age* (New York: Harper & Row, 1985).

The same perspective is seen in an essay by Tod Lindberg, an editor of *Public Interest*, published recently in *Commentary*. Lindberg writes with a certain bitter nostalgia of New York's decline as a center of learned opinion. The main evidence of this punitive decline is that several neoconservative journals and journalists have moved from New York to Washington, thereby causing, from Lindberg's standpoint, a veritable *translatio imperii* within the world of political commentary.

Professor Shapiro emphasized that neoconservatives draw from the social sciences and statistical research more heavily than do the older conservatives. This is undoubtedly true as even a superficial comparison of *Public Interest* and *Modern Age* should make clear, yet this generalization must be qualified. Most popular neoconservative journalists like Newhouse, Decter, Kristol, Novak, and Podhoretz present their views without fussing over statistics. Indeed, part of the appeal of neoconservative arguments among the business community is their avoidance of the highbrow. For example, Nathan Glazer opposes minority quotas as inconsistent with the 1964 Civil Rights Act and with the individualism that he associates with American democracy. The conservative humanistic perception of quotas is infinitely more complex. It is based on a view of unchanging human nature and on various authorities from Aristotle to sociobiology. Conservatives believe in the corporeal nature of man and the intrinsic soundness of sexual roles. Defending these propositions requires more intellectual energy and makes greater demands on the listener than the neoconservative argument about whether quotas really produce equality and are consistent with 1960s-type liberalism.

There are admittedly more neoconservatives than old conservatives at prestigious universities. One reason for this, that I myself have mentioned on other occasions, is that conservatives ever since the 1960s have fled universities for political careers. This tendency, which Stephen Tonsor has called the politicization of second-generation conservatism, has definite consequences. It has caused movement conservatives to lose contact with the world of thought and ultimately forget their philosophic roots. Yet this tendency did not develop without external pressure. While at Yale, I heard conservative students discussing the ostracism of Willmoore Kendall, which I myself remembered. Indeed, I myself recall a productive scholar, Charles Moser, being denied tenure by the Department of Slavic Languages. Moser's colleagues made no secret of the fact that his anti-Soviet views had directly affected the tenure decisions. Neoconservatives were then on the Left and were generally less subject to such professional setbacks. And though there were obvious exceptions like Walter Berns, many neoconservatives protected their left flank even while they quarreled with the Left by opposing the war in Vietnam.

I suppose in view of the late hour, perhaps I should come rapidly to my conclusion. Many of these remarks may seem petulant and even spiteful, but perhaps are long overdue. A Marxist friend explained to me that all movements have their Trotskyists and survive only by periodically expelling them. Theologians tell us that religious communities can only endure by recognizing and condemning heresy, yet the Marxist analogy may be more apt in the present circumstances. There is a close relationship between Trotskyism and certain neoconservative attitudes and values. Attention has been given to the background of Irving Kristol and other older neoconservatives as former members of a Marxist-Leninist group at war with Moscow. I believe this Trotskyist connection is of more than antiquarian interest. A Trotskyist mindset has surfaced in the neoconservative movement as seen by its emphasis on global revolution and democratic universalism. For American radical intellectuals of the twenties and thirties, Leon Trotsky, who had been driven from Russia by Stalin, incarnated the idealism of a Bolshevik Revolution. Although Trotsky was a brutal killer who had supported the mass execution of, among others, Russian social democrats, he was a flamboyant Marxist intellectual and he viewed the Russian upheaval of November 1917 as merely the first step in an imminent global socialist revolution. Abjuring all forms of nationalism, including Russian, Trotsky looked forward to a world society established through shared revolutionary ideals. An intellectual vanguard would lead mankind into the new age.

It is not hard to recognize the link between this vision shared by the Marxist sectarians at City College of New York and the global democracy now preached by the younger neoconservatives. James Burnham may have been looking only at surfaces when in '73 he perceived the liberal gestalt behind neoconservative rhetoric. In my opinion, globalist revolutionary idealism is a common characteristic of both Trotskyists and neoconservatives. So too is the view that these groups have of themselves as occupying a middle ground between reactionaries and misguided revolutionaries who are derailing historical progress. This last point is crucial for understanding why neoconservatives think and combine presentism with what Theodore Draper has called the messianic and guilt-ridden treatment of history. Like the Trotskyists who offered qualified support for Soviet socialism, two cheers but not three, the neoconservatives defend the present American society in comparison to earlier or alternative ones. Though not as the fulfillment of all their hopes, such a fulfillment would only be possible in a world without Soviet Communism and its threat to a global democratic welfare state order —(Break in audio)— that account for the hand wringing of neoconservative polemicists. Contrary to Draper's assertions, the neoconservatives do scold the Right for insufficient enthusiasm about democracy as well as the pro-Soviet Left. If neoconservatives fight the Left more vehemently than they do the unconverted Right, however, it is not because of their rightist orientation. Neoconservatives view the Right as an unpleasant but useful base to be occupied in pursuing their love-hate struggle with old comrades. At stake in the struggle are related visions of progress in global revolution.

One may observe among the neoconservatives the typical Trotskyist ardor for revolutionary purity. Michael Ledeen, writing in *Commentary*, deplores the fact that reactionary South Africa as well as Soviet Russia has thus far resisted democratic revolution. Democratic globalists are not interested in mere allies against a common totalitarian enemy. Like Revel, Ledeen, and the National Endowment for Democracy, they seek ideological soulmates for a world crusade on behalf of democratic ideals. In responding to those of his readers who objected to his partial defense of Solzhenitsyn as a critic of the liberal West, Norman Podhoretz proudly called himself an idolater of democracy. One might respond by reminding Podhoretz and other neoconservatives that there is a biblical injunction against idolatry. One might also remind conservatives what Eric Voegelin said about the gnostic glorification of the here and now. Such warnings may be useful as long as conservatives look to neoconservatives for self-validation. What the neoconservatives can really offer the intellectual Right is not self-validation, but an example of self-respect. The Right may desperately need that in both the long and short runs. Thank you.

The Neoconservatives: The Species and Their Origins

By Burton Yale Pines

When Mel Bradford first called me several months ago and asked me to speak to this group, he asked me to address the proposition of whether differences between the varieties of conservatives are narrowing. And then in Bradford tradition, he suggested that I argue that indeed they are narrowing. Well, not only am I susceptible to pressure from Mel Bradford, but also it's a proposition which I welcome. It's the kind of offer I found difficult to refuse because I indeed do believe that the various strands of conservatism increasingly have more in common and less separating them than ever before. To be sure, as we have just heard, we still have our honorable and distinguished differences. We here know what those differences are and we have spent more hours and more days debating them than we can count. We relish every minute of the debate. We celebrate these differences. They are, after all, extremely important, centering fundamentally on man's place in the world and the world's place in the cosmos. And these differences continue among young conservatives. I see this every fortnight at the Heritage Foundation's Third Generation lecture series, gatherings of a hundred or so conservatives in their twenties and very, very early thirties, too early thirties. These are lively, intense, passionate debates among young conservatives about their differences. The debates among us have enriched us individually, and certainly have enriched our nation.

In this room, perhaps more than anyplace else, we have known the joys of the tensions between the libertarians' passion for freedom and the classical conservatives' deep concern for order. The libertarian has something to teach us about individual freedom and the dangers of authority of any kind. The neoconservative teaches us about the nature of our enemy. The neoconservative reminds us about the grand and proud tradition of compassion within conservative ranks. And I think the ability to analyze the welfare state and talk about the welfare state merely reflects a very grand tradition among conservatives of compassion. I hope that we have not given up to the Left a monopoly of compassion. If anything, the Left has abandoned the individual to the cold of nature whilst the conservative recognizes that those who are better endowed than others have a responsibility to fellow man and the neoconservatives remind us of that tradition. The neoconservatives, by giving two cheers for capitalism, let's be frank about it, that's one cheer more than we hear from some classical conservatives. The traditional conservative reminds us of Edmund Burke's lessons of the virtue of order and the cautious approach to history and, perhaps most important as you well know, of our compact with preceding and subsequent generations.

But while differences remain, I believe that these differences today make less of a difference than ever before. American conservatives seem, by and large, more harmonious than ever before. The reason for this is obvious: the experience which we have shared as we've been transformed from a movement, or movements, in opposition, to one which governs. It is this which also has transformed our focus. Instead of being almost obsessed, as we were in opposition, with what divides us, we have had to focus more on what we have in common. In this, we have discovered much about us that we share–perhaps more than many of us suspected.

Our narrowing of differences even began before we governed. It began in the 1970s, a decade so terrible that it mobilized, or frightened, or awakened all kinds of conservatives to a common danger and gave us at least a common determination to battle a common enemy and a determination to save this republic. It gave us all, in short, a determination to repeal the 1970s. That was a dreadful decade. The United States was on the retreat on almost every front. We surrendered to high taxes, to bracket creep, to inflation, gas lines, government meddling evermore in our lives. We surrendered to street crime and the coddling of criminals, to falling educational standards, to steady erosion of traditional values and traditional morality. We surrendered to the ridicule of religion and of the religious and to functional illiteracy. And we surrendered to the notion that America's children no longer are entitled to believe that they will lead lives better than their parents. We retreated in Vietnam, Angola, Ethiopia, Nicaragua, and in the face of OPEC. We surrendered the Panama Canal, closed our eyes to Soviet treaty violations, and at the United Nations apologized obsessively for being America and daring to have national interest. We squirmed helplessly as Iranian fanatics humiliated us and held us hostage for 444 days, and we saw one president after another–Nixon and Ford and Carter–defeated by the problems they faced and turned haggard by the burdens of presidency. America in the 1970s seemed to have grown used to soaring inflation and interest rates, shrinking economic opportunities, abuse and humiliation overseas, and leaders who told us that less is more, small is beautiful, and yesterday was better than tomorrow ever will be.

Well, it was a dreadful, dreadful decade in what happened and what it symbolized. And we became convinced, each in our own way, that what we had to do was oppose that decade and repeal it. This conviction swelled our ranks. It swelled our ranks. It spawned a New Right, the Christian Right, the legions of politically active fundamentalists, the neoconservatives, the ethnic conservatives, the blue-collar Right, the politicized homemakers and others still emerging such as Hispanic and Black conservatives. This conviction also transformed much of the traditionally-cerebral Right into activists.

What gradually happened to each of us in this process is that we realized, perhaps more than we ever had before, that what we were doing was fighting the battle to save the West. In that battle against the 1970s, it became clear to us and to our enemies that we are the West, that we are the affirmation of 3,000 years of tradition, of wrestling with the most basic and profound of issues, with definitions of right and wrong, of human limitations, of good and evil. Unlike the philosophies of the Left, which are a conscious effort to reject and destroy Western tradition, we learned in the 1970s, many of us, that the varieties of conservatives affirmed this tradition. We knew what we wanted to conserve. The Left merely knew what it needed to destroy.

In the 1970s, a searing experience, we found that we pretty much could agree on who were the West's enemies. While each of us had our own hierarchy of who was the worst and which was the worst enemy–and our hierarchies differed then and differ now–we by and large concluded that among the varieties of enemies the West faced, and against which we must battle, were the Soviet Union, big government, big taxers, radical feminists, secular humanists, moral and value relativists, the State Department, the elite media, the new class, United Nations, the Blame America First establishment, and others.

Well, if our differences began narrowing in the 1970s as we fought the common enemy, we became more conscious of what we share as we began to govern in the 1980s. We had no choice but to do so. In opposition, understandably, we had the luxury of being able to take pure, uncompromising positions. But given the chance to make public policy, to serve in government, to provide the analyses and advice to which officials look for guidance–in short, to pursue that broad array of activities of those who govern–we have been forced to bend and compromise where we had not thought possible before. We have realized, as we did not have to do while we were in opposition, we have realized that the best really is the enemy of the good. That the important really often must be sacrificed to the urgent, and that it is essential, above all, to forge alliances. Now, I am not implying that fundamental principles have been abandoned. I don't want to be misunderstood. I simply am stating that we seem to be learning that a fundamental principle need not be the litmus test of every single action. Thus, we have learned to build coalitions on the Right. We find that neocons can work with libertarians on economic issues, even if tensions exist regarding defense policy. We find that traditional conservatives can work with the Christian Right on education and cultural issues, even if tensions remain on the legitimate role of government or in such matters as free trade.

More importantly, we have found that we have begun educating each other. The Christian Right, for example, rarely, very rarely have thought about foreign policy. By working with other conservatives, however, the Christian Right first came to appreciate why the neocons and traditionalists are so concerned about the Soviet threat. And then, as the Christian Right learned more about the Soviet threat, we began to find that members of the Christian Right began supporting a get-tough-with-Moscow foreign policy. On issues of individual liberty, libertarians are growing to understand, though certainly not to support, but at least growing to understand, why the Christian Right so ferociously battles abortion and pornography. And the Christian Right in turn is coming to appreciate why the libertarians so passionately worry about government sanctions against such individual transactions as purchasing publications which may be regarded as pornographic or obtaining an abortion.

The result of this is not enthusiastic support for each other's position. It may not even be support of any kind for each other's position. More typical is friendly tolerance, a word that may offend some, indeed. But what has happened, I see, is a kind of friendly tolerance. And this has meant a significant waning of the testy, even vitriolic confrontation within conservative ranks. Not everywhere to be sure, but most everywhere. Disappearing is the snide reference, at least in public, by one kind of conservative of another. Gone almost entirely, at least in public, is ridicule and animosity. This is extremely significant because it has spawned a kind of mutual respect which allows much closer and more effective cooperation on those issues on which various conservatives do agree, and it keeps eroding the areas of disagreement.

Now, something else has been eroding as well, something which may have contributed to, significantly and still to some extent, the friction between various conservatives. And though it may be improper to bring this up in polite society, I don't think it can be ignored. I'm talking about class, class differences. It's understandable that the cosmopolitan, or academic, or intellectual conservative may have balked at embracing and welcoming into conservative ranks the low church, pulpit-thumping, Bible-waving preacher. Or the activist who mobilized tens of thousands of homemakers against the Equal Rights Amendment or those who make life miserable for abortion advocates. There is a world of difference in tone and education and perhaps upbringing and manners between those gentile conservatives who long have waged the battle of ideas and those street-smart conservatives who have recruited legions of activists for the battle. There is a world of difference between those who chose to spend their lives in the cozy, though embattled, confines of the campus and those who relish life in the trenches. Between those exhilarated by turning a phrase or impaling an adversary on a non sequitur and those who may regard parsing a sentence as an unnatural act. And I think that we can admit it. Some of us enjoyed being a tiny band of intellectual warriors, bereft of political power but comforted by the thought that we were of the elect. There may be some resentment of those who are transforming us from an elite into a majoritarian movement. After all, forty million Frenchmen can't possibly be right. In opposition, these very real differences in class–and I think lifestyle is not quite the right word, class I think is–these differences in class kept some conservatives at arms' length from others. Understandably. Predictably.

The requirements of governing, however, have eroded these barriers considerably. Class frictions within conservative ranks today are much less than they were as recently as 1980. And of course differences have been narrowed because of the Reagan presidency. I'm not only talking about Reagan's policies and actions and how our support for many, but certainly not all of them, forced us to focus on what we have in common. I am reminded of Elliot Abrams' presentation last night of why it's good for the morale of Nicaraguans for us to recognize their country and the Sandinista regime. I'm not sure that's a policy on which we would support the Reagan administration. And recognize our many policies we don't support. I'm talking more about Reagan's style and Reagan's rhetoric, which expresses so much of what we believe.

As conservatives, we long have recognized the importance of rhetoric. And Ronald Reagan's is conservative rhetoric, in many ways, at its best. He says what we want said. And hearing it, I will argue, hearing it has brought us together. His use of the Oval Office as a bully pulpit reflects the conservative ideal of the nation's leader as teacher. Reagan mounts the bully pulpit to inspire and educate. His rhetoric gives us confidence in our system of government, it nurtures America's intrinsic optimism and patriotism, it contrasts extraordinarily with the whining of Nixon, the pessimism of Kissinger, and the self-flagellation of Jimmy Carter. Very few here in fact may fail to be thrilled by the Reagan rhetoric. Many few here may fail to feel a conservative kinship to other conservatives when we hear Reagan talk about America as the last best hope of man on earth, as a Zion in the wilderness, as a city on the hill.

And let me take a moment to recall some of the other things that Reagan says, which I think in fact helps blur some of the differences between conservatives and make it easier for us to work together. In his second inaugural, Reagan asked, "If not us, who? And if not now, when?" He has told us that there are no limits to growth in human progress; our nation is poised for greatness. He has dared brand the Soviet Union an evil empire. And in his recent State of the Union speech, he spoke bluntly of the threat from Soviet forces, from the Soviet drive for domination, from the increase in espionage and state terrorism. Need we remind ourselves of what Cyrus Vance said, in contrast to Reagan's statement, with Cyrus Vance telling us that Carter and Brezhnev "share similar dreams and aspirations on all important issues." And they probably did. In his first inaugural, Reagan concluded with the kind of statement which has echoed through America through its entire history except in the 1970s, a statement which every kind of conservative could make with confidence. He said, "And after all, why shouldn't we believe that? We are Americans."

To be sure, conservatives continue to have differences. We must neither sacrifice our differences nor abandon them. But what we have learned to do is to recognize and focus on more of what we share than on what would divide us. In the recent issue of *Policy Review*, George Nash tells us that this is the moment of conservative opportunity. And I would like to add that this is the moment of conservative challenge. If we are to meet this challenge and exploit this opportunity, we should work together more and we have to work together harder on what we share.

If we are serious about governing, we must move forcefully, let me suggest, on three specific areas in which I believe we have broad agreement. First, we must fight to reduce the role of government in American lives. This means in a very policy-specific way using our various talents to support those policies which cut the government, such as lower taxes, a balanced budget, privatization of services. Second, we must challenge the Soviet Union. This means working together for a policy of rollback based on support for anti-communist, national liberation movements in Angola, Nicaragua, Afghanistan, Mozambique, and elsewhere. It means backing measures which hurt the Soviet Union such as denying them Western credits. It means backing measures which makes maintaining the Soviet Union more costly. It means backing Reagan's Strategic Defense Program, which will deprive the Kremlin of its current ability to brandish nuclear weapons to intimidate or blackmail us. And third, and this I think is most important, we must identify and defeat our enemies here in the United States. We must do a better job of that. We must name, as Midge Decter has advised us, we must name more names. We must identify and defeat our enemies in this country.

At the same time, we must translate our conservative vision and promise, our conservative heritage into a form comprehensible and appealing to whole new groups. In a way, we must become better evangelists. Ours is the good-news gospel and we can be more successful than we have been in explaining to Jews, Blacks, and Hispanics why conservative principles and programs offer them a better economic, social, and political future. With our help, Ronald Reagan has launched a conservative revolution, but only we can make this revolution triumph and only we can make this revolution survive beyond the Reagan presidency. And we can do this only if we prevent our differences from getting in the way of the very much we have in common. If we are to govern, then we must want to govern. And we then must be ready to open our ranks to those whom we need to govern. As an elite, we may be able to lead. But to govern, we must become a majority. Thank you very much.

The Neoconservatives: The Species and Their Origins

By Stephen Tonsor

I feel, ladies and gentlemen, somewhat like Mr. Creedy in the Midas muffler television ad; the engine of the old model of conservatism which I drive is still running well, and I believe that if it ain't broke, don't fix it. I have come to view conservatism as a perennial political philosophy which does not admit of neos or Saturn models. Moreover, my parents and grandparents belong to a generation which had difficulties with hyphenated names, and I am not about to retrace their steps. I became a conservative in 1954. Rather, I should say that I discovered I was a conservative in 1954. The event was not a conversion experience, but a moment of self-revelation and identification. It was not unlike the experience of a friend of mine, a Catholic, who one day on entering a Catholic church reached out his hand to dip it into the holy water font and said with sudden clarity of mind, "My God, what am I doing here?" He left the church and never returned. I dipped my hand in the holy water font of Russell Kirk, and I said, "Home at last."

Whether or not one is a neoconservative is not simply a generational matter. It's not that I am an old party comrade and knew the twelve apostles and those neos who came after us belong to a new and different age. After all, Irving Kristol must be nearly as old as I am. No, there are still young, big-C Conservatives who enter the movement every day and who are as far from "neodom" as I am. Nor is the great divide the consequence of changing times and altered political and economic circumstances. It is not that most neoconservatives think that Barry

Goldwater is cute and ought to be honored and revered and humored now and then, but think that we ought to realize that he belongs to the paleolithic age of conservatism and the Conservative movement. If that indeed is the case, then I too am a paleoconservative, in contrast to the self-styled neoconservatives. It can't simply be that neoconservatives read and often write for *Commentary* magazine. I read *Commentary* and have done so for years. I find myself often in agreement, always stimulated, and now and then put off by *Commentary*. However, I don't think *Commentary* is a reliable test. It often publishes what I consider big-C Conservatives. Age, changed circumstance, and an identifiable literary connection have little or nothing to do with the ideological identity of those on the Right. There, I've uttered that awful word which is usually prefaced by far Right.

No, these differences which separate neoconservatives from Conservatives are differences which have, for nearly a hundred years, divided the Right itself. I have made these personal references because I believe that the way in which I became a conservative, my starting point, was very different from the way in which one becomes a neoconservative. One's starting point, and the way in which one achieves an identity, has very important implications for what one becomes. These differences among conservatives, these differences in the Right are grounded in the relationship of conservatism to modernity.

Increasingly, our culture is becoming aware that it is no longer modern, though it is totally uncertain just why it is. This cultural break with modernity presents us with the preconditions for an accurate assessment of our relationship to modernity. By modernity, I mean that revolutionary movement in culture which derived from a belief in man's radical alienation, in God's unknowability or nonexistence, and in man's capacity to transform or remake the conditions of his existence. The thronging secularism, the attack upon the past, religious and social, aristocratic or bourgeois, the utopian dream of alienation overcome and innocence restored are all linked together in the modernist sensibility. To be up-to-date was for a hundred years to be an alienated person. Indeed, authenticity was another word for alienation. The world was viewed as anarchic chaos upon which man, now become God, imposed his own particular dream of order. Often as not, that order of human invention was an inverted order, an á rebours, against the grain, against nature. Prometheanism and satanism were one and the same order of man's invention. The romantic satanic hero is the same man as the Prometheus of Shelley and Marx, the Zarathustra of Nietzsche. To pretend that the Right and the Conservative movement has been immune to modernity is self-delusion.

On the whole, the Right has been much more modernist than the Left because the Right has dared to think consequentially, because the Right knows that he who says A must also say B. It is for this reason that the modernists of the Right have been almost without exception fascists and totalitarians, for they know that when things fall apart and the center does not hold, the only recourse is to an invented or an imposed order. Now that we are able to gain some perspective on the last century, we recognize that the social and political consequences of modernity are in fact totalitarianism. We can see that the denial of the existence of order as the ground of being and the rejection of the transcendent are a one-way street–a one-way street to Dachau. If everything is permitted and the will to power is the only reality, then the gulag is as logical as an Euler diagram. Those who do not refuse to think the unthinkable have known this for a long while. Hitler did not need to give a written command, no, not even a verbal command for the Final Solution. Hitler and the members of the SS Einsatzgruppen knew the Final Solution was implicit in their conception of reality. It is on the ground of modernity that Right and Left are merged and the differences between them are only differences of style and slogans. The Right, which is born of modernity, is a radical, a revolutionary Right which cannot in any important degree be distinguished from the revolutionary Left.

Now, it is a matter of fact that most of those who describe themselves as neoconservatives are or have been cultural modernists. They have been, to use Peter Berger's telling phrase, baptized in the fiery brook. Peter Berger was making an elegant pun on the name of Ludwig Feuerbach, the left-Hegelian inspiration of Marx and the church father of alienation theory. We conservatives have been baptized in the Jordan, and there is a vast difference between the Jordan and the fiery brook. That is the telling difference which separates conservatives from neoconservatives.

It has always struck me as odd and even perverse that former Marxists have been permitted, yes, invited to play such a leading role in the Conservative movement in the 20th century. It is splendid when the town whore gets religion and joins the church. Now and then, they make good choir directors. But when she begins to tell the minister what he ought to say in his Sunday sermons, matters have been carried too far.

Conservatism has had some strange camp followers in these last thirty years. I once remarked to Glen Campbell that had Stalin spared Leon Trotsky and not had him murdered in Mexico by Frank Jackson, he would no doubt have spent his declining days in an office in the Hoover Library, writing memoirs and contributing articles of a faintly neoconservative flavor for *Encounter* magazine and *Commentary*.

Is it ungracious of me to suggest that political and even religious conversion does not often improve the mind's capacity for a sound judgment? Whittaker Chambers, whom I find one of the most beguiling intellectuals of the 20th century, had a flawed judgment. He had a flawed judgment as a Marxist, and he said some very silly things on the subject of conservatism when he became a convert. All of which is not to say that the rejection of Marxism is unimportant and that the piecemeal rejection of various articles of faith shared with left-liberal modernists is unimportant, nor do I wish to imply that the assistance of neoconservatives is unwelcome in the work of dismantling the failed political structures erected by modernity. Conservatives have made common cause with classical liberals, and there is no reason why they should not make common cause with neoconservatives. When the wagon train is attacked, we arm the women and the children even though they may in their ineptitude occasionally mistake the friend for the foe.

Still, halfway from modernity is not far enough. Politics has always been inseparable from culture, and both derive ultimately from religion. It is absurd to believe that one can remain a modernist in culture and reject the implications of modernism in politics. Unbelief is incompatible with conservatism. Conserve what and to what end? Werner Dannhauser, writing in the December 1985 number of *Commentary* tells us, and I quote, "Too many conservatives have failed to come to terms with Nietzsche's thought, thank God, dismissing it as an embarrassing attempt to outflank them on the right, but the challenge he represents will not go away." Dannhauser continues, "Nietzsche went far beyond Burke, who held out the hope of a time when atheism might cease to be fashionable. Nietzsche postulated an irreversible loss of naivete in western civilization. To put the matter crudely, he argued that the cat of atheism was out of the bag. The meanest capacities could learn that religion was a myth. And when a myth is exposed for what it is, it can no longer serve to provide a unified horizon." Dannhauser continues further, "Too many conservatives whose own belief is weak and nonexistent, who will privately admit that religion is for the troops, continued to try to teach the catechism to those troops, forgetting that the latter have by now been thoroughly exposed to the Enlightenment and its lessons." There you have it. The dividing line between conservatives and neoconservatives is the line separating Burke from Nietzsche. Let me say parenthetically that I could never understand the reasoning processes, and I came even to doubt the ability of these men to read, of Jews who are Nietzscheans.

Walter Kaufmann, who was on the whole both more honest and more sophisticated than Dannhauser, was quite unable to discern that while Nietzsche was not a biological racist, he was a philosophical antisemite. If Nietzsche's antisemitism was less vulgar than that of Julius Schrecker or of Nietzsche's friend, Richard Wagner, it was no less deadly. One is struck again by the true and forceful portrait Thomas Mann gives us of the Nietzschean modernist in the person of Adrian Leverkuhn in Mann's great novel *Doctor Faustus*. Adrian's music is modernist music. Adrian is a composer. Not only as a style, as a musical style, but in terms of the metaphysical conception out of which the music is constructed. It is also demonic music. It can only come into existence through the ruin of a soul, the destruction of a mind. And as the work of the composer reaches fruition, Germany is destroyed philosophically and sinks into ruin beneath the rain of Allied bombs.

Mann, who made the character of Adrian Leverkuhn of a composite of Nietzsche and Arnold Schoenberg, intended in this–the greatest novel I think of the 20th century–to tell us something about the cultural reality of our age. The narrator, Serenus Zeitblom, is a religious and pious conservative, one I take it who had missed the Enlightenment of which Dannhauser is so fond. I sometimes imagine myself and my fellow conservatives to be of the type of Serenus Zeitblom. We have a loving regard for our age and our fellow men, and we realize that we must often forgo intervention and permit the tragic drama to play itself out. Because Adrian Leverkuhn could not accept an order which, modernist that he was, he felt to be meaningless, he imposed a new order, rational and cleanly articulated as the music of Bach. But lacking Bach's attachment to the divine and reconciliation to the human, Leverkuhn's achievement was a great technical triumph, but only a triumph of technique. It is fitting funeral music for a culture which died of pride. Rational technique and the pursuit of irrational ends, that suggests the modernist condition.

That is why neoconservatives are so inventive and often correct in dealing with the realm of technique. But when push comes to shove, as it always does in society and culture, ends are of ultimate importance and will finally determine the appropriate technique. What the neoconservatives have done is to divorce techniques from ends in an effort to maintain their cultural modernism while rejecting its social and political implications. This I say is quite impossible and, in the long run, dangerous. It is easy to see that the utopian social and political programs of the last hundred years have failed. It is not the cat of atheism that has been let out of the bag, but the failure of the Enlightenment in all its forms. Neoconservatives are, as Irving Kristol remarked, liberals who had been mugged by reality. But while they have been detached from their social and political myths, they have not located themselves in a body of principle which makes life worth living or that one would die defending. Much as I admire the views of Irving Kristol, which I find regularly propounded in the *Wall Street Journal*, I would not, to quote Whittaker Chambers, storm up a beach defending those views.

It is important to remember that neoconservatism is made up of those liberals who were mugged by reality, though that phrase is only a part of the truth about neoconservatism. It is above all a transmogrification of what has been called the New York Intellectuals. The New York Intellectuals, in turn, were a reflection of the instantiation of modernity among secularized Jewish intellectuals. Neoconservatism is culturally unthinkable aside from the history of the Jewish intellectual in America in the 20th century. When the New York intellectuals turned from the beguilements of left-wing revolutionary utopianism, they did not in fact become conservatives, but attached themselves to positions which were neoliberal in the sense that Mises and von Hayek were neoliberals. And just as Mises and von Hayek are, above all, philosophical and cultural modernists, so too New York intellectuals who now call themselves neoconservatives are modernists.

Conservatism has its roots in a much older tradition. It's a worldview which is essentially Roman and Anglo-Catholic. Its political philosophy is Aristotelian and Thomist, its concerns moral and ethical, its culture that of Christian humanism. Most old-fashioned conservatives are free of metaphysical anxiety and as happy as clams in a world which bares the unmistakable imprint of God's ordering hand. They are free of alienation. They believe that human institutions and human culture are subject to the judgment of God, and they hold that the most effective political instrument is prayer and a commitment to try and understand and do the will of God. If neoconservatives wish us to take their conservatism seriously, they must return to their religious roots, the religious roots, beliefs, and values of our common heritage. They cannot dither in the halfway house of modernity and offer us technical solutions which touch the symptoms, but which never deal with the causes of contemporary disorder.

CHAPTER 2

The Future of Reaganomics

April 7-9, 1989
Philadelphia, Pennsylvania

Saturday, April 8
10:00-11:30

The Future of Reaganomics

Edwin J. Feulner, Jr.

Martin Anderson

Allan H. Meltzer

The Future of Reaganomics

By Martin Anderson

[The opening of Anderson's talk is indiscernible]

There's been some more reports that taxes must go up, will go up, despite what President Bush pledged during the campaign. And many people I know believe that a major recession is coming soon for sure. That's not a pretty picture. Deficits are everywhere as far as you can see, and the dollar is falling. Taxes are about to be raised a lot with a major recession knocking at the door, not to mention state and local (indiscernible). And yet there's something that's not quite right about this difficult picture in the American economy including (indiscernible). In fact, sometimes I get the uneasy feeling that things are pretty good and might even get better.

There's nothing more frustrating than psyching yourself up for the worst and then being overwhelmed by good news. First point to note is that the economy is remarkably frisky in spite of all the reports of doom and gloom. And following all the economic forecasters, the United States economy has had at least seventy-five straight months of economic growth. That's the longest stretch of steady and sustained economic growth that we have ever had in the United States, at least since they started keeping statistics back in 1824. And nobody saw it coming, not even President Reagan's most optimistic advisors back in 1981, 1982, had any idea that by 1989, we'd be basking in the glow of record economic growth.

While economic growth was moving along, another record was set. Since November of 1982, we've created something in the order of nineteen million new jobs in the United States. And that's more jobs than ever before created during a like period of time. And, contrary to popular wisdom, they were good jobs by and large. Fifty percent paid more than $20,000 a year. And the amount of goods and services produced was phenomenal. For the past five years, we have produced over 20 billion dollars' worth of goods and services. And that's an amount greater than that ever produced by any other country on the earth. It's an amount almost too large to comprehend. Congress likes to measure things like economic recessions and depressions and economic expansions. When they do so, like in the Great Depression of the 1930s, they usually apply three measuring sticks. So, it's the amount of goods and services produced, we look at the number of jobs created, we look at the number of months during which economic growth increased steadily, and we also look a little bit at the stock market. So, by those standards, by those criteria, we have just witnessed, during the past six years, the greatest economic expansion in the history of the world.

And during this great expansion, we also did some other unusual things. Inflation was driven down, and it stayed down. Interest rates dropped. People's real incomes, after inflation and taxes, began to rise. And then let's take a little look at the stock market values, a very interesting real index of how people feel about (indiscernible). The American press was traumatized by the 1987 crash. They often portray the stock market as shaky and declining. But if you step back and look at the entire record over the last twenty years or so, look at the sweep, the picture is much, much more reassuring. For example, using the Standard and Poor's stock price index, back in the early 1970s, the index grew at about 100. Ten years later, after Watergate, four years of Jimmy Carter and his liberal friends, the index had climbed all the way up to 125. And it's roughly, on average, about 25 percent gain over ten years, averaging about 2.5 percent a year. As we entered the 1980s, the market slowed temporarily and by the summer of 1982, it was almost as low as it was in the early 1970s. Then look at what happened. Beginning in the summer of 1982, the stock market, like some giant rocket, went sharply up and took off. The trend for the last six years has been remarkably consistent and strong. And today, even after the shock of the 1987 crash, the index sits around 285 last time I looked, which is over 250 percent higher than it was in the summer of 1982, just six years ago. How can this be? How can things be so good when they were just so bad?

I think there are two basic reasons that explain how we did so well when so many are convinced we're doing badly. I think first of all, some of the bad news is not quite as bad as it seems. And then there are some things going on which have been largely ignored in terms of the impact they have on the economy. First, the bad news: the federal deficit. Yes, it is too large, and we must make every effort to reduce it. But contrary to some popular impressions, it is not increasing, and it is not dangerously high. The best professional judgment now shows the federal deficit declining in the years ahead depending on whether you accept the administration's forecast or CBO's forecast, it is expected to decline to a level that is somewhere between 40 billion dollars and 130 billion dollars a year by 1993. I know that's a wide range, but that's pretty good for [economic forecasters]. The important thing is it's declining. And as a percentage of GNP, the deficit is now expected to drop to what I would call manageable levels. We tend to forget something. The size of our economy is now approaching 5 trillion dollars a year. By 1993, projections show that the deficit will lie somewhere between 1 and 2 percent of the GNP. And that's a deficit range we had during the administration of John F. Kennedy, Lyndon Johnson, and Richard Nixon.

Perhaps the most important factor that's contributing to the unexpectedly good economy are the government's policies on taxes and regulation. Last year, the effective marginal tax rate dropped from 38 percent to 28 percent. Now that's a whopping 26 percent decline. As far as I know, not many econometric models tried to calculate the effect this tax rate cut would have on people's decisions to invest money, to save money, and to produce. So obviously this does have a significant impact, and it may be, may be the most important reason, why the economy continues to thunder along. In addition to the government regulations that have changed, I think the most important factor on the regulatory front has been the improvement of the general climate for business regulation. The prospects for new, intrusive regulation of business have declined dramatically. In recent years, government regulations of business have stabilized. People have little fear of new, unexpected regulations. So, I would say on the home front, there are three things that are declining and when combined together have a major impact: one, declining tax rates; two, declining deficits; and three, declining business regulations. And all three together have combined to provide a stimulus for an unexpectedly strong economy.

But then there have been other factors. In fact, I think there are two other major factors that have contributed to our economic prosperity more than the ones I've mentioned so far. They never get incorporated into economic forecast models, and they are possible (indiscernible). First, there are revolutionary political changes taking place in many countries. Literally, a new wave of capitalism is sweeping across the face of the world. In the last ten years, country after country has begun to move away from centrally planned economies towards freer markets. The government controls have been swept away wholesale, tax rates lowered, trade barriers reduced, and government-owned businesses have been privatized. We have seen it happen in Canada and in England. It has happened in France, Australia, and New Zealand. And there have been truly revolutionary changes in the Communist China as over one billion people have begun to move towards a freer economy.

Perhaps the most extraordinary of all is what's going on in the Soviet Union and Gorbachev's perestroika, which, by the way, every time I read about it in the press it's defined as economic restructuring. When Gorbachev, himself, in around page fifty in his book, defined it himself.[26] He says, "You know, most people would look at this word and interpret it literally as economic restructuring, but I do not mean it that way. I mean in its full sense: revolution." The key elements of the Communist economy have been thrown overboard and replaced with some of the building blocks of capitalism. Even in countries such as Angola and Vietnam they are decentralizing and moving towards a greater degree of capitalism.

In fact, so much has happened so fast in so many places, it's literally breathtaking. And no one is systematically keeping track of it all. The clues that you get from daily newspapers, television, magazines tell a tremendous story. For example, just a small thing. About a month ago, Iraq started a stock market. And the paper reports that the reason they started the stock market was they started privatizing and selling things off, they suddenly had a shortage of capital, and they started the stock market. Even Sweden, where most of my ancestors came from, the Holy Mother of socialism. It's stunning, the sudden reversal of ideology, adopted key elements of Reaganomics. They announced tax reform that includes a reduction in personal income tax rates by as much as fifty percent. And then, one of my favorite stories: Recently, the *Wall Street Journal* carried the story that the Soviet Union had just issued a new coin. The design of the coin celebrates Christianity, depicting Vladimir I, the man who introduced Christianity to Russia, holding a large cross. Now that's something that was unthinkable a few years ago. It's a symbol of a small degree of revolutionary changes that are occurring in country after country. Basically, we are in the midst of a profound worldwide change in our political and economic institutions. A freer world economy is good for the United States of America.

And there's one final factor on the world scene that, maybe, I think, the most important of all and the effect it's having on our current and future economic prosperity, and that is world peace. Peace is breaking

26 Mikhail Gorbachev, *Perestroika: New Thinking for Our Country and the World* (New York: Harper Collins, 1987).

out all over. When historians ten to fifteen years from now look back at the eight years of the Reagan administration, I think they will conclude that Ronald Reagan's most important achievement was this: he turned the nuclear arms race around. Today, both the United States and Soviet Union are busily engaged in bilateral nuclear disarmament. Under the terms of the INF Treaty, some 2,611 nuclear missiles are being destroyed. There are prospects in the START negotiations that it is possible we may even destroy up to 50 percent of those nuclear missiles that threaten to annihilate us all. The Soviet Union pulled its troops out of Afghanistan now (indiscernible). Iran and Iraq have declared a ceasefire and on and on.

I think that what has happened is attributable to two things. The first has been the powerful buildup in our national defenses, tremendous increase in military spending, which was largely made possible by the sound economic policies the government has been following for the last eight or nine years. And also by—which I think will be looked at as another major achievement of the Reagan administration—the reintroduction of an old idea called defense and beginning of SDI, building our protective missile system.

By the way, I've got to mention one thing. Last night when I was listening to Ed Meese speak and heard other people talking about him—I want to tell you a secret about Ed Meese. Back in 1981, '82, he was the fellow that pulled together and chaired a small committee inside the White House to set the stage for SDI, modern experts had a meeting with President Reagan. He never gets credit for being a nuclear (indiscernible).

And why is world peace so important to economic growth? Because of how people view the future. As the prospects of war, and possibly nuclear annihilation, fade, people's time horizons tend to lengthen, they tend to plan further out in the future. And any time the discount rate drops, we all know, that affects long term interest rates (indiscernible). The end result is what is going on is going to be very good for the U.S. economy.

And just summing up, I argue there are some very strong powerful reasons why the U.S. economy has been so strong, why the stock market has surged up since 1982. And it is not a coincidence. It goes directly to economic expansion and the tremendous upward movement in the stock market that began that same year, 1982. It just happened to be the same year that President Reagan's comprehensive economic policy was put in place and implemented. And during that same time that the general economic climate was improving in the United States, it has also begun to improve all across the world—primarily because of the gradual, slow freeing up of so many closed statist societies. And now, in the last year or two, another vital element has been added: the sharply improving prospects for a greater degree of world peace. If that trend continues and if the superpowers continue to pursue effective nuclear disarmament, the effect on the world economy can only be positive.

So, there are three things I think that determine what the future of economic prosperity in the United States is going to be. The first is sound economic policy. Keeping tax rates low, cutting some existing taxes such as the capital gains tax even further, controlling the federal deficit by controlling the growth of federal spending, and moving towards less, not more, government regulation of business. Bush's election in 1988 ensured the continuation and advancement of Reagan's economic policy. The second is the spread of capitalism around the world. And third is world peace.

And I just want to say one final word. A lot of people have referred to this as the Reagan Revolution. It was not. Reagan was part of the revolution. He became its political leader, but he did not give it life. All you're seeing is the result of a political and intellectual revolution that has been sweeping not only across the United States, but across the entire globe. It was caused by not a handful of people or hundreds of people. It wasn't caused by millions of people either. It was caused by thousands of people, people who worked long and hard for at least the last twenty-five, thirty, forty years. And these are the people who wrote the books and the articles, who talked about economic issues, politics, law, philosophy. These are the people who published the magazines, the newspapers, and worked in radio and television. These are people who taught in the universities and worked in the think tanks. These are the people who worked on the political campaign, and a few actually ran for public office. These are people who accepted political appointments and tried to make government work. Working alone, none of them could have made it happen. But together, it was the efforts of thousands of people that did make it happen.

And today, we are in the midst of a profound intellectual political revolution that is still developing. In the twenty-five years of the Philadelphia Society, the men and women who comprise it, have been on the cutting edge of this movement. I think that's the real heritage of the Philadelphia Society. The best is yet to come. As Ronald Reagan has often said: "You ain't seen nothing yet."

Is America Big Enough for Conservatives, Too?

By Allan Meltzer

Thank you. It's hard to follow Martin Anderson when you're talking about Ronald Reagan because few people know as much about Ronald Reagan or had as much experience with Ronald Reagan as Martin Anderson (indiscernible).

Anthony Downs in his classic work on political economy told us that politicians are not elected to choose programs.[27] They choose programs to get elected. In this view of politics, principle or vision has little role. And in the ordinary making of politics, or the ordinary workings of politics, perhaps this cynical view is apparent.

President Reagan had a vision. At times, he was able to translate that vision into a strategy and even to develop some tactical procedures for moving that vision and its strategy into legislation. The areas in which he was most successful, his administration was most successful, were things like tax cuts, tax changes, the large defense buildup, the Strategic Defense Initiative. But there were areas where he was less successful or not very successful at all, where he failed to accomplish his purposes. Deregulation would be a case, I believe, where the vision of a deregulated society was not put forward in the same strategic way, or the same strategy that might have been developed, for example, for translating the idea of a smaller tax share through a program for tax deduction and finally getting that program implemented. In Central

27 Anthony Downs, *An Economic Theory of Democracy* (New York: Harper & Row, 1957).

America, as Ed Meese said last night, the administration was not very good at converting its vision into a strategy and the strategy into a tactic. So in those areas, the administration was less than successful or not very successful at all.

The role of academics and speakers is to shape the vision and perhaps to develop the strategy. To create a demand in the polity for the vision, or at least for the strategy—and there may be a difference. Whether the public shares our vision, they may be willing at times to accept our strategy. But that will only happen if we, in fact, do the hard work of developing the vision, developing the strategy, and finding people who are able to translate it into a tactical program that succeeds.

In the eight years that Ronald Reagan occupied the White House, and his administration helped power Washington, they enacted large parts of the vision that he had originally announced in his 1981 campaign and subsequently developed. Our task is not to wait for another Reagan, it is to shape the popular vision and develop strategies for the future that will be eventually translated into those parts of the program which the Reagan administration was unable to carry forward and those parts of the program which the Reagan administration, or others, have simply not paid attention to. We have plenty of time, I think.

When I listened to President Bush—since our topic today is the Reagan Revolution and how long it will last, I thought about listening to President Bush deliver his State of the Union address sometime in February. The vision that came to me from that talk was the vision of government as a problem solver. There were programs for the environment, programs for daycare, and a host of others. I was reminded of an impoverished Lyndon Johnson, who described his purse as empty, but his heart filled with the programs that could, with governmental action, improve the way in which society operated. To extend the (indiscernible) initiatives in areas like savings and loans, where there is an absence of any incentives, where government assumes responsibilities, perhaps necessarily, for mistakes of the past without developing a set of incentives that would be important to making sure that the mistakes of the past would not be repeated. Or in areas like the international debt or government proposals to simply tear up or twist arms to remove some of the long-term, developed features of contracts in order to achieve some temporary aid, for example, things like sharing clause, or subordination clause in contracts which the banks are asked to, or told to, give up.

The greater vision, perhaps best enunciated in his [Reagan's] Moscow University speech, freedom and the role of the individual were paramount. Well, it's not anti-government, but it was a vision of limiting government. Government had a role in society, but it was ultimately individuals that mattered. It is difficult to hear that vision being enunciated, or put forward, in the current policy-making (indiscernible). Reagan spoke at Moscow about freedom and "the continuing revolution of the marketplace," or a reform, if it is not institutionalized, will always be insecure. He understood that that vision had to be institutionalized and there had to be a strategy and a means of carrying it forward, as well as a tactic, that he sometimes would win or lose in trying to implement the strategy. What is George Bush's vision? What is the vision of his administration? They see government, as I said, as a problem solver. There are no signs of vision, at least I see no signs of vision that guided Ronald Reagan and at its best, guided his administration. What we have are mainly tactics.

So many of the achievements of the Reagan administration are at risk, but many of them will survive. They will survive principally because on many of the issues, the public has what it wants. It wanted lower taxes, and it has lower taxes. And if you ask them, as they often are asked like in media campaigns, whether they would like to see taxes raised, overwhelmingly they answer no. In the two elections, they have translated their view of policy, or recent tax policy, at the polls. In areas like defense, they perhaps face greater risk.

Reaganomics, at least as I understood it, consisted of four particular programs. Principally: lower taxes, reduced role of government, lower inflation, and a stronger defense. So, as we look forward, we want to ask: What is likely to survive? As I understand in my view, there are no large tax increases likely without an emergency. Without a tax increase, there will be no large increase in government spending. There will be limits. There will be limits to the size of the cuts in the past. The reason I believe that is that the Reagan program, large parts of the Reagan program, appeal to the public. Voters, as I pointed out, do not favor tax increases. Most assume when they are asked that Congress has the main responsibility for the deficit and therefore [plays] the key role in trying to bring it down. Most favor a solution in which the deficit is reduced by seeing government spending reduced. Seventy percent of the population thinks that more taxes will mean more spending. We've been successful in translating that view, policy, into a program that the public has bought. So, they want spending reduction. Of course, they don't agree on which spending should be cut. So, not much will be done to cut spending or raise taxes. That vision, or that aspect, of the Reagan Revolution is likely to continue. There are some minor exceptions: cigarette taxes, liquor taxes, or senior (indiscernible). You may see some changes in those areas. But on the broad issue of taxation, the public largely has accepted the policy views, the vision, the strategy, that marked the early years, particularly, in the Reagan administration.

Defense is quite another matter. The last time I spoke here I emphasized, some years ago, there are major issues, such as the size of government, taxes, defense, the political system works when the public gets what it wants. That doesn't mean that our role is simply to carry out what the voters express in the polls. We can make a difference on the margin, but only on the margin, by trying to convince them to raise their sights and to look forward to a society of liberty and freedom.

To remove from the American scene, to the British scene, one sees a different, more aggressive, larger vision of what can be accomplished through the political system. Margaret Thatcher has, I think, demonstrated clearly that in the political process there is still a lot that can be accomplished. Like politicians with that, we were able to translate the vision into a strategy, and the strategy into a tactical program, for reforming virtually all the institutions with that (indiscernible). So, we have much to do in our future work trying to catch up to some of the reforms in education, healthcare, regulation, privatization where our British cousins have in many ways taken the lead from us.

Finally, it is important not to neglect what has been accomplished so far. Martin Anderson gave, I think, a very good picture of some of the achievements of the Reagan administration, and I won't repeat them. The bigger question that we want to face is not how well we can glory in what we've achieved in the 1980s, but what we can look forward to achieving by the year 2000.

And one of those achievements, quite apart from the economics but I want to emphasize, is to look back and think about what a professor of economic development might have told his classes in the 1950s through the 1960s. To use an ordinary textbook, he would have assured them that there were two ways for economic development. There was the planned economy and the market economy. And there were these and these advantages of the planned economy and these and these advantages of the market economy. The great change that has taken place since the '50s and '60s, I believe, is that no one any longer believes that. Some are stuck with a system that they don't want, but no one believes that those two systems are going to be equally powerful and useful in developing income or raising standards of living. The reason for that is not just the work that we've done, but the way in which events have worked out. No one can ignore the experiment that has been run, the powerful experiment that is visible to everyone, most of all to people who live in that other system. And that's the experiment where you compare North and South Korea, East and West Germany, Hong Kong, Taiwan, Singapore, and mainland China, Where you have the same people, the same history, and the same culture, and vastly different standards of living at the end of the last forty years.

Those events have made a difference, just as, in a more modest way, the events that we celebrate in the Reagan Revolution have made an important difference in people's attitudes toward the role of government, the size of taxes, importance of defense, the kinds of things that we would like to celebrate when we think about the achievements of the Reagan Revolution. Thank you.

CHAPTER 3

Conservative Reflections on the End of the Cold War

April 26-28, 1991
Boston, Massachusetts

Friday, April 26
7:00-9:00PM

Conservative Reflections on the End of the Cold War

Lowell C. Smith, Chairman

William F. Buckley Jr.,
"A Few Reflections on War & Peace"

Saturday, April 27
12:00-2:00

Charles Heatherly, Chairman

Edwin Meese III,
"Success Is the Best Revenge: Looking Back on the Eighties"

A Few Reflections on the End of the Cold War

By William F. Buckley

Thank you, ladies and gentlemen, and thank you, President Lowell Smith. I'm happy to be among my fellow truth seekers. All of us are very much animated by the successes which we have had in our common ventures. It isn't often, is it, that we get such a gratifying testimony as we recently had. I think of Robert Heilbroner writing in *Dissent*. He said, as I'm sure all of you noticed in your regular reading of *Dissent*—and those of you who didn't see it, they may have picked it up when republished in the *Wall Street Journal*. He wrote, "Capitalism has been as unmistakable a success as socialism has been a failure." Here is the part that's hard to swallow: "It has been the Friedmans, Hayeks, von Miseses who have maintained that capitalism would flourish, and that socialism would develop incurable ailments. All three have regarded capitalism as the natural system of free man. All have maintained that left to its own devices, capitalism would achieve material growth more successfully than any other system. From this admittedly impressionistic and incomplete sampling, I draw the following discomforting generalization: The further to the right one looks, the more prescient has been the historical foresight; the further to the left, the less so."

It is good to know that we in Philadelphia Society have been here all these years, this little priesthood, irradiating the little illumination that is the ember of the Philadelphia Society. Tom Wolfe said, at the 35th anniversary of *National Review*—he saw nothing wrong in gloating from time to time. I'm not sure I'd use the same word, but what is exactly the right word to describe the pleasures one takes in empirical verification of postulates we've held leading to conclusions we've insisted lie at the other end of soritical exercises leading from those postulates. We're entitled to celebrate. A celebration is prescribed, indeed, even scheduled, in the Lenten season. In our world, it is always a Lenten season, in that there is nothing even the Philadelphia Society can do to root out either invincible ignorance or the wreckage that ensues from the writhings and thrashings of the iconoclastic imperative. But every now and again, we have our (indiscernible) Sundays, in which we rejoice, and there is much to rejoice over, even as we know that when the clock strikes twelve, we'll need to redouble our efforts merely to maintain the ground we have achieved, because doubters tend to breed faster than believers—it being a human temptation to take shortcuts in attempting to realize utopia. And shortcuts are almost always attempted through the instrumentality of the state, which at once can organize armies of soldiers to fight for liberty, and armies of soldiers, and policemen, and bureaucrats to attenuate liberty and to enslave.

Having arrived quite by accident into the use of martial language, I remind myself that when our commodore, Don Lipsett, asked me in February to give a title to my "speech," as he insisted on calling it, I paused to remark that it is a relief to hear something I say referred to as a speech. It is almost universally now referred to as a presentation, as in, "We all thank Mr. Buckley for his fine presentation." I'm always tempted, when that happens to me, which is almost always, to rise and say that I give presentations only when I'm attempting to persuade a corporation to advertise in *National Review*. You will note from the scarcity of such ads that, self-evidently, Mr. Buckley does not make fine presentations. In any event, as many of you have known, Don Lipsett, through prestidigitative techniques not equally mastered by any other human being on earth, with the exception of Mother Theresa, manages to deploy muscles of steel which are guaranteed to prevail over your own inclinations. In this case, as in every other—in my case—to defer to the last minute the selection of the title and text of any presentation. So insistent was he that I finally blurted out over electronic MCI from Switzerland last February: "Call it 'Reflections on War and Peace.'" Indeed, that is how he has advertised my remarks to this, my favorite forum. And lo, what is on my mind is questions of war and peace.

I will proceed as I am given to doing by affirming a few propositions, with some of which I hope many of you will agree. If not, I have known rejection before. Once upon a time, I was even rejected by Robert Heilbroner. My first proposition is that our victory in the Cold War gives us ground for great satisfaction, but satisfaction diluted by historical humility. All the joy that effloresced during the months after the Berlin Wall came down was heartfelt. We were, after all, talking about 110 million people who lived behind the Iron Curtain, not counting the Soviet Union's 250 million. But what these people can't reasonably be expected to have is a large appetite for the great gurgles of self-satisfaction coming up from Western opinion brewers, who, filing their fingernails, are advised, as to paraphrase Anthony Lewis, "We told you it would be all okay if we just waited it out." The human tendency is to forget quickly, and conveniently, past suffering, especially if it was other people's suffering—most especially if you were conceivably responsible for it, as we were in major ways responsible for suffering behind the Iron Curtain, beginning in Yalta and up through the failure over the decades of successive administrations to pursue liberationist strategic analysis. And looking over the dead wall—if there is contrition going on among the hundreds of thousands of Soviet agents, including Mr. Gorbachev, who imprisoned, tortured, and killed during the past forty years—their grief is stoically self-contained. The Jewish community will never let the world forget about the Holocaust, understandably so. Every living German is aware of that Holocaust—most of them unborn when it happened. By contrast, not one in 500 Westerners could answer the question: "How many Ukrainians were starved to death by Stalin in 1932, '33?" And not one in 1,000 would know that that figure is higher than that for all those killed during the Holocaust. One wonders how many Oliver Stones, so mindful of the suffering associated with Vietnam, will, during the next ten years, devote their splendid indignant energies to dramatizing the fate of Eastern Europe during the forty-four years just past.

We can sleep better for knowing that our cousins have regained their freedom, but we can't bring back to life those who lost their lives, nor bring back lifetimes in freedom to those who spent theirs without civil liberty. Like the Jews who survived the Holocaust, we are left only with the moral mandate, "It must not happen again, to the extent that we can prevent it," which raises instantly such vexing questions as: Might we have prevented the slaughter among the Kurds? And derivatively, because the answer is, of course, yes, we could have prevented it, would it have been prudent to do so? Strategically sophisticated? Historically mature? Politically advisable?

Before opining on this question, I am drawn to probe the future of those so recently emancipated, and accordingly proffer my next proposition, which is that it is unlikely that Adam Smith can save the East European states, let alone the Soviet Union. In *National Review*, a year ago, Milton Friedman told us that—in his habitually unassailable judgment—the newly-liberated East European states need to take drastically anti-statist steps in order to make substantial economic progress. What he says, of course, applies *a fortiori* to the Soviet Union. Mr. Friedman believes that any state that has suffered from so protracted an experience with socialism cannot handle the problem of economic resuscitation while simultaneously taking on the welfare load routinely accepted by affluent Western democracies. If Mr. Friedman is correct, the alternatives faced by Poland, Bulgaria, Romania, Czechoslovakia, are of international consequence. We may find ourselves dealing with people who have a vision of liberty and prosperity, who, then denied prosperity, are attracted to false utopianism. Hermann Göring testified at Nuremberg that it was as simple as this: that in 1933, Germany had no alternative than to move in the direction that it did. Within the Soviet

Union, the situation is somewhere between desperate and chaotic. In Germany, it is the socialists who in the past few weeks have profited from the hard realism Mr. Friedman speaks of as necessary.

It's worth it to travel in the Soviet Union, as many of you have, of course, done—sometimes, to be sure, voyeuristically. Personal experiences stay usefully in the memory. There are, of course, significant changes brought on by glasnost. Yet although the marketplace has been officially acclaimed as to be preferred to a command economy, it isn't only in the public sector that it fails to work. It is even in the little recesses of the private sector. The cultural ignorance of the free market, and of course, deficiency, is very quickly apparent. For instance, to guests of the Intourist Hotel in Moscow, the economic idea of arbitrage, the process that prompts people to buy a product where it is cheap and sell it where it is dear until prices level out, has not even worked its wonders within the Intourist Hotel in Moscow, let alone in greater Moscow, let alone in greater Russia. On the second floor of the Intourist Hotel, you can buy five ounces of caviar for $29.00. On the first floor, the same can cost $44.00.

Outside, the five of you who are traveling together ask for a taxi to go to a museum. You're told that five passengers are too many for one taxi—that you will need two taxis. And to take you to where you are going will be $5.00 per cab. You hesitate ever so briefly to digest alternatives, and the Russian driver becomes an entrepreneur in the Russian style. "Well," he tells you grandly, "You're not to worry." He will make an exception and take all five of you in his one cab for $10.00.

You need to telephone a companion staying in another room. You call the operator. It rings busy. It rings busy for an hour. It's very important, so you descend to the hotel reception desk and ask the woman at the desk: "Where is Mr. Peter Samara staying?" What then happens is on the order of asking your grandmother to come up with a picture of her high-school graduation. The receptionist holds up a lapful of yellow slips and begins to go over them one by one. At the end, she says, "He is not here." "Yes, he is here," you insist, "he's been here for two days." "He is not here," she repeats. At that moment, Peter shows up. You exchange intelligence, and ask for his room number, which is 601, so that from now on, you can dial him directly. The next morning, you wish to call 601. You follow the hotel dialing instructions. To call 601, you must dial 2032097. Well, you can handle that. Does that mean that to call 602, you would dial 2032098? No, 2035040. At 3:30 p.m., on your way out, you report to the concierge that your toilet has stopped up. You come in at 11:00 p.m. and note that it is still stopped up. At 9:00 a.m., it is still stopped up. It occurs to anyone scheduled to check out of the hotel that morning that there is an obvious way to leave the mark of his displeasure.

The airport in Moscow is an extension of hotel life. You arrive three hours before flight time, as you are told to do. You need to complete a form which reminds you of Professor Parkinson's book, *One-Upmanship*, because you are not given, where crucial, room enough to supply the information Moscow desires in its glasnostian fury to get from you. If you're carrying $87.00, you're required to write out not merely 87, but eighty-seven dollars in approximately a third of an inch of space on a form which no Russian in his right mind, which includes some Russians, is ever going to read. Somehow, it is not as it was in previous visits. There is the occasional smile—not universal, granted. Gorbachev hasn't in a couple of years made Moscow into Tahiti. His popularity, according to a recent poll, is about the equal of Lyndon LaRouche in the United States. What exactly is the voice of the Russian people is not easy to determine. It would be presumptuous to infer from the popularity of Mr. Yeltsin that their voice is the same as the voice of those who, two hundred years ago, were instructed by the insights of Adam Smith.

My ensuing proposition is that the decline of the Soviet Union cannot be arrested by United States foreign policy. Late in December, the Soviet government instituted rationing in the city of Leningrad for the first time since the Nazi invasion in 1942. That is a measure of current Soviet hardship. Nine months ago, I was told in Moscow that the Russian harvest was overflowing, but that less than one-half of it would be recovered, owing to the collapse of all rail and road transportation. It's been nearly two years since the then Prime Minister Ryzhkov, facing an audience of seven hundred economists, announced that in his judgment, the Soviet Union had eighteen months left to live "unless drastic alternative courses are taken." We know that drastic alternative courses have not been taken, and that we are indeed seeing the dissolution of the Soviet Union.

Over the course of the year up until the summer, I advocated extravagant purchases by the United States of Soviet military equipment, aggressive in character and redundant in quantity. What the Soviet Union needed, I reasoned, was $100 billion USD a year for three years until they could turn their country around, and that what we needed to secure the peace was the end of the destructive potential of the Soviet aggressive state. My reading of events persuades me that the Soviet Union cannot really use the money. Its problems are organic.

I'm reminded of the short story by Oscar Wilde. The young man with the disfigured face pays a large sum of money to a sculptor to make him a mask to hide his ugliness. This is done, and the man with the mask grows into old age, although all the world knows only the fine young face of the master sculptor; and the man with the mask devotes his life to ennobling work, spending his time and resources to relieve the misery of others. In old age, he falls sick, and his doctor diagnoses the need to remove the mask, does so, and to the astonishment of the actor's company, discovers young and beautiful features. The old unsightly face has been transfigured by the nobility of the life he led, and now the mask has become reality.

The Soviet economy can't work its way out of the cesspool it has lived in unless it shrives its past, and this can't be done by a transfusion of foreign money. There is certainly an urgent case to be made for stimulating our SDI program, indeed, for persuading the Soviet Union that in respect of protection from incoming missiles, we have interests in common. But short of pressing those, we have primarily only to stand and wait.

I'll move to the related question touching on the ultimate alternative in foreign policy, debated so extensively last January. My next proposition is that no useful exchange on war and peace can be had when one party to it insists on the inviolability of human life. Our tradition teaches us that human life is sacrosanct, but not that it is inviolable. The United States, all conservatives and most libertarians agree, has the authority to risk the life of an American soldier. It isn't possible to argue with someone whose meanings are inchoately pacifist. There is no negotiable analytical tender. Those who abjure pacifist doctrine but continue to press the primacy of human life need to be convinced that a sacrifice undertaken today will convincingly diminish the magnitude of a sacrifice probable tomorrow. The anti-war people never really found a persuasive doctrine after using up the argument that in the Persian Gulf we should continue with the sanctions until they ran dry. Perhaps in recognition of how straightened their arguments were, we began to hear in mid-February the reductionist argument about a single human life. Anna Quindlen of the *New York Times*, scoffing at those who took comfort in the low casualty figures during the first four weeks of our engagement, said, "Sure. It doesn't matter that only six American aviators have been killed, unless one of them is Joe, and he happens to be your father, your brother, your husband, or your lover." And from Arthur Schlesinger Jr. the comment made in January that the Gulf War is "not worth one human life." The attempt to write policy over the corpse of the kid over there who just got married, the younger son of proud and devoted parents, is a sentimentalization of calculations necessarily made, so to speak, in cold blood.

"Liberty," Jefferson once said, "needs to be watered regularly by the blood of tyrants and patriots." That formulation scares some of us off, sounding as it does like the Charge of the Light Brigade with march music by John Phillips Sousa. But you can draw out that observation and ask: Is it or is it not historically the case that free societies have had to defend their freedom at the cost of human life and, short of a happy ending to human history, are likely to continue to have to do so? If the answer is, "Yes, this does need to be done," then you can accost the second question: "Does the threat to your freedom begin on the day that the Nazi trooper deposits you on a train to Buchenwald, or does it begin a little before that time—say, when Hitler took over the Rhineland and it was still just possible to stop him?" Because of course it wasn't just Joey who died finally stopping Hitler. It was fifty million Joeys.

A mature society alert to timely action against destroyers of the peace makes its bid. We lost 500,000 men between Pearl Harbor and the flight from Saigon. It was calculations of that order that armed us psychologically for the casualty figures we feared lay ahead for us last January, a thundercloud of fear that all but passed over us. We were ready—and that didn't mean that the death of Joey wasn't heartbreaking to those who loved him—but our responsibility then, and our responsibility as we face international perspectives in the future, is always to satisfy ourselves on the basic question.

Accordingly, my next proposition is that in the Persian Gulf, our vital interests were at stake. America baiters, but also some of our best friends, have done their best to sully our policy by saying that it all had to do with oil—the mere mention of which justifies the disdain of far-seeing men of large heart. The mere mention of oil in this context is shorthand for rank materialism. It is worthwhile exploring quite directly the fastidious distinctions here implied. The distinction between oil and, oh, poetry, or whatever it is that it is okay to use force to secure—affirmative action, maybe. Oil may be thought of as that murky stuff that produces rich and vulgar Texans. The trouble is that to think about it in that way is the equivalent of thinking about an unemployed man seeking a job as a materialist. Until another form of efficient energy is developed, the industrial world needs oil, even as the unemployed man needs a job. But those who are indifferent to the universal availability of oil might as well be indifferent to the universal unavailability of employment. Saudi Arabia has one-quarter of the world's reserves of oil, which, combined with Kuwait and Iraq, add up to more than 40 percent. If we grant that the United States has a vital interest in world peace, then we grant that it had a vital interest in seeing to it that the Persian Gulf should not become either an instrument of extortion or a pit of anarchy around which armed vultures of the world would likely gather to make other than love. Indeed, a strong case might have been made for threatening military force against the cartel that, until it self-destructed by reason of avarice among constituent parts, waged economic war against the West for a decade, beginning in 1973.

The isolationist tradition against entangling alliances was not bad geopolitical thought in other days, other times. The notion that we depended on any particular commodity that could be produced only in the Mid East or in China, or in Australia, was quaint. The United States was never a fully-realized autarchic, dreamy nation that produced for itself everything that it consumed. From our earliest days, we were a nation of traders, and throughout the 19th century, we were busy exporting our goods and importing others. But it wasn't really until World War II that we faced a scarcity of a critical commodity so agonizingly that only doctors and generals were permitted to buy a new rubber tire. What then happened so suddenly by American historical standards was a prospect not only of running out of something that we didn't ourselves have enough of—oil or molybdenum, or whatever—but also at about the same time, we came within the range of weapons we could not cope with, because nobody can cope with nuclear weapons after they have landed. We can only either (A) get in the way of their being manufactured, as Israel did by bombing Iraq's gestating nuclear plant in 1981, or else, (B) deter a nation from dispatching its bombs by threatening insupportable retaliation, or (C) stop the bomb mid-way by SDI.

The stated objective of Iraq in the current exercises was to annex Kuwait, in order to force it to limit production, in order to increase the price of oil; and OPEC tends to work or not to work according as

Saudi Arabia cooperates or does not cooperate. It is only Saudi Arabia that produces, or can do so, so much oil that it uniquely has the power to affect the world price. That is why we went to war, and the moment is past due when the Bush administration approaches King Fahd of Saudi Arabia with such words as these: "Now, look, Your Majesty. We bail you out of a no-win situation. Except for the United States Marines, you and your court would be sitting in Monaco right now. Now, we don't want to take over your country, but we don't want either to become your economic subjects. And that means that we have to look upon your oil as the whole world is slowly coming to look upon pollution—that the source of the pollution is in Detroit or in Chernobyl isn't the point. It is the point that the impact of what happens in Detroit or Chernobyl can affect Manitoba and Norway. So, as a sign of permanent solidarity between the great people of Saudi Arabia and the great people of the United States of America, and the great people of the NATO powers, and of the defunct Warsaw powers, we will now execute this here agreement, binding the price of Saudi Arabian oil for 50 years to the price of free-market oil at Galveston, Texas." If sometime in the very near future such an agreement is announced, we will have amply documented our motives for going into the Persian Gulf in August of 1990. Our perspectives will establish that we have protected our vital interests and those of the industrial world through the lifetime of my grandchild and King Fahd's 10,000 grandchildren.

My final proposition on the war-and-peace question is that circumstances argue the wisdom of pressing forward during that first week in March to unseat Saddam Hussein. Conservatives properly distinguish between principles and ideology. Principles become ideologized when they are applied without reference to circumstances. What were the relevant principles, President Bush defending his inactivity in mid-April? Put it this way: "The United States is not going to intervene militarily in Iraq's internal affairs and risk being drawn into a Vietnam-style quagmire." There are problems in defending this proposition. (1) It requires a great imagination just to begin with to suppose that the United States had not been intervening militarily in Iraq's internal affairs. We mobilized and instituted a worldwide quarantine of Iraq, just to begin with. If not directly military, it was certainly paramilitary, and indeed, in some respects more directly an intervention in Iraq's internal affairs than the subsequent smart bombing of its military installations. When the local stationer can't import pencils, we do right to think of this as an intervention in internal affairs. (2) We correctly and charitably dismissed the analogy to Vietnam and spared Mr. Bush the embarrassment of submitting it to licentious dissection. Suffice simply to say that our ventures in Vietnam and Iraq had only in common the existence of American military in the field. (3) Mr. Bush might have ordered the Army to go forward to Baghdad, stopping short of the capital only if Saddam Hussein fled before the American troops arrived. In giving that order, President Bush was leaning on the American tradition of keeping one hand away from other people's internal problems—in failing to give that order.

Now, this tradition, however short-lived, is entirely honorable. I have myself been guided ever since I first came upon it by the maxim Senator Fulbright framed twenty-five years ago: "Insofar as a nation is content to practice its doctrines within its own frontiers, that nation, however repugnant its ideology, is one with which we have no proper quarrel." It was under the patronage of this distinction, for instance, that we felt it appropriate in 1965 to land the Marines in the eastern half of Hispaniola to interdict what looked to us what looked like a threatened extension of the Soviet Empire, while entirely ignoring the western half of that island, where Papa Doc Duvalier was committing atrocities against human beings as voraciously as his Communist counterparts. We've come a long way since Woodrow Wilson charged us with making the world safe for democracy and John F. Kennedy hailed the American opportunity to bring freedom to the remotest corner of the world.

President Bush and his spokesmen, including General Schwarzkopf—the post–David Frost Schwarzkopf—also stressed the explicitness of the United Nations' mandate, which was indeed concerned primarily with the liberation of Kuwait. In doing so, the administration was treating the United Nations mandate with such frugal specificity as to satisfy Neanderthal strict constructionism. Floating about in Resolution 678 is a sentence enjoining the coalition forces to "use all necessary means to uphold and implement Security Council Resolution 660, et cetera, and all subsequent relevant resolutions, and to restore international peace and security in the area." It is inconceivable that anyone this side of the Ramsey Clark wing of public opinion would have held that our forces were legally immobilized on midnight, February the twenty-eighth simply because effective resistance had been overcome. A military column sufficient in strength to have ousted Saddam Hussein could have reached Baghdad within thirty-six hours. Military judgment seems to concur.

What is absolutely plain, given the events of the ensuing seven weeks, is that we did not restore international peace and security in the area. It can hardly be maintained that we did so, when during that period over one million Kurds were ravaged and effectively exiled. Even if the entente cordiale concluded the day before yesterday endures longer than preceding pacts between the Iraqi government and the Kurds, these slaughters in the south and in the north will not be undone. It is not at this point hyperbolic to say that international peace and security are inconsistent with the continuation of Saddam Hussein in power.

(4) From all of which, we correctly deduce the following, which is that the United States should have consummated its operation in liberating Kuwait by dispossessing the government that enslaved Kuwait. Call it, if one seeks a formal dispensation, a prudential or controlled improvisation. It is, in my judgment, profoundly conservative to argue at first from definition, and to argue after a certain point from circumstance. The first step requires that we absolutely affirm the principle in this case: No use of force except when vital interests are at stake. The second step permits us to seize the moment, catching the tide of favorable geopolitical momentums in order to advance policies that

inure not only to our own interests, but to humane interests in general. In seizing the opportunity in saving the Kurds we'd have exhibited that same respect for the decent opinions of mankind on whose relevance we insisted when we first put together our national enterprise in the Declaration of Independence.

The justification here given for going ahead with controlled improvisation is intended to explore the theoretical structure of US government military policy, but we should add that there is geopolitical justification. The image of America can translate into the influence of America. The image of America plummeted during the past month as we were seen standing platonically by, in Sunday-suited primness, when we uniquely had the reserves easily to stop Saddam Hussein. Had we followed through, it is likely that we'd be facing a less degree of intractability in our current search for arrangements that would provide at once for Israeli security and Palestine nation.

And so, I close by saluting you all. It was almost thirty years ago that Ed Feulner and I each put up $50.00 to incorporate the Philadelphia Society. I swear I never knew a bigger bang for a buck. Don Lipsett has been our Big Bertha. We owe him the kind of debt only sincerely convinced free men can give—a debt of gratitude. He has been the organization's catalyst. I am sure you share with me the sense, as I have suggested, of being his creature. But I would guess that we are docile servants sharply contrasting with that dumb servitude our enemy, the state, organically desires to impose on us. I wish you a spirited weekend, which I wish I could share with you. That would mean sharing with you my wife, and this the Supreme Court has not yet demanded. Good night.

Success Is the Best Revenge: Looking Back at the Eighties

By Edwin Meese

Thank you very much, ladies and gentlemen, for that very graciously warm welcome. And thank you, Joe, for that magnificent introduction. As a matter of fact, in gratitude for your very generous words about me, I will not try to challenge you for the Lyn Nofziger conservative humor award today. It is great to be here with so many friends at the Philadelphia Society. It is a little awesome, however, to be interposed between Joe Morris, whose abilities as a raconteur has just been demonstrated, and Dan Oliver, who is no mean speaker himself. I remember it was at a Philadelphia Society meeting a few years ago, where Dan introduced me to give the keynote address, but it was his introduction that was credited in all the magazines.

Commodore Lipsett, some months ago, asked me if I would take a few moments here and speak briefly about the 1980s, which, as we all recognize, was a decade of tremendous change in the world—perhaps one of the most significant decades in this century, with the exception, perhaps, of World War II. He said particularly he thought it would be appropriate to talk about the '80s in view of the tendency, nowadays, to have historical revisionists thinking about what really went on during that era that started with the inauguration of Ronald Reagan in 1981. And I agreed to do this. Little did I realize that just within the last week we would have an example of this historical revisionism. I'm quoting now from *USA Today* in yesterday's edition, in which it says, and I quote, "Former President Jimmy Carter called Thursday for a formal investigation into charges Ronald Reagan's campaign cut a secret deal with Iran to delay the release of U.S. hostages until after the 1980 election." And then, later, it goes on to explain where these charges are coming from. It said, "Former Carter administration official Gary Sick went public with the rumors last week. He wrote that Reagan's campaign staff may have worked out a deal with Iran in an effort to undercut Carter's reelection chances."

Now, I suspect that the voters of the United States in 1980 had other things on their minds which more particularly affected the reelection chances of Jimmy Carter that year. Now, you may remember the inflation, the interest rates, and all the other things that we were going through, which Jimmy Carter charitably referred to as our malaise. As a matter of fact, having insight into this episode, which as I'll mention in a moment was untrue. But anyway, it's kind of like a bank robber complaining to the police for putting a parking ticket on his getaway car. Now, the story that Carter is referring to has been discredited so many times since 1980, but nevertheless, the news media allows a Carter partisan to raise the issue again. It's given banner treatment in the *New York Times*, and then is given considerable attention on television as well. And then, the former president himself, who was recently described in the news media as a highly competent carpenter, attempts to capitalize on this rash of news coverage to discredit his successor. Now, some would be so unkind as to suggest that Carter is speaking out in order to distract attention from the obvious and not-too favorable comparisons between his Desert I and President Bush's Desert Storm. In any event, Jimmy Carter is not alone. There has been a steady stream of books, articles, television programs, and so on that have turned the facts upside down and have highlighted imaginative but untrue conclusions and have attempted to transform rumor, innuendo, and speculation as the uncontradicted—or what they would call uncontradicted—truth.

It reminds me a little bit of a story that was told in my early days in Washington. I'm sure many of you have heard it, some of you even from me. But it illustrates kind of the attitude of the news media towards the Reagan administration, which persists to the present day. This is that story about the scientists at the National Ocean and Atmospheric Administration, that bureau that we used to call the Weather Bureau. And they had their telescopes—they were monitoring the weather—and they happened to notice there was a meteor hurtling towards United States at such a speed, and with such force, they calculated that within twenty-four hours it would strike the Earth and all life on our planet would be extinguished. And the report there this morning goes on to tell them how this would be reported by the objective media: The *New York Times* would have a box on the front page that would say, "World Ends Tomorrow, see Page 14." The *Wall Street Journal* would have a notice on the front page that says, "World Ends Tomorrow: Markets to Close Early." *USA Today*, with their marvelous colored graphs, would have a story that says: "World to End: How We Really Feel About It." And last but by no means least, the *Washington Post*, in its inimitable way, would have banner headlines that say: "World to End Tomorrow: Reagan Policies Blamed."

Well, as we seriously consider the historical revisionism, and perhaps look at what we must remember from the '80s, I would suggest it's not really much to worry about with (indiscernible). The literary equivalent of the *National Enquirer* is not really what would attract the attention of either serious political scientists or future historians. But I'm much more concerned about books by people like James Johnson of the *Washington Post*, Bob Schaeffer of CBS, or even the thrust of Lou Cannon's new book, because all of these people, for whatever reason, appear to misperceive, or at least in some cases, more probably, misinterpret critical truths about presidential leadership and its impact on national and world affairs during the 1980s.[28] I suspect

28 Meese is referring to Lou Cannon's *President Reagan: The Role of a Lifetime* (New York: Simon & Schuster, 1991). It remains a very influential book among historians on the subject of Ronald Reagan and his presidency.

that one of the reasons, at least for those notorious liberal pundits who are taking this view or trying to reshape these views, is that they have been outraged by the success of conservative principles and by conservative actions during the decade of the '80s.

I think it is really a great service to all of us to have the posters being displayed—and I'm sure many of you have seen it—that's being displayed by the Young Americans Foundation, and it's been in a number of our conservative publications. But where they compare what Ronald Reagan said in 1981 and 1982—in his various speeches, like the commencement at Notre Dame, or the address to Parliament in Westminster in Great Britain—and then, what the liberal pundits were saying at the same time or during the same decade. I won't repeat the Reagan quotes because they're well-known to most of you. But it is amazing when Lester Thurow, the so-called eminent economist, would say as late as 1989: "Can economic command significantly compress and accelerate the growth process? The remarkable performance of the Soviet Union suggests that it can. In 1920, Russia was but a minor figure in the economic councils of the world." Now, this is 1989, folks. "Today, it is a country whose economic achievements bear comparison with those of the United States." They have been compared, and only this morning, you've heard the results. And then, in the field of political science we have equally astute educators here. Seweryn Bialer, the professor of political science at Columbia University in the earlier part of the decade, 1982, 1983, wrote: "The Soviet Union is not now, nor will it be during the next decade, in the throes of a true systemic crisis, for it boasts enormous unused reserves of political and social stability that suffice to endure it even in its difficulties." I hope that Paul Weyrich and his colleagues on the panel this morning will be quick to send that quote back to the Soviets so they can find out where these untapped reserves of stability are hiding.

Well, I think it's important today that we do spend just a little time looking at the Reagan presidency and the decade of the '80s, and the fact that there were several components of that presidency, which were very important to what happened. First of all, the fact that the president represented, in his campaign and his presidency, certain basic values that recognized some critical and essential precepts of the American people. Secondly, that the president had some specific, defined objectives in terms of what he wanted to do in this country and what he wanted to do in world affairs. And thirdly, that there was a well-thought-out strategy for achieving those goals. I think we only have to refer to Marty Anderson's paperback version of his book, *Revolution*, in which he recounts a conversation with President Reagan in which the strategy, for example, in dealing with the Communist world was well sat out and in view.[29]

Now, obviously, we know that President Reagan didn't solve all the problems, mistakes were made, and human frailty was not repealed during this period, and that a number of opportunities were lost. But I think we also have to recognize that there were some significant accomplishments, and that there were certain economic, political, and national security principles that were verified during this period, so that an accurate portrayal of what occurred during the 1980s is very important, both to provide a fair depiction of history and also to provide some useful lessons for the future as far as our country is concerned.

Now in the few moments that are allotted to me I can't even begin to summarize all the events or even the types of events that occurred during this period, but I think it might be important to mention a couple of highlights. First of all, the fact that the economic policies of tax reduction, of slowing the growth of federal spending, and indeed the average growth in percentage terms during the Reagan administration was less than a third the average growth over the presidents on either side of him. The regulatory reform and the stable monetary policies of this period ended a recession, reduced dramatically the misery index that was made up of a combination of inflation and unemployment,

29 Martin Anderson, *Revolution: The Reagan Legacy* (New York: Harcourt, 1988).

produced nearly twenty million new jobs, and sparked the longest peacetime economic expansion since World War II, and probably the longest in our history, which lasted some 92 months.

In the foreign affairs and national security field, President Reagan's willingness to recognize the Soviet Union as an evil empire, and to say as much; his challenge to the West, when he was before the British Parliament, to consign Communism to the ash-heap of history; his rebuilding of the military forces, developing the new technologies and inspiring the highest quality of personnel and the highest morale in our history, gave meaning to the phrase "peace through strength" and coincidentally enabled us to obtain the smashing successes that were achieved during the Persian Gulf War. Inaugurating the Strategic Defense Initiative and reasserting the United States' leadership in the world, as well as having a rational program or approach to arms control and arms reduction were all instrumental in bringing about the conditions that formed the basis of many of the deliberations in this meeting. Namely, the changes in the eastern part of the world.

I think perhaps the results and the credit for that, in terms of world affairs, were best summarized by Margaret Thatcher in a speech she gave, and I'm sure many of you attended in Washington, D.C., on the 8th of March of this year at a luncheon sponsored by Heritage and several other conservative organizations. Mrs. Thatcher said that in the decade of the '80s Western values were placed in the crucible and they emerged with greater purity and strength. She said, "Much of the credit goes to President Reagan. Of him, it can be said," she said, "as Canning said of Pitt, that he was the pilot to weather the storm." She goes on to proclaim that "the world owes him an enormous debt, and it saddens me that there are some who refuse to acknowledge these achievements." And then, she described how the world has changed—and I just want to summarize this—in the world since the decade of the '80s. In her words, "The Cold War was won without a shot being fired. Eastern Europe regained its freedom. Its peoples elected democratic governments and they announced their intention to leave the Warsaw Pact, and indeed, today, the Warsaw Pact is no more. The Berlin Wall came down, and Germany was reunified within NATO. Germany and Japan, the vanquished nations in the Second World War, prospered mightily, and ironically became the (indiscernible) in the new world peace." She went on to say, "A weakened Soviet Union was compelled by the West's economic and military competition to reform itself. A new, more realistic and clear-sighted leadership came to the top." As we've heard this morning that story is still playing out as they say. But she goes on, "Glasnost was launched, perestroika was started, and we saw the beginnings of democratic politics. As the Soviet Union abandoned its revolutionary role in the world, the United Nations became a more effective forum for actual diplomacy." And she says, finally, "and the United States once again became the preeminent power in the world."

Well, in closing, as we review the decade of the '80s, under the title that success is the best revenge, I would suggest to you that it is not only success in actual terms, but it is important that we reaffirm—at every opportunity we have—what really happened in the '80s, so that success will be perceived as well as having actually occurred. Reviewing the 1980s is not just an opportunity to set the record straight in regard to the Reagan presidency—although some of us, at least, think that might be a worthy goal in itself. But it is even more important, I would suggest to you, to reaffirm the lesson that conservative principles and conservative actions do produce beneficial results. And it is the following of those principles that undergirded the achievements of the '80s and I think we would all agree in this room that it is those principles which deserve greater observance in the '90s. Thank you.

CHAPTER 4

Should America Be the World's Policeman?

April 26-28, 1991
Boston, Massachusetts

Saturday, April 27
4:30-5:30

Should America Be the World's Policeman?

Joseph A. Morris, Chairman

Midge Decter

Doug Bandow

Should America Be the World's Policeman?

By Midge Decter

Joe told you that we've debated before. The last time they stood us on opposite sides of the stage, like we were presidential candidates, and we had a contest. And that reminded me what I hate about debates, and I think Doug agrees with me on that point, because I don't want to score points against him and you all keep score. I want to convince him that I am right and that he was mistaken, and that's what he wants to do to me, I'm sure. In other words, I hope that we can have a much more serious and useful discussion between us than a debate, and among us, than a debate. The proper way to do that, it seems to me, would be to begin with the many things we have in common, like love of country, and like impatience with many other countries, particularly in Europe, for their niggardliness in repaying the United States' loyalty to their safety and wellbeing. This we both agree about. There are many other things to add to this list, but I don't have time, except to say that they would confirm my old conviction that the only important disagreements are those between people who agree on fundamentals.

Having said that, I turn to the assigned topic: Should America be the world's policeman? Some people might find this a rather crude and oversimplified formulation of the question of isolationism versus interventionism. I don't. Indeed, I believe that I, myself, suggested to Don Lipsett that it be put this way. Nor do I believe that my unqualified yes to that question is itself either crude or simplistic. I live in New

York City. I like policemen. I like knowing they are around. I feel a whole lot better every time I see one, and the world I daily inhabit, which is chaotic and dangerous enough with them, would be an unimaginable hell without them. And if it is that way with me, a member of the class of the deserving affluent, it is ten times that way with the poor, whose real complaint against the cops—*pace* the middle-class activist who presumes to speak for the poor all the time—is that there are not enough of them.

Do I offer this as an analogy with the wide world? You bet I do. In any case, the truth is that America is the world's policeman, whether you, I, and/or the American government like it or not. We are now the greatest single power in the world. Thus, everything we do, or decide not to do, or simply fail to do, has immense consequences for world order. Notice I do not say "New World Order." There is no New World Order, nor, in my opinion, can there be. I think we are all in agreement on that so I sense in the room this afternoon. There is only world order or world disorder. What is new is that this "New World Order," partial at best, and frequently very disordered, used to be for a long time presided over in the main by two massive military powers: the United States and the U.S.S.R. And now one of them, reduced by desperate need and encroaching disaster to suing for the favor of the other, has withdrawn in certain significant ways from the field. That leaves us, as I said, willy-nilly. And willy-nilly again, our withdrawing from an active role in the world will be as much an intervention in it as would be sending our warships to roam the high seas. So, my first point is, let us not kid ourselves: For us to remain "neutral" in significant foreign conflicts or struggles is just a way of our siding with the stronger parties to those conflicts—as in staying out of the Balkans' pursuit of independence.

To be sure, there are many conflicts of no significance to anyone but the parties involved. I don't know, a civil war in Liberia, I guess, would be pretty close to what I mean by that. There are other conflicts we should, in my opinion, feel morally bound to keep out of, except on our knees in penance like the civil war in Cambodia. Where, in addition, the only people it is not a human scandal to support have less than a snowball's chance in hell. There are conflicts—Iran and Iraq should have been one such, but alas, wasn't—where our staying out would be the expression of the proper hope that both governments would eventually fall. And obviously, this list of situations where our proper role would be to stay out is not exhaustive. I could probably think of many more. The lady may be an activist, but that doesn't mean she's crazy.

Nevertheless, we have to face the fact that for the United States to make known by word or deed its unconcern about the action of another power becomes a sanction of that power. Witness Iraq's invasion of Kuwait, which would almost certainly not have happened if Secretary Baker's message to Saddam Hussein had been that the United States would not tolerate it. There's no use, either, in saying that others should share this burden of responsibility with us or be damned. Much as my heart reverberates to the argument that it's time we stopped begging the Europeans say, or the Japanese, for permission to let us look after their vital interests. And I believe that possibly the worst thing George Bush will have done—in an administration that already boasts quite a few candidates for that award—is revivify and reenergize the U.N. But much as I feel this way in my mind, I know these resentments are foolish. The road to hell, as any parent of an adolescent can tell you, is paved with "shoulds." The point is that any condition in the world, from oil blackmail to political subversion, that is inimical to the vitality and security of Europe will before long be inimical to us too.

Nothing was more blind—morally, economically, and politically blind—than the argument offered during the Gulf mobilization, and then during the war, that we were sending boys to die for gas guzzlers. Oil is not just what we put in our cars to make them run. It is what lubricates the economic health of the whole world. It is not a luxury—not for us, and not for anybody else. It is a staple in much the way wheat and water are staples. Then, there is the mutual moral dependence of

Europe and the United States to be ignored only at everybody's risk. Don't make light of that entity called the West. The moral energy of liberty is in too short supply as it is. So, we have no choice other than the choice to fulfill our responsibility or to shirk it.

There is a second thing to be said, and it's way more important than the first. And that has to do not with the effect on world affairs of American participation or lack of participation, but of the effect on us. You see, we have not, for more than five or six years at a time, made up our minds as a nation to be on Doug's side of this debate or on mine. Often, we intervene, but on the cheap, and end up making a mess: from Cuba, to Vietnam, to Nicaragua, to Iraq. At other periods—the 1920s will serve as a pretty good example here—we tried to turn our backs on the world and ended up making a mess. The rationale for our withdrawing from the world is, at bottom, reducible to the proposition: "Every man for himself." Not only is this an unworkable proposition, it undercuts the whole of public value and morality. In the case of those who advocate such a posture it is difficult, both in logic and in psychology, to determine what would ever under any circumstance be worth putting up a fight for. But if the isolationist's arguments always dangerously skirt the edge of nihilism, undertaking to engage the world with only half a heart is not only dangerous to others—as the Contras and the South Vietnamese could tell you—but it's spiritually injurious to us. We spend much and contrive to get nothing back in the way of energy, pride, and morale.

The world is, after all, lucky to have us for its leading power. We cannot, I think, bring democracy to everyone—not by a long shot. But we have proven ourselves—on the whole [and in] particular by comparison with all the other leading powers in history—a decent and generous people. And we provide an example of prosperity, social equity, and civic harmony that could, if we ourselves uplift, be a harbinger of hope. The world is lucky in us, and we can—please finally—be lucky in ourselves. But what is more energizing and inspiriting than taking on the chores that life has assigned you, without complaint and without reservation, and in good grace? How else to give thanks for our incomparable blessings? And how else but by giving thanks for them, and being willing to share them, protect them, and if need be, fight to keep the world safe for them, will we be able to ensure the blessings of liberty as we are told we are supposed to do for our posterity?

SHOULD AMERICA BE THE WORLD'S POLICEMAN?

By Doug Bandow

We really are living in exciting times. Who could have imagined a couple of years ago that the Berlin Wall would fall, Germany would be reunited, that Communist governments would be swept out of Eastern Europe, that the Jaruzelski regime would even be overthrown? Who could have imagined that the Russian Republic was sending a foreign minister abroad? Who, indeed, could have imagined that the chairman of the Joint Chiefs of Staff, when asked about why is it so easy to talk about cutting the budget today, would answer, "I'm running out of demons. I'm running out of villains. I'm down to Castro and Kim Il Sung." In this changed world we need to reconsider our foreign policy.

Just as Midge Decter, in fact, closed down the Committee for a Free World in response to changed circumstances, so should we change the interventionist foreign policy we've adopted over the past four decades. The question that is facing the U.S. very much is: What kind of a power are we going to be? The U.S. is and will remain a global power. The question, though, is: Should we pretend to be a military empire—the world's policeman or 911 number, as one person referred to it—or should we go back to being what Jeanne Kirkpatrick commented as "a normal country"?

Today, the U.S. has its military spread all over the globe. We have tens of thousands of troops still in Iraq, potentially tied down to a long-term occupation to protect the Kurds. President Bush has said we need to maintain at least 195,000 troops in Western Europe. The administration seems committed to maintaining at least 100,000 troops in the East Pacific, despite the fact that the Soviet president is now globetrotting across the Pacific visiting Western capitals not Eastern capitals—not North Korea, not Beijing. And though Midge recoils at the thought of, say, intervening in the Liberian civil war, in fact, conservative columnist Bruce Fein advocated just that last fall. John Copper of Rhodes College wrote an article saying the U.S. had to guarantee Taiwan's security. Poland recently requested that the U.S. come to a treaty with it, to protect it in the instance that something happens with the Soviet Union falling apart—when it becomes embroiled in some conflict. Indeed, this morning, it was reported in the *New York Times* that the U.S. government is now telling Americans to get out of Addis Ababa, get out of Ethiopia, because chaos is coming. My guess is that there will probably soon be a call for American intervention in Ethiopia to prevent a genuine human holocaust.

Well, the U.S. continues to provide money to virtually every nation around the world, and as Midge said, the administration believes that it's rejuvenated the United Nations. The administration now wants Congress to make up on past (indiscernible) to the U.N., because you know, in the past, we've gotten our money's worth out of that body. And Ronald Reagan, despite his conservative reputation, pushed through increased funding for virtually every multilateral lending institution in existence: the International Monetary Fund, the World Bank, the Inter-American Development Bank, the African Development Bank. Across the board, the Bush administration has followed their policy, agreeing to a 50 percent hike in the IMF funding, agreeing to the creation of a new European bank, which the U.S. will provide most of the funding for, that the French will run. The U.S. spends about $20 billion of its own money in bilateral aid in various ways, which goes to a variety of leftist dictators, socialists—all sorts of regimes around the world.

I think that what we have to ask, in looking at this very interventionist foreign policy, is: Is there anything for which Americans are not expected to pay? Is there anything for which young American men—and now, potentially, women—are not expected to die? Should we have an interventionist foreign policy? There are certainly lots of high-sounding reasons to have one: promotion of democracy; protection of human rights; to stop aggression; to enforce international law. One of the most unusual, in my view, is Ben Lautenberg's suggestion: "It's important we remain number one in the spiritual sense, and that to spend money on the military preserves that sense of being number one."

If for all the idealism that comes out of many of the justifications for American intervention, there's usually a sense of realpolitik behind it. Let's be honest, the reason President Bush initially sent troops to the Gulf was not because of Kuwait, it was because of the oil. He may have transformed in his mind later on the question of human rights abuses, but had it been Tanzania that invaded its neighbor there would have been no U.S. response. There was a very real realpolitik reason for having done so. We see that all over. Why does President Mobutu, a man of grievous human rights violations—a socialist, a man who's wrecked his economy—receive aid from the United States? Because of a sense of geopolitical interest. Again and again, what we find is that our intervention is animated not by high-sounding ideals, but by all sorts of different sorts of reasons we can wrap in nice rhetoric.

For this reason, I think we have to look very closely at the benefits of intervention versus the costs. This is certainly not nihilism. It's a question of frank and enlightened self-interest. What is the purpose of this nation? Because there really are enormous costs associated with intervention. Part of that is obviously financial. Depending upon the analysis you look at, including the Defense Department's own analysis, NATO accounts for nearly half the U.S. defense budget. The defense of the Pacific costs around $40 billion. And what you find is a very real financial drain, year after year, on the United States.

Our domestic freedoms also suffer. Midge said we have to look kind of at us. But let's very much understand, war is the health of the state. If you look at World War I and World War II [there was] a massive assault on human freedom in this country—where we even incarcerate 100,000 people on some alleged threat, and then hold them until after the next presidential election, before we release them. The vast expansion of the government's economic power is commons World Wars I and II. New York rent control was a temporary measure adopted during World War II—it is still with us. We find massive expansion in any conflict—the Korean War, Vietnam—of the government's power to take economic resources and control our lives.

Our interventionist foreign policy has also malformed our constitutional system, which I would suggest is the most important aspect of our form of government. How far we have come should be obvious to the fact that we have serious thinkers who claim to believe in a jurisprudential philosophy of original intent, who argue that the president had the unilateral authority to take one-fourth of the U.S. military, transport it across the globe, and attack another nation without congressional authority. While there are certainly arguments to be made in some gray areas, to me, if the Constitution means anything, it is in this case that clearly Congress had to declare war.

Further, I think interventionism has some very real human costs, which we should never let get away from us. Woodrow Wilson had fantasies of a new world order himself in World War I. What that led to was an American intervention in a mindless slugfest that killed millions, resulted in 116,000 dead Americans, as well as a disastrous peace treaty that led directly to another, even worse war that killed over 400,000 Americans—an obvious example of deleterious, dangerous intervention. Meddling is the cause of far worse than it has solved. 112,000 young men have died in two undeclared wars since World War II, and though we were certainly lucky in the Persian Gulf, tens of thousands did die, but they were not primarily Americans.

There is a very real cost of intervening, especially with troops. It's one thing to ask young Americans to die for their country; to die defending the constitutional liberties of this system; to die for their fellow citizens. It's quite another to ask them to die for what? The cause of a monarchy in the Middle East? For maintaining stability in Europe? Or trying to preserve some sort of freedom somewhere else? And finally, in today's world, there's a very real risk of intervention, in terms of our own nation, because of the proliferation of ballistic missiles, as well as nuclear weapons and biological chemical weapons. I think we need a Strategic Defense Initiative, for this alone, irrespective of what one has to worry about the Soviets—the fact that we're running into a world of potentially small states around the world having a devastating ability to inflict harm. But that shows, I think, the potentially disastrous results of foreign entanglements, because we're getting to a stage where, indeed, some crazy fellow somewhere could take umbrage at our action and take out an American city. At some point, that will be a real possibility, and that will be very dangerous, and we have to recognize there's a very real cost again to intervening.

How should we formulate a foreign policy, then? I think the purpose of a foreign policy has to be to serve the purpose of the U.S. government. What is the purpose of the government? What should it be doing? It's to serve the interests of the society; to serve the interests of the citizens who created that system; the citizens who live in it; the citizens who support it. It's not to provide pots of cash for Secretary Baker to hand out so foreign despots return his phone calls. It's not to run global crusades around the world on behalf of whatever ideals we might think are important in our moment. We shouldn't sacrifice American lives to stop even hideous suffering of others—as horrible as those sorts of things may be. The money and lives of the American people do not belong to policymakers to be thrust around.

The purpose, I think, is that those lives—our money, our treasure—should be sacrificed only in the defense of the interests of this country, of this society. What are the primary duties of the U.S. government? What really are our interests? I think the first is to safeguard this nation's security: to preserve the people's lives, the property in this country. It's also to preserve the constitutional system that we have: our liberties, a sense of ordered liberties, and freedom. The values, in fact, which have spread around the country; the sorts of values which have really animated people in Eastern Europe and elsewhere. Those sorts of values are very important for the United States to protect, for its citizens, for those who live here. I'd say there's no higher duty for U.S. or other officials. It's not to say there are not higher, transcendent norms, in terms of personal sacrifice.

The problem with foreign policy is it's not an individual act. To advocate sacrifice to help others means you're advocating the sacrifice of other people. You're asking others in your society to die. You're asking others in your society…you're not asking them, you're telling others in society to pay to put bombs on planes to bomb other countries. It's not a question of, "Aren't there higher norms?" Of course, there are. And indeed however misguided one might think the Lincoln Brigade was in the Spanish Civil War, there we saw individuals acting out in what they perceived to be their highest ideals—their willingness to put their own lives on the line.

And we have to look differently, in terms of a foreign policy that encompasses our national community, everyone in our community; and when should we risk their lives? When should we put our fellow citizens' lives at risk? It's a very different standard. I think that to decide on a specific intervention it's not enough just to say, "Well, does this fit the contours of American government, the purposes of American government?" That's necessary, but it's not sufficient. The second question, then, is an alternative means to achieve the goal? Well, let's look at Europe. I mean today, I would argue, of course there's an alternative means. The Soviet Union remains a public problem, but I think the possibility of it becoming an aggressive power again—roaming throughout Eastern Europe, taking on united Germany, taking on France, whatever—is very small. The alternative that we have today is to tell the Europeans, "You all defend yourselves." It's not a difficult proposition. The Soviet Union is in ruins. Its economic system is a disaster. It's facing potential civil war at home, depending upon how this recent accord comes out between the republics. It would have to go past all of its former allies; it no longer has an East German ally. The world has changed. These countries don't need an American defense shield anymore.

South Korea has ten times the GNP and twice the population of North Korea. I find it absolutely astonishing, the notion that the United States has to remain putting its troops at risk, for a country that is fully capable of building up its own defense. When I've talked to South Korean officials, the reaction was, "We don't want to spend more." But quite honestly, I don't care. The question is what should American taxpayers fund? When should American soldiers be at risk? Not to relieve South Korean taxpayers of defending themselves. There's an obvious alternative here to American intervention. You can find it in many different cases.

Of course, it may be difficult to fashion alternative solutions. I think there was an alternative solution in the Gulf. Probably not of liberating Kuwait. I don't see Syria and Saudi Arabia as working together to liberate Kuwait, but I think there was real interest in other parties in the region to provide some sort of defense for Saudi Arabia. These sorts of alternatives are going to be unpleasant at times. They won't give us as much as we want, but it's unrealistic, I think, to expect the United States to maintain a perfect global order; a world order—this new whatever. We should be focusing on developing policies that are cost-effective means of protecting our interests, of fulfilling the purpose of our government, and protecting our citizens.

And even if we think there's no alternative, let's at least look and decide when the costs and the benefits are worth it. We look, for example, at Vietnam. There may have been no other alternative back in the '60s if you really want to preserve South Vietnam, and say you've decided it's a vital interest. What is an alternative? I think we have to sit down and say, "What happens if we don't intervene? What happens if we lose?" The arguments then, it's fascinating to go back and read some of the arguments that came out: "This would be horrible if South Vietnam fell: the whole of East Asia would go communist; Japan would go neutral; all those things." When we look back sixteen years ago, and lo and behold, South Vietnam fell. And what's happened? Japan is now the second-ranking economic power in the world; the Soviet Union has opened up diplomatic relations with South Korea, and is telling the North not to build nuclear weapons; Vietnamese officials have been talking about inviting the U.S. back in, they desperately want recognition, they want aid; the Soviets are downplaying their presence in Cam Ranh Bay, pulling some of their both navy and airplanes back. What we found is that the absolutely worst happened in Vietnam, and indeed, there was no disaster. There was a human tragedy, no doubt, but the question is, trying to prevent that human tragedy, was that worth 58,000 young American lives, especially when they were told to go? We weren't even talking about people who had volunteered. They were told to go, face jail, or you go over. Fifty-eight thousand did not live through it. I think one could look around the world again at places where, yes, it's going to be an untidy world.

The point is, we shouldn't be apologetic about our nation's many advantages. They really give us an opportunity not to intervene. Relative geographic isolation is very important. It doesn't protect us from ballistic missiles, which is why I think we need an SDI, but it does give us a lot of advantages. In other countries, I mean France on the verge of World War II had a very real incentive to forge an alliance, to be involved in these sorts of things, in a way that we don't have to. The fact that we're the world's largest economic market. And the question of the fall of Japan—even the fall of Japan or of Germany would have far less impact on the United States, because of the size of our market. It gives us an ability to step back and say, "We don't have to intervene in every case."

Now, this sort of position has been denounced—in print, in fact—of being cold and heartless. Well, let me suggest it's cold and more heartless to send young Americans to die for purposes that it's not in their interest to defend. It's more cold and heartless to demand that Americans die for causes around the world rather than their own constitutional system. That's the true cold and heartless sort of thing.

I think that Midge and I, as she said, share a lot of ideals in common. But I think the best thing for us is the presumption that we shouldn't be intervening. Yes, there may be a case where we've decided in our absolute national interests, vital interests, we have to go to defend our security and to defend our constitutional system. But I think that case is very rare. We have very real advantages today. I think that we should take advantage of them. Old men have been thinking of new ways for young men to die for centuries. I think it's time we came up with fewer reasons. Thank you.

CHAPTER 5

Immigration and the Obligations of U.S. Citizenship: Melting Pot or Meltdown

APRIL 22-24, 1994
CHICAGO, ILLINOIS

SUNDAY, APRIL 24
8:30-11:00AM

Immigration and the Obligations of U.S.Citizenship: Melting Pot or Meltdown

Larry P. Arnn, Chairman

Tim W. Feguson

Thomas Fleming

Michael Vlahos

Stephen Moore

Peter Brimelow

Immigration and the Obligations of U.S. Citizenship: Melting Pot or Meltdown

By Tim W. Ferguson

Thanks very much. Larry and I are, I believe, the only members of this panel who are currently Californians, and therefore able to report from the front on this issue, although the front is spreading, isn't it? I don't think there are too many parts of America for whom this is purely an academic subject.

I returned to California in 1990 after spending most of the 1980s in New York City, where, by my reading, nearly everyone, and certainly those who are advocates of the free market, seemed to support open immigration. If my friends at *National Review* were at that time on the battlements against it, I apologize. I didn't notice. But in any case, at that time, I didn't sense there was too much debate on the issue among the circles that I ran in, in any case. And I think even today in New York City, there would be widespread agreement that the overall effect of a fairly open immigration policy has been to the advancement of that city. That may reflect certain peculiarities of the New York City welfare state, but nevertheless, I would argue that it is still true today.

At that time, of course, as Ed Meese noted yesterday, we were also in the thrall of the Reagan optimism, and that was generally open to the idea of welcoming newcomers to the country. The *Wall Street Journal*, as most of you are aware, during that period advocated open borders, a stance from which it has never retreated. That was the culture from which I came back to California in 1990.

California during those same '80s had enjoyed an unsurpassed boom. Its population had increased by six million people. Upon becoming reacquainted with my family, including my three siblings, who all work for the government, conscientiously providing services that citizens have no choice but to receive, I discovered that there was indeed another side to the immigration story. My family is a pretty good read for me on the attitudes of middle-class America that escaped me in my ivory tower. And my family, though never particularly tolerant on this subject, was positively fulminating on the subject of immigration.

I discovered shortly thereafter that they weren't alone, that there were lots of citizen groups springing up in California and around the country, genuine grassroots groups with no commercial interest behind them that were advocating a toughening of the immigration restrictions. As a result, I started to write a bit on this subject. And then, following Peter Brimelow's seminal article in *National Review*, I began to write more about it, including an article at the end of 1992 in the *Journal*, which I somehow got past the editorial palace guard, that suggested that immigration was about to explode as a political issue in California. And I think, at least on that score, though Anna took the Pulitzer away from me, I was right.

My personal history in this is perhaps helpful to some of you, as it might–the outlines of my odyssey might somehow mirror yours, perhaps, in the sense that I have, if not changed my opinion on the issue–and I don't think, basically, I have; nevertheless, I have been sensitized, in the '90s vernacular, to a certain kind of reservation, to put it mildly, that a lot of people have on this subject. So, if I'm no longer quite the pure libertarian that I was, I am still leaning in that direction, but willing to concede that during certain times and in certain places, there may be something to the argument that what we have long referred to as a "breather" might have some merit.

However, in terms of our discussion today, because of the breakdown of the panel the way it is, I sense that if I were to indeed try to advance my qualified opinion, that I would be standing between two express trains going in opposite directions, and that did not seem like a particularly good place to stand. So, I'm going to hop aboard the train that is closer to my heart, which is the libertarian one, but perhaps take a little bit different twist, in the sense that the title of our session today makes reference to the obligations of U.S. citizenship. And I'm going to use that to argue for an aggressive Americanization campaign for immigrants; past, present, and future immigrants; immigrants that I would like to see arrive in the future.

I think both the paleocons and the neocons have advocated for some years now the expression of a confidence in American culture that ought to reassert itself. And it seems to me that nowhere ought it to be more willing to do so than to those persons most willing to accept the expression of that confidence in one's culture, and that is those people who are choosing to come to the United States. The Americanization idea is a throwback to some programs early in this century, during the previous peak period of immigration. These programs, which I will not go into in any depth here, were, I believe, essentially products of the Progressive Era, and also casualties of it, in the sense that there was a belief that we could make this country better for everyone, but a certain sense of shame in advancing what some people believe were quaint notions of the sort of purebred Americanism that has always bothered some elements of the American elite.

What I have in mind by an Americanization effort—an aggressive, positive Americanization effort—is an effort both to welcome and to teach those newly arriving residents of our country, primarily using the nonprofit, voluntary sector. And this was the case also in the early part of this century, when these programs were in force; the use of local service clubs, for example. I recently checked, by the way. Occasionally, I'll be interested in whether certain barometers of traditional culture are on the rise or on the wane, and my sense was that the Rotary Clubs and the Kiwanis Clubs of the United States were perhaps dying on the vine, because of various cultural trends. And what I found was that in actual membership terms, they are both growing, and have been growing steadily through the last three decades. To me, that's an indication that we have, in that limited sense, a ready and waiting body of people who perhaps could be called on to participate in an Americanization effort. The PTA, in its more laudable days, was involved in this kind of effort, and I believe that kind of organization, if not the PTA itself these days, could also play a role. There are many others.

I would like to use this effort to promote the idea of an earned citizenship. That is, I suppose, the middle ground. If we are ever to find middle ground between the camps that are represented in this room, perhaps that is it, and that is the emphasis that I would want to place on it. Citizenship would then be, in turn, key to the reception of, or the enjoyment of many of the benefits in the United States which are in some way touched by the state in some official capacity. And that applies, of course, not only to the receipt of outright benefits, but to various transactions. And you can think of them as you remember your own day-to-day life of cases in which a Social Security number is called upon for approval of loans or various financial transactions, and numerous other ways in which you just simply live your day-to-day life. That's the kind of reach that I have in mind, in terms of using this earned citizenship as a reward and inducement for those.

It would still be possible for people who arrive legally and illegally in this country under my scenario to continue to live here in this sort of detached outer existence; the cash economy and what have you, in which many immigrants live today; but they would no longer be entitled to the sort of official sanction and receptivity that they are increasingly being given. How might this system work? Well, the first problem it seems to me you have to grapple with is the problem of the babies, those infants granted citizenship upon birth. Obviously, my system–my idea here, my modest proposal–cannot begin to take account of that. It seems to me, therefore, it is reasonable to deal with this problem.

We're talking about tens, perhaps hundreds of thousands of babies being born in this country for the purpose of obtaining instant citizenship. I don't think a constitutional amendment that some people have in mind on that score is likely to succeed. If it somehow did, that would be years off. So, therefore, the challenge, I think, in the interim, is to somehow limit the arrival of mothers in their eighth and ninth month of pregnancy, so that we simply don't have the births here. In this area, I am willing–this is the one area, perhaps, that I am open to the use of expanded Border Patrol activity. I think the Border Patrol is futile in a lot of ways, but one group that it probably could succeed in screening out of the country are women in their ninth month of pregnancy. I don't think there's too many ways for them to get around the border check station. But that's it, as far as the Border Patrol is concerned, for me.

For the others, I have in mind a sort of—if you will, if this is not too corny–a merit badge kind of approach to earning citizenship. It's not entirely easy right now. It's not insubstantial, the barriers that the INS places in front of people trying to obtain citizenship. I would, in fact, relax some of those. I think the INS ought to be a customer service agency. And for those who are genuinely seeking to become citizens of the U.S., it ought to be made easier, in terms of the official bureaucracy. But I think there ought to be certain substantial tests beyond simply mastering the certain rote memory of citizenship documents that are now part of the process.

For example, let me offer these suggestions. I think it ought to be a qualification that one during one's probationary, provisional period in the United States, ought to have worked steadily, and to have provided support and supervision for one's family members, if they are also in the United States. This would include, of course, having none of the family on any form of relief.

In school, I think it is reasonable to expect the attainment of good grades. Let me say something about schools. There is the thought that the burden of immigration on the school systems is an overwhelming one. And certainly, in the way we are trying to do it in the United States, especially in California right now, it is. However, that has a lot to do with the inflexibility and bureaucratic nature of the schools. If you think of the adult school programs providing English-language training for the new arrivals in the United States, these programs, I think, are rather models of how schooling can, in fact, be provided to large numbers of people at reasonable costs in a very concentrated form. So, I don't think the burden of schooling, to those who really wish to seek it, is necessarily as overwhelming as some have suggested.

A third qualification would be not to get in trouble—that seems almost obvious—not in trouble with the law, and neither should your children be in trouble with the law. A fourth would be—and this is an area where it obviously would need to be fleshed out—but I think it's a very important area that ought not to be overlooked, and that is to show some kind of commitment to your community, in terms of service. Right now, there are active ethnic business organizations in most major metropolitan areas, and as we have heard discussed this weekend, there are very active legal rights organizations. But I don't believe there are so many active actual service organizations. That is, providing a backdrop of help to your fellow ethnic community members, as well as the rest of the people in the towns where you live. And I think it's reasonable to expect of our probationary or provisional citizens that they are active on that front, including service to one's church. In my mind, that would qualify as long as it meets some kind of church-and-state test that we care to impose on it.

A fifth qualification would be that one learn English. In addition to the citizenship test that I mentioned earlier, where English language proficiency of some kind is expected, I believe it's worth gauging one's awareness of civic activities and current events in one's local area. In other words, can you do a reasonable job of reading your local newspaper? Are you aware of what's going on in your place of residence? I think that's another thing to ask of people who want to be American citizens.

And finally–and this is perhaps the most novel, and maybe unworkable part of this idea—is the provision of credits for living in certain places. That is to say, it would be easier to become a citizen were you to have spent your probationary time in certain areas of the

United States, and not in others. And the basis for suggesting that is my sense that there is something of a Laffer Curve that applies to immigration, which is to say, that rising to a certain point on the parabola, there are net gains to be had from an increase in immigration to a particular area, but past the apex on the parabola, there begin to be accumulating detriments to the area. And therefore, what I am suggesting is a somewhat incentive-based method for spreading out immigration across the country.

I do believe that there is plenty of room in the United States—when you think of it in its entirety–plenty of room for newcomers, especially those who are ambitious and productive, and desiring to be good citizens. And through this sort of incentive plan, to spread the wealth as it were, I think that we could obtain more of the benefits of immigration, and minimize the downside of it. I am, as I hope comes across, a believer in the idea—I side, I guess, with the idea that the United States is an idea, not, in the narrow sense, strictly a place. I believe it's an idea that's impressed on and absorbed by its people.

I will use this one occasion to make reference to John O'Sullivan's keynote the other night, in terms of the Battle of the Bulge story that he recounted. It seems to me today that the situation has changed somewhat. Back then, perhaps, there were certain cultural peculiarities of the United States that were not recognized widely. I would argue by virtue of the expanded communication around the world that in fact a lot of our cultural secrets, as it were, are out. The many political scandals in our country are now familiar to many people around the world, by virtue of CNN and other methods. Michael Jordan's scoring average is probably also well known. I expect that Madonna's panty habits are now familiar in most parts of the world. But I think what is less shared, actually less shared, is the notion not only of tolerance of free speech, but also–and this, perhaps, is equally peculiar to the United States and to some other Western democracies—and that is that the tolerance that some people will rise economically above the native population; the willingness to accept that the other, the outsider, will actually be the most successful, in an economic sense—those are ideas that I think are special to America, and which can in fact be a better sort of shared code than the sort of cultural nuances that perhaps served that in the past.

Let me close by putting this idea another way. This organization has had many rancorous debates in the past about exporting liberal democracy and other values of the United States around the world. I tend to line up on the side of those who do think that that effort is futile, and sometimes dangerous. I believe that through the sort of program that I'm advancing here, that it is possible, in a sense, to spread those ideas and values not by exporting, but by importing, if you will; and that there is a powerful potential in that, that will redound not only to the benefit of the world, but of the United States. Thank you.

Immigration and the Obligations of U.S. Citizenship: Melting Pot or Meltdown

By Thomas Fleming

I am not going to talk to you today about the economics of immigration. That's an extremely important subject, but over the past year or two it's become almost safe to talk about. And rather than talk about a safe subject, I think I'll talk about something that's more dangerous; that is, the culture of our national identity.

As I was getting ready to prepare this talk, I thought of something Alain de Benoist, the French right-winger, told me a year ago when he was in Chicago. We were discussing the problem of Islamic immigrants in Paris. And Benoist said quite pointedly, "The problem is not with the Muslims. The problem is with we French who have forgotten who we are."

I'd like to begin by recalling a passage quoted yesterday at length by Professor Kopf from a recent work by Christian Meyer, an ancient historian. And Christian Meyer observes that no ancient Greek, whatever else he doubted, ever questioned the absolute right of a community to restrict its political and social privileges to those who were born into that community. Now, why were the Greeks so insistent upon this?

Well, first of all, because most of these Greek communities, these city-states, were autonomous, self-governing republics, and they regarded the population of these autonomous republics as simply a family writ large; that across the generations, the bones of their ancestors were all planted there, and that they regarded it not as some kind of abstract fantasy such as we sometimes hear America discussed as. As Greek city-states became more democratic, this sentiment—this intense local, parochial patriotism—increased, rather than decreasing. Pericles, for example, Professor Kopf also pointed out, restricted citizenship to persons who had two citizen parents. Perhaps this was an attempt to restrict the provision of Athenian welfare, or perhaps it was simply a new, deeper sense of national identity.

The Athenians thought of themselves as an autochthonous people, meaning that they were not immigrants; they had always lived on the territory of Attica; but they also believed that their autochthony was a question of having been born from the land itself; that their ancestors were somehow sprung from the ground. They had an intense feeling of localism. We, on the other hand—we are, just as Britain is—we are a nation of immigrants, of people who had to make this land their own.

In the famous line of Robert Frost, "The land was ours before we were the land's," and that it was a process of war and civil war that resulted in making us Americans, not just possessors of the land. And as a result, at least by 1800, Americans had—or in fact, before 1800—Americans had much of the same blood and soil mentality, the same kind of rooted localism, which was enjoyed by thirteenth-century Italians or fifth-century Greeks. And as late as even the turn of this century, someone like the novelist Owen Wister, a good Philadelphian, was able to argue–much to the disgust of his friend, Teddy Roosevelt–that it was time for the North and South to heal their wounds. And he says very movingly in a novel, which takes place in Charleston, South Carolina—he says, "We were a family once." We Americans, North and South.

Now, to a republican—whether it's an Athenian like Thucydides, a Roman like Cicero, an Italian like Macchiavelli, or an American like George Washington or Senator Robert Taft—this notion of citizenship is extremely important. And it's usually discussed as a question of rights and duties, and I will not depart from that. What are the duties of citizenship in a republic, as conventionally considered?

Well, first of all, they're duties of defense. A man is supposed to serve in the militia, or serve in the army. They're also judicial obligations. For example, one should sit on juries and be law-abiding. There are political obligations: to vote, to attend assemblies, and to take part in the political life of the community. Aristotle, in fact, defines citizenship as the right and obligation to participate in the political life of the community. There's also economic obligations, that one be a contributor economically to society, rather than a mere consumer of resources. And finally, there are social obligations—namely, primarily, the obligation to have a stable marriage, take care of your own children, and not, again, let your own personal preferences lead to social pathology.

Now, corresponding to these duties are a set of rights. If we have the obligation to serve in the militia and the army, we also have the right to be protected in our persons from those who would violate our property or our persons, and safe from foreign enemies. We also have the right to get justice under the law, and with equal justice under the law, as citizens, as guaranteed by our constitution—not on an equal footing with non-citizens.

We have political rights, as well, which is the right to participate in the political process according to our abilities. And we have economic rights—the right to work, to trade, to buy, and to sell, in a free manner—and these rights are not uniformly extended to non-citizens in a republican society. We also have social rights, namely the right to intermarry. In a republic, it is forbidden to prohibit citizens from marrying each other. The right to intermarry is one of the definitions of citizenship.

Now, some of these rights of citizenship may be granted as special privileges to immigrants and to visitors, especially if there are reciprocal agreements between the various countries. I'm speaking historically now, of course. But there's never been, in a republican society, a question of equality between citizens and non-citizens. Aristotle remarks that it is the characteristic of tyrants to accord equal rights to immigrants. That is the nature of tyranny, because the effect of that is to diminish the actual rights of citizenship.

Now, as republics grow and spread–in Robertson Jeffers's memorable phrase, "and thicken into empire"–there is a tendency to spread citizenship more broadly. And the notion of citizenship turns inevitably into that of subjection. It was the genius of the Romans to extend citizenship to their Latin neighbors, and eventually to the Italians, and they used an interesting two-step process, granting certain social and economic rights, the Latin right to near allies, as a preparatory move to granting them full citizenship rights, which would be the right to participate in the political process, only as these people generally became part of the Roman world.

Now, in America, this kind of discussion may sound very alien, but what I'm describing would have been as true of South Carolina and Vermont in 1800 as it was true of the ancient Romans or the ancient Greeks. Unfortunately, the Romans were too successful. They were destroyed by their own success, and they found themselves in the possession of a great, multinational, polyglot empire. And by the end of the first century, they were in the process of granting full citizenship to anybody who happened by accident to be born within the empire.

You all are probably familiar with the great passage in the Acts of the Apostles, where St. Paul, rather than face torture, which was a regular routine for extracting evidence from noncitizens, appeals to the emperor as a Roman citizen; and being a Roman citizen actually conveyed that kind of right. A hundred years later, this would have been more-or-less impossible, because gradually, social classes took the place of the distinction between citizenship and non-citizenship; and by the third century, you could torture Roman citizens, so long as they came from a more humble background, and that is unfortunately the problem of republics turning into empires.

Now, inevitably, the broader the citizenship is extended within a society, the thinner it is; and that is true as well of Rome as it is of the United States. This problem began to be discussed in terms of the slavery issue in the 1850s, and in the *Dred Scott* case, it was argued by the abolitionists that simply because blacks did not have the right to vote, or sit on juries, or hold public office, in states like Massachusetts and New York, that didn't mean they were not citizens. It only meant they were second-class citizens. And the attempt to erect this notion of second-class citizens, like the ancient Roman *humiliores*, was given a sound drubbing by the brilliant Jacksonian Chief Justice, Roger Taney, a man whose memory we should revere—and instead, because, I fear, of the ignorance of the American people, we are fond of attacking.

Now, what is the problem of immigration within this context of republican citizenship? America was, of course, founded as a classical republic, and anyone who has read Adams and Jefferson, or George Mason, will understand how much classical notions of citizenship were at the root of our society. But as colonies with wide open spaces, Americans were eager for people to fill in the land. Although Thomas Jefferson and Franklin, among many others, were very suspicious of any influx of Central Europeans–they were suspicious, for example, of Germans and others, because they thought they did not have the habits of responsible self-government. But as a practical consideration, the continent was open, and there was plenty of room for ethnic communities to come en masse and settle; whole settlements, whole villages of Germans settling in the Dakotas, or Norwegians in Minnesota.

Now, the United States inherited one defect of the English [audio cuts out] meant to be a subject of the Crown, based simply on the fact of birth within the island of Britain, the fact of birth. On the Continent, the notion was of *jus sanguinis*, that is, the right of blood, which meant that if you were descended from citizens, this made you a citizen. In England, this was not adopted, because of the problem of–it was an island, and second of all, the king had land on both sides of the channel; and so, there was a problem of loyalty. So, where you were born became important.

Today, in the United States, we stand at a crossroads, now, in thinking both of the notion of citizenship and the notion of immigration.

We have massive legal and illegal immigration from non-Western cultures, which is threatening the identity of the American nation; we have a leftist self-hating culture that is devoted to destroying everything that we grew up believing in; and this has led to a phenomenon at our universities known as multiculturalism, which is the attempt to marginalize Western and American culture. If immigration constitutes an invasion into the United States, multiculturalism constitutes a fifth column.

Now, if we want to preserve or restore a republican form of government and a republican institution such as the republican conception of citizenship, then we have to perhaps consider the following immodest proposal, which in fact bears a lot of resemblance to certain things which Tim Ferguson said. Citizenship will have to, in the future–if it is going to mean anything–it will have to be restricted, for example, to those who will serve in the army or the militia when called upon; this would make our current president, for example, a non-citizen.

Citizenship will have to be restricted to persons who are law-abiding and who are willing to serve on juries, and this will exclude the wealthy doctors who prefer not to do jury duty. Citizenship will have to be restricted to those who pay taxes rather than merely consume them. This would exclude shirkers, draft dodgers, deserters, many rich people, felons, and career criminals, welfare recipients, and government employees, including congressmen, public school teachers, and social workers. [Audience member]: Judges and policemen. [Fleming resumes]: Judges and policemen. Secondly, I would like to propose the restoration of *jus sanguinis*. That is, you're a citizen if you're descended from citizens, not if you happen casually to be born here. Germany still has the *jus sanguinis*, and the French are in the process of restoring it. The changing realities of the American immigration picture makes this absolutely essential.

I think also that we must deny all forms of welfare, as broadly as we can define that, to non-citizens, other than a one-way ticket back to where they came from, if they wish to come here and consume our resources. I think we also need tough naturalization requirements, some of which Tim Ferguson has already referred to. Proficiency in English, American history, European history, and the Constitution should be taken for granted.

A clean criminal record should be absolutely a prerequisite. And America is suffering from an incredible crime wave right now, much of which is orchestrated by ethnic gangs of recent immigrants; Jamaicans who run the drug traffic–and of course, there's the historic mafia–but there are many other groups, including, according to the FBI, the worst of them are so-called Russian Jews, who mostly aren't Jews, but who got in here under false arrangements.

They should be self-supporting, and I think that we should also revive a notion which is in Switzerland, which is that citizens should not just be accepted by the national government, and then imposed on the rest of us; they should have to be accepted by a state, by a local community, and I would like to say every new citizen has got to find 100 American citizens to go surety for him as a bond, as a guarantee of his good behavior in the future. Thank you.

Immigration and the Obligations of U.S. Citizenship: Melting Pot or Meltdown

By Michael Vlahos

Why does immigration bother us? Aren't we a nation of immigrants? I think the problem of immigration is embedded in a larger misconception that most of us share about America, a misconception that I think is implicit in the thematic title for our convocation here, because America is really neither an idea nor a people alone, but a tribe; or, more properly, a band of tribes.

David Hackett Fischer wrote an interesting book, which many of you may have read, called *Albion's Seed.*[30] And he posited, I think fairly persuasively, that America grew from four original tribes. He gave them these rubrics: Puritan, Cavalier, Quaker, Back Country. And he said that these tribes not only persist, but that they still have cultural hegemony in America, and in fact, that they created the American idea. He says, "The American idea of freedom developed from indigenous folkways which were deeply embedded in the inherited culture of the English-speaking world." Folkways. The American idea is rooted in a dominant group of folkways.

This is extremely important, and I'll give you four or five things that have flowed from this. One is that these folkways became regional identities, and that they shared the same overarching ethos—that is to say, language, religion, concepts of the family, and ultimately, a

30 David Hackett Fischer, *Albion's Seed: Four British Folkways in America,* (New York: Oxford University Press, 1989).

larger concept of liberty vested in a republic. However, number two: They have very different approaches; approaches flowing from their folkways, toward liberty, toward the nature of conduct within the polity. Third, that this led to conflict; that in fact, these folkways, these different groups as they became regionally attached to various pieces of the American soil, were to themselves very different, initially. They sensed that difference as much as they sensed their kinship, and this led inevitably to conflict culminating in the Civil War.

But they also shared enough to create a shared, single republican system, and that these groups together achieved a hegemony, culturally, in America. There were no other tribes. They banded together, in effect, in times of challenge from other tribes, to keep their dominance. And in effect, they created a system where other tribes, other groups, whether they came as groups or as individuals, in order to become members of America, had to become essentially culturally members of this tribe, especially to advance; and that, also, these tribes over the course of two centuries–more than that, because they were here before we were a nation–grew together. They were fused, in effect. And so, they've not only kept their hegemony—only two of our presidents have been outside of these four tribes—but that folkways hegemony, in cultural terms, has equaled stability, and a kind of solidity of the civic idea of America.

Now, there have been some crisis times, and I've mentioned the Civil War. And one of the interesting things about the pre-Civil War period, the period we call Sectionalism, was that seven-eighths of the immigrants coming to the U.S. at that time went to the North. In other words, immigration and that cultural influx heightened the sense of sectionalism. What happened, though, in the Civil War, was that one of these folkways achieved dominance over—well, one or two—achieved dominance over the other two, and you had a period of resolution worked out there, through the process of this conflict, and the way in which this conflict led ultimately to a reconciliation.

The second crisis in the 1890s was a little different. There, you had a much larger influx of people from very different tribes coming to the United States, who weren't easily assimilated. That was the perception at the time. It was a much larger percentage of the American population, and it was very unsettling. And so the question was, would the dominance of these four tribes be maintained? In effect, it was maintained. In effect, as others have pointed out, like O'Sullivan, there were barriers put down at a certain point, and in fact, the barriers themselves were followed by an interesting period in American cultural life, in which nativism renewed and recreated a sense of Americanness. This was what was so powerful about this great period of cultural efflorescence in the 1930s.

Now, today, it's interesting. You don't just simply have the new tribes coming in, new folkways, but that they're taking a regional identity that wasn't necessarily true in the 1890s, when the new tribes that were coming in were more fluid and more able to move within American society. You have also–which you didn't have in the 1890s–you have from within the elite in America a deconstructionist philosophy flowing from postmodernism, which essentially is dismantling the very essence of the idea of the dominance of these four tribes and their hegemony. And finally, this elite is a national elite that is networked nationally, and is no longer rooted in the tribes that they were once a part of. And I ask the question of how did we get to this point?

I want to return to Rome. It's interesting that Tom Fleming spent so much time on Greece and Rome, because Greece and Rome have always been important metaphors, even models, to American leaders. The founders were extremely infused with this sense of what they were creating going back, leaping back, to the only model that they could see in the past, which was Rome. And Rome was a nation. A city-state was a nation. But we forget that the Latin word, *natione*, means "tribe," essentially, and Rome was a city-state not of one group, but of several groups, several tribes; and Rome went through its period of conflict between these tribes. But eventually, it established a culture of its own, and that culture only began to lose itself as Rome became successful. The success of Rome as a warrior state, a warrior republic, was its undoing. And as Tom mentioned, it began to lose its sense of itself as it became an empire.

The wholeness of Rome was lost, not when it incorporated the Latins, not even the Italians, necessarily; because again, these were people who could invest themselves with the same language–that wasn't too difficult for Italians, certainly not for Latins—and they could invest themselves with the same culture as Rome. But when Rome went beyond its capacity to be itself, and became an empire, it broke down. And the empire became a situation where you had a unitary Roman elite–it was unitary in cultural terms—presiding over many fractious nations.

Now, I return to the original question: How did we get to this point? American elites have always worried that we were in danger of going through the same process that Rome did. You can look at *The Education of Henry Adams*,[31] where he writes about America in the 1890s as going through the same process of cultural and political disintegration that the Roman Republic did in the days of Marius and Sulla. We worried about the corruption of imperialism in the postwar era, and with good reason. We worried about it, because that's what was happening.

In effect, the period after World War II saw the creation of an American empire. And I've been wrestling with how we reached this point where America and the American idea as a cultural concept seemed to be so much under attack. The first of these issues that comes home to me is that America became an empire after World War II—an empire of good, no doubt about that, but that empire created—it necessitated, because it was a mobilization state–necessitated the creation of a national elite, a new elite. And I would argue that this elite was a fusion of the elites of the various folkways that Fischer describes—and that this elite, in effect, became comfortable with the

31 Henry Adams, *The Education of Henry Adams*, (New York: The Modern Library, 1931).

notion that they were born to rule, and that their capacity to rule the world became the basis for a same kind of approach domestically. And I think you began to see this by the 1960s, and that the way in which the Civil Rights Movement was perverted is the second aspect of what's happened in America.

The problem of assimilating, embracing, elevating to equal the black community, black society, created an enormous problem for the elite. It didn't want to assimilate. Even though blacks were willing and ready to assimilate into these four folkways, as they still roughly existed in America, it was easier to create a situation, I would argue, where you could bring into the fold of this cultural elite, a black elite, and at the same time maintain under your larger rule the nation as a nation of separate tribes. In effect, you began to see, starting in the 1960s, the developing concept that we saw in the Roman Empire, for example, of America transforming itself from a fused group of tribes culturally identified with those folkways, with a political system and concept of civic virtue that flowed from that, into a very different kind of society, a society ruled by an elite that was culturally homogeneous, but redefining the rest of the population as a set of separate nations by law; and that, in effect, using black society and the difficulties of assimilating black society was the entering wedge for recreating America in this new image; and that, in effect, what you see when people talk about diversity is: You see diversity of face, but unity of culture in the elite.

When you look at the Clinton cabinet, the people who are not of the original four tribes, who are not of the four Anglo tribes, if you want to call them that, are culturally the same. They are assimilated into it, just like you could be Syrian or an Egyptian in the third century; if you were rich enough, and you learned Latin, and you assimilated into that elite, you became part of the Roman elite. Philip the Arab was emperor of Rome in 235, and celebrated the 1,000th anniversary of Rome; but the people were kept–and especially what were once Roman people were essentially stripped. And Tom described this nicely. By the time you reach the point where Caracalla in 212 gave citizenship to all of the people of the Roman Empire, it was no longer Rome. Rome ceased to exist long before it fell. Long before it reached its pinnacle of power, it had died. It died as an idea.

And essentially, what we see today is the creation of the concept of a multinational empire presided over by an elite that retains the folkways of those four original tribes—a perversion of the American idea. And I would argue that we're afraid of immigration because immigration is now seen by Americans as a way of encouraging and making final this process, because immigrants are painted by this national elite as essentially being new nations coming to America; no longer are they individuals whose proclamation of themselves as Americans makes them Americans. No longer are they the kind of people who come here wanting to be American.

And let me just give you the example of my father, who is Greek. He couldn't speak English until he was five, even though he was born here, because he grew up in a hermetic little Greek world in Springfield, Ohio. The first thing he did was to get—he was given as a gift *The Count of Monte Cristo* when he was five years old, and he proceeded to start reading it. And he read that book as a five- or six-year-old. He taught himself English. He left the Greek Orthodox Church when he was nine to become an Episcopalian. That was a remarkably courageous act, not only if you know my grandmother, but if you think about what those communities of immigrants were like in America. And they continually broke down. Immigrants wanted to become American, and wanted to become American not in the civic, abstract sense, but in the cultural sense of the four folkways.

Now, however, the national elite—and you can see them doing this on things like National Public Radio—provide an individual set of graduated rewards, in what I call a political group spoils system, to encourage new immigrants to be persistent in their original nationality, their original culture. And you see them being asked to come up and talk about their culture, and how wonderful that culture is. The entire concept of multiculturalism thus becomes a beautiful mechanism of control, where the control of this national elite is embedded; and those among the people who are able to rise into it are then accepted. They're the only ones who still go through the process of assimilation. It's a perverse system, and it's one that we have to stop.

We are part of the elite, but whenever you have periods of reform in America, it is those elites who've retained the most powerful vision of what America is that are able to actually make the reform happen. That's what we need to do, because even though we are a minority among the national elite, the dominant national elite is focused on a very different vision. We have the people with us, and the Perot insurgency showed how much hatred of the elite exists in America, and how much Americans, I think, below the surface, understand what's going on. They may not be able to articulate it very well, but they understand it. They understand the fact that they're being marginalized in politics; they understand how they're being stripped, like the Roman citizen, who is progressively stripped of his capacity to have any role in the system.

The stratification in America that goes along with this process, in terms of class, culture, and wealth, is also evident. The only way this can change is for a group from within the elite who are aware of this to come forward, and to stop it. So, my role here, if there is any, is to bring this to your attention, as sort of an adjuration. I have no policy, except that the vision which must come from within us and from within a renewed Republican Party must be one that tells this story, because this is the story of America—not an idea alone, nor a people, but a tribe; that there is a set of specific cultural values that others want to be a part of, but that we have to be able to lead Americans to this, not just offer policies, but offer, as well, a vision that they can relate to. Thank you.

Immigration and the Obligations of U.S. Citizenship: Melting Pot or Meltdown

By Stephen Moore

Thank you very much. [Larry] mentioned the fact that I started an organization with a couple of other people a couple of years ago to promote immigration, and to celebrate immigration; and we thought long and hard about what we should call this group. One of the purposes of the group was to take on the major anti-immigration group in Washington, D.C., in America, FAIR. So, our original name of the group was "UNFAIR," but we decided to change that to the American Immigration Institute.

I get up every morning at about 7:30, and at 8:00 in the morning, a woman named Lilian comes to our house. Lilian is a Guatemalan, and she is our daycare worker. She takes care of our one- and three-year-old. We tried to get American workers. In fact, we went through about five Americans to do this job. They were all not good workers. Lilian is probably the best worker that we've seen, and she's extraordinarily successful. She goes to graduate school at night, and so forth. We don't know how we would run our lives without Lilian. And it's a very typical thing. Daycare workers are very commonly immigrants, today. I think a lot of the conservatives who are against immigration don't have children.

Second of all, when I go to work, when I walk out the door—we have a private garbage collection service where I live, which is extraordinarily successful, and these Mexicans who do the work are the hardest–they look like they're sprinters. They run and they pick up the garbage every day, and it's very different from when I lived in Washington, D.C., where we didn't have private garbage collection, and so forth. And that's a really great benefit for us.

Third, when I walk to work every day, I go by a Korean deli. I think probably there's one like this in virtually every neighborhood in America, where you live, and so forth. And every day, Mr. Kim is behind the counter. Mr. Kim is one of these people who insists on calling it a "woobin." Mr. Kim, it's a Reuben, a Reuben. He insists on calling it a "woobin." I keep telling him we have a culture and language we're trying to preserve here. But he's the kind of person who is there virtually every day behind the counter, and he brightens up my life.

And then, I go to work, and when I get to the bus station, if I miss the bus—this is one of the great benefits—if I miss the bus, there's a Pakistani cab driver who sits by the bus stop every day, and if I miss it, he smiles, because he knows I'm going to take his cab. It's a great benefit to me, because I know he's a backstop. If I miss the bus, I can take this bus.

Then, I get to work. We just opened a new office building at the Cato Institute. If any of you are in Washington, I urge you to come by and see. We're in a–not a very good–it's a beautiful building, but we're in a very bad location of Washington, one of the most dangerous areas. We're also very secluded. We're not near anything, which is a little bit frustrating, and we always thought, "What are we going to do for lunch around here?" And what has happened is that an Indian woman has set up a hotdog stand, right in front of our building, every day. And it's extraordinary to me. I don't know how she possibly sells enough hotdogs every day to remain in business, but for everyone in Cato, it's been a great benefit, especially during days when it's pouring down rain, where we'd have to walk literally eight blocks or a mile to get to anywhere to eat. She is always out there. And in fact, even when Washington, D.C. was virtually closed down for a week during the middle of winter, when we had a huge winter storm, this Indian woman had her stand open in front of our building, when virtually nothing else was open in the city.

And then, when I go home at night, we have a one-year-old, who– any of you who have young children can relate to this, that every once in a while, we run out of milk in the middle of the night, and this is a crisis. I know we often overuse the term "crisis" in Washington, but this is a crisis when you have a screaming child in the middle of the night, and you don't have milk. And so, thank God, about four blocks away, there's a 7 Eleven where, of course, any of you who've seen *The Simpsons* knows that Abdul is always behind the counter there.

It was very funny. Sam Francis, who—I think he's a marvelous man; he's very misguided on immigration policy—wrote a column a few months ago, saying, "You know, you just can't go to a 7 Eleven anymore and not have an Arab behind the counter," as if this was some kind of a problem with the American culture, that all the Arabs had taken over the 7 Elevens. The point I'm trying to make here, though, is I'm going to give a presentation on why immigration is good, and I'm just trying to tell you that this is all self-interest motivated, because the only people I know who work in America are immigrants.

Now, what is it about this issue of immigration that makes really brilliant people like John O'Sullivan and Peter Brimelow and others say some of the silliest things? I have total respect—I work for John on a daily—a very weekly basis, and so forth; I think Peter is probably the top investigative reporter, probably, in the country, and so forth. But on this issue, it's very frustrating to me, because for the last ten years or so, I have been debating the left on this issue. I debated people from the AFL-CIO, the Sierra Club, FAIR; people like Garret Harden and Paul Erlich; people who don't share any of the values of any of us in this room, and they have used very fallacious arguments and relied on junk science and so forth to make their claim. And I must say, it's very distressing and depressing to me to see now, the right enter this debate, or many on the right, and use many of these same arguments, in fact, to promote immigration.

Now, I am an economist, and one of the points that I would disagree strongly with John O'Sullivan about is when John said that there is a difference of opinion among economists whether immigration is good or not for the economy. Ladies and gentlemen, there is no difference of opinion. In fact, the economic literature is—I could have a stack of studies from here to the ceiling on the economic effects of immigration, and it all points in the same direction—virtually all. And in fact, to prove this point, what I did two years ago was I did a survey of the top forty economists in the country; past presidents of the American Economic Association; the Nobel Prize winners, and so forth; and I just asked them, "What's the impact of immigration on America?"

And we asked four questions. The first was, "What impact has twentieth-century immigration had on America?" And the choices were very positive, positive, negative, very negative. Eighty percent said "very positive impact," and the other 20 percent said "positive impact." None of them said that immigration in this century has had a negative impact. And remember, we're talking here about people like George Stigler and Milton Friedman, and the very finest economists in the country; the people who've risen to the top of their profession.

And then, interestingly enough, we asked them, "Well, what about illegal immigration?" because everyone's against illegal immigration. What's the impact of illegal immigration? And 75 percent of these eminent economists said that even illegal immigration has a very positive impact on the American economy. Only about 11 percent said that immigration is having a negative impact.

Now, it is true, however, that there are some economists who make the case that immigration is having a negative impact on the economy, and in fact, this is what I find most frustrating; is that the people who are promoting–let me tell you the major economist in the country who is promoting an anti-immigration position. This is a man by the name of Donald Huddle. Don Huddle—I would never say this about a colleague, but I've read through all of his stuff: He is truly a crackpot. And let me just tell you some of the things that this man argues.

For instance, Don Huddle published a study about five years ago, which got an enormous amount of publicity, which said that for every one hundred immigrants in the country, they displace between twenty-five and fifty American workers; not just in the year that the immigrant comes, but forever. That is, that these people are permanently displaced from the American workforce. And he has–just to give you an indication of what this fellow is like—he has quotes in there saying things like, that these immigrants are being exploited by greedy employers, and so forth.

And then, he published a study about a year ago, which has gotten an enormous amount of publicity; in fact, it was front-page news in papers all over the country, which said that immigrants use more in public services than they pay in taxes. And he indicated that by his reckoning, that the result was that there was about $40 billion more in public services used by immigrants than immigrants pay in taxes. So, Julian Simon and I, and others, started to look at this research, because it got so much publicity.

By the way, Donald Huddle–we got his curriculum vitae—has never had a paper published in a scientific journal in his life, whereas people like Julian Simon and so forth, who argue the opposite, have had huge numbers of articles. Now, I'm not saying that having an article published in a scientific academic journal is the greatest gatekeeper mechanism that we have to keep out junk science, but it is a fairly—let me put it like this: A lot of good research doesn't get published, but at least it does keep out some of the worst junk science that is being promoted.

Now, here are some of the things that Donald Huddle says in his study, for example. Donald Huddle said that there were about twelve million immigrants who entered the country in the 1980s, and this was a very—we couldn't figure out how he got this number, twelve million immigrants, because it's way higher than the Census Bureau and so forth indicates. And what we found out was that Don Huddle made an incredible error in his study: He double-counted the immigrants–remember in the mid-1980s, we had a legalization program, where in effect, we had about two to three million people who had been in the country illegally, who we legalized. What Don Huddle did in his study was he double-counted these people. He counted them when they entered the country, then he counted them again when they were legalized. I'm just trying to tell you this because a lot of conservatives do go around citing Don Huddle's study.

Then, Don Huddle said that he–another mistake that he made was he said that there are about nine million illegal immigrants in the United States. Well, in fact, the Census Bureau, the National Academy of Sciences, and so forth have done many, many studies on this, and they indicate that it's probably about half that many illegal immigrants in the country. But Huddle used a figure about twice as large. It's very reminiscent, by the way, of what the Left has done on this homelessness issue, remember, where they went around saying, "Oh, there's four, eight, ten million homeless people in the United States," even when we had Census Bureau data and so forth which indicated that the numbers were much, much smaller.

Then, Huddle left out the major form of taxes that immigrants pay, which is Social Security. The major form of—in fact, the major form most of us pay, in terms of taxes, is Social Security taxes. So, in fact, if you use Don Huddle's methodology, everyone in this room uses more public services than we pay in taxes, because the major form of taxes that we pay is Social Security.

Now, let me quickly go to this question of historical pause on immigration. Now, one of the issues that's been an issue of confusion in this conference is the idea that we are under siege by immigrants and that we are at a historic high level of immigration. Well, it is true that if you look at the number of people coming in at any given year, of course we let in about one million immigrants per year; but of course, that's an irrelevant statistic, because what's important—especially if we are talking about the impact of immigrants on our culture—is how many immigrants are we letting in as related to how many people are already here.

And what you see here is that we are at a very low level of immigration right now. In fact, we would have to allow in about five times as many immigrants as we do today to have the same impact that we did, for instance, at the turn of the century, during the period of the Ellis Island immigrants. And I want you to notice one other thing about this figure. One of the points that a lot of conservatives are making is it's time for an historic pause on immigration. And we have had historic pauses. For example, in the 1860s and so forth—and we had a historic pause right before the turn of the century, and so forth—the interesting thing about these historic pauses is that even during these periods of historic pause, we let in fewer immigrants than we do now. So, I would argue that, in fact, [what] we have today is an historic pause in immigration. In fact, maybe it's time to bring this historic pause to an end.

This just shows foreign-born population as a percentage of immigration. There has been a large increase since the 1960s, but again, we're still well below the historic average for immigration. So, the point I'm trying to make here is, we are less a country of immigrants today than we have been in virtually throughout our history, except for some periods.

Could you put up the next figure, please? This is the population explosion in America. This shows basically population growth over the last five decades. And a lot of conservatives, and a lot of liberals are concerned about American population growing out of control. This shows, even if we let in one million immigrants per year in the 1990s, which is probably a little bit more than we will allow in, that the U.S. population will grow at a slower pace in this decade than it has in any decade since the '50s.

Who knows what this is? Population growth. This is basically population growth. We've all seen this very scary statistic. But this curve also represents something else. Does anyone know what this curve represents? That's pretty—no, what this represents is life expectancy. One of the great triumphs of human history is that in the last one hundred years or so, life expectancy in the United States has about doubled, and in fact, from about 1800, it's had a huge upswing. Now, the reason I make this point is that many people are concerned about the "population explosion," but there are two reasons that the U.S. population and world population are growing, and they're both evidence of human triumphs.

The first reason is life expectancy. People are living longer. That's a good thing, I would think. Second of all, if you turn that curve around, what you'd see is the other reason that population is growing in the world, and in the United States, is infant mortality. Infant mortality has been cut by about two-thirds since the turn of the century, which is, again, a human triumph. Now, what this means, of course, is that world population is growing because people are living longer, and children are living at birth. This is a great human triumph, and yet we see many conservatives and many liberals alike basically decrying this, when this is probably one of the greatest triumphs that we see. Now, the point I'm trying to make here is that population growth is not a reason to be concerned about immigration.

And finally, I'm sure that most of you are aware of this, but some people make the claim that the reason we don't want immigration is because of scarce natural resources, and so forth. And this is emblematic of virtually any natural resource that you want to look at. Natural resources are becoming much and much less scarce over time. In fact, tomorrow, when Peter Brimelow and I go to San Francisco, to again debate this issue, one of the people on the panel is a woman, Virginia Abernethy, who's written a book talking about how we need no more immigration because America is running out of energy. So, anyways, the point I'm just trying to make here is that in terms of the demographic impact, there's really nothing to be worried about immigration, and this basically is the same thing. It's just food prices. It shows the historic decline in food.

Now, let me make one last point about the cultural argument about immigration, and then conclude this. Now, the argument is made that we have a culture to preserve, and so forth, and that multiculturalism is a large problem in the United States. I don't think that anyone in this room would deny the fact that multiculturalism is a huge, huge problem, and I don't think that many people in this room would dispute the fact that our culture is under siege. But I would argue that the people who are promoting multiculturalism are not immigrants. They're not Asians. Asians are out there too busy making money to worry about multiculturalism. It's basically fifth-generation, white, pinheaded liberals on university campuses.

Multiculturalism will continue to exist, and the whole idea of quotas and so forth will continue to exist, even if we don't continue to accept immigrants. I would argue, also, that to the extent–the greatest threat to our culture are not the 535 next immigrants who escape over the border illegally, but the 535 people in the U.S. Congress who are destroying our culture. So, let's keep our eye on who the enemy is, here.

Now, in terms of solutions: What should we do? I'm very interested to learn that, in fact, just from the first four speakers—I don't know what Peter is saying, but I'd like to put this to him to see how he would respond to it—but I agree with virtually almost everything that the previous speakers have said. We don't want people to come into this country who commit crimes. We don't people to come into this country who are going to go on welfare. We don't want, necessarily, people who are going to come into this country and not learn English, and so forth.

So, what I would propose is a program where essentially, what we do is double the number of legal immigrants per year, from about one million per year to about two million per year, which would still put us at a historic low, in term—well, put us below the national average, in terms of what we've had in the past. But in a sense, what we do is with the additional one million immigrants we let in per year, we do this on a skill-tested basis, so that the one million additional immigrants are essentially—you see, in the United States, we have the greatest economic opportunity in the history of mankind. What we can do, if we want to, is basically skim the cream, drain the brains from the rest of the world, basically be selective.

We can take the [audio cuts out] Silicon Valleys in the United States, and so forth. And so, basically, the condition, however, of taking these two million immigrants, is that over five years–a kind of residency requirement–any immigrant who goes on welfare is deported. Any immigrant who commits a crime or felony is deported. Any immigrant after five years who hasn't learned the English language and so forth, should leave. And this should be our policy, and I would wonder what Peter would think about that. Thank you.

Immigration and the Obligations of U.S. Citizenship: Melting Pot or Meltdown

By Peter Brimelow

Thank you, Larry. Thank you, ladies and gentlemen. One of the problems immigrants, of course, is that they speak with funny accents and nobody can understand them. Particularly when they just have their time cut in half. If any of you don't understand, please raise a fiery cross and I'll try to respond.

I feel uniquely qualified really to talk about the obligations of U.S. citizenship because I have, in fact, just become one. So I can tell you what they ask you. It took me a long time to get up the courage to tell my mother, that was the problem. He asked me "What country did the U.S. break away from in 1776?" She said, "I guess you know that." I did know that, but I was relieved. I thought they're going to ask me about the name of some obscure American boxer. I'm not interested in sports.

The great thing about immigration, as Steve said, is that you get to argue with your friends. It's even better than arguing with your wife. It seems to me that immigration is an issue on which reasonable men can disagree. I say reasonable men because I never expect to hold public office. So, I don't worry about this reasonable person stuff, but we can also agree.

We can agree on this, for example. I think this goes directly to what George was saying earlier. I think all of us here will be uneasy about this. Sam Donaldson on *This Week with David Brinkley*, "Native-born

Americans don't have any more right to this country, in my view than people who came here yesterday." Yesterday. Not the five years that you need to get citizenship, yesterday. Cokie Roberts: "That's right." I think that's no way to run a railroad.

I have another quote from Cokie Roberts, which goes directly to what George was saying. She has spoken out very forcefully against the term limitation movement. She says that some experience is sort of necessary in Congress to provide institutional memory. She says. "To say that we want only non-professionals governing us is to show a basic disrespect for government. And though that sentiment may be popular, it is dangerous." And this is the particularly important part. "We have nothing binding us together as a nation. No common ethnicity, no history, religion, or even language, except the Constitution and the situations it created." I don't think Cokie Roberts would recognize the Constitution if it bit her on the big toe. What she means is what the political elite happens to want by the Constitution. And of course this is completely untrue. America has considerable continuity. It is, in fact, I think, a nation.

Let's look at what reasonable people can agree on. We can agree, I stipulate, that immigration can be a good thing. It's a great benefit to you that the U.S. can get skilled people. At the same time, we can also agree that it's not that much of a good thing and here I think Steve is just not looking at literature. I mean the literature of the economic history is very clear that the impact of immigration is marginal in the U.S. The consensus is that it didn't increase per capita growth after 1850. The tremendous wave of immigration after 1850 did not increase per capita growth in the U.S. It didn't even increase overall growth that much by a factor of maybe five to fifteen years' worth of growth. This is very surprising to me. I'm doing a book on this subject right now just like Steve. I was astounded to find this, but that's what the literature reflects. Why do economists not reflect this when Steve polls them? It's because they're almost human. Economists are almost human. I've seen similar polls taken on rent control, and you find exactly the same result that economists will not follow the logic of their analysis when it comes to something which is highly politicized.

We can also—and I got Julian Simon to agree to this—the point is immigration is a luxury for the U.S., it is not a necessity. And the reason is very simple, labor is just not that important as a factor of production. And that's why the Japanese have been able to grow so fast since 1955, for example, ten times, as opposed to the U.S. three times, although they have virtually no immigration at all. I think if I can get Julian Simon to agree to that I ought to get Steve to agree to it.

I think another point is—and I think Steve has conceded this already—is that while we can like immigration in principle what we're looking at is immigration in practice. And the '65 Act and the subsequent policy has had some very dramatic effects, both in terms of the way it skews immigration in flow and its tremendous effect on skill levels. Immigrants on balance now are less skilled than the native born, the 1990 census shows. I don't think Steve's looking at the literature here. I would say the most prominent economist is George Borjas, who is a Cuban immigrant, and he's been looking at the 1970 census, and that's what his work shows.

Of course, we can all agree, it's not the immigrants' fault that a lot of these problems like welfare participation, and so on, occur. It's not the immigrants' fault. It is the fault of the fifth-generation pinheaded liberals, and so on and so forth. But, you know, that's like saying we've got a cold and we say to ourselves, "Well, there's a thunderstorm outside, and if we didn't have this cold we could go out in the thunderstorm, so we're going to go out into the thunderstorm anyway, even though we've got the cold," and we get pneumonia. You can get two problems interacting here and you have to deal with them both.

Finally, I'd say we can always agree that America is a nation state in general, and American in particular is an interlacing of ethnicity and culture. It's not exclusively political as Cokie Roberts thinks, and it's not exclusively ethnic. Both matter. Now, the important thing about immigration, what do you think about immigration to a nation state, is how effective assimilation is? And that's a function of the numbers coming in. It's a function of the time involved, and it's a function of the type, how dissimilar the immigrants are from people coming in already.

I could play a very elaborate statistical game with Steve but I'm afraid you'll have to wait until my book comes out because I want to go up to zero time left now. But the fundamental point to grasp is this: the Census Bureau has said that in 2050, when my child is going to be 59 years old, the U.S. will have a population of just 390 million. 130 million of those will be descendants of post-1970 immigrants and the immigrants themselves. 130 million will be immigrants and their descendants. If it wasn't for this immigration, which is all brought about by public policy, the U.S. population would stabilize. That's a remarkable thing for a public party to do, particularly when there is no economic need for it. The U.S. could grow perfectly well without immigration. Now, I know people like Steve are highly optimistic about this, that they think that the strain on American institutions is not that serious, and that it has happened before, although the numbers don't indicate that, not on that scale. And they may be right, but what I can say, ladies and gentlemen, is that they'd better be. Thanks very much.

CHAPTER 6

The Conscience of a Conservative in the 1990s

April 28-30, 1995
Philadelphia, Pennsylvania

Sunday, April 30
8:30-11:00

The Conscience of a Conservative in the 1990s

T. Kenneth Cribb Jr., Chairman

Lee Edwards

Morton C. Blackwell

Ronald E. Robinson

Donald Devine

The Conscience of a Conservative in the 1990s

By Lee Edwards

Thank you, Ken. Good morning, ladies and gentlemen. Like many conservatives, my life was changed by 1964. And I was fortunate to work closely with an extraordinary man: courageous and cantankerous, inspiring and infuriating, profound and profane.

I remember, when I went to him as his new direction of information, I was excited and full of plans to promote him personally, and his many personal interests–his flying, his photography, his ham radio, his specially-equipped Thunderbird, his love for the American Indian, his heroism during World War II. His blunt response, as I outlined this program to me was, "If you have any of that crap, I'll throw your ass out of this campaign. This will be a campaign," he said, "... not of personalities but principles." He would not be packaged or positioned or compromised. And he refused to take himself seriously. Asked what he would do if the Soviets attacked, he replied, "Circle the wagons." Queried about a rumor that a film would be made about him, he conceded it was true, by Eighteenth Century Fox. He was, in fact, *sui generis*.

"Listen, I have little interest in streamlining government or in making it more efficient, for I mean to reduce its size. I do not undertake to promote welfare, for I propose to extend freedom. My aim is not to pass laws, but to repeal them; it's not to inaugurate new programs, but to cancel old ones that do violence to the Constitution, or that have failed in their purpose, or that impose on the people an unwarranted financial burden. I will not attempt to discover whether legislation is needed before I have first determined whether it is constitutionally permissible. And if I should later be attacked for neglecting my constituents' interests, I shall reply that I was informed that their main interest is liberty, and in that cause, I am doing the very best I can."

Newt Gingrich, Dick Armey, Phil Gramm–no, that's Barry Goldwater. Contract with America, [no] *Conscience of a Conservative.*[32] Proclaimed in 1995; no, written in 1960. Thirty-five years after it was first published, that passage retains its amazing power; it's ability to make one say yes, that's the kind of legislator we need. We can imagine its electrifying impact on young conservatives in the year 1960, after eight years of President Eisenhower's dime store New Deal, and in the middle of the 1960 presidential race between tweedle-dum Kennedy and tweedle-dum-dee Nixon.

Now, the link between these uncompromising words, my aim is not to pass laws but to repeal them, and the historic Republican win last November is direct and unmistakable. Indeed, Senator Gramm, chairman of the Republican Senatorial Campaign Committee that helped produce the Republican majority in the Senate has said, quote, "My first political thoughts in the 11th grade, came from *The Conscience of a Conservative.*" In his usual grandiloquent style, House Majority Leader Dick Armey calls Goldwater the great progenitor, the patriarch to whom we proudly trace our lineage. And Duncan Hunter, former chairman of the House Republican Conference, states that the seventy-three new Republican congressmen live by the Goldwaterite message government is too big and spends too much.

What is most remarkable about Barry Goldwater is that he not only had a conscience, but that he acted on it, and constantly. He felt obligated to do right, guided by the traditional virtues of prudence, courage and justice—although rarely, it must be admitted, moderation.

32 Barry Goldwater, *The Conscience of a Conservative* (Shephersdville, KY: Victor Publishing Company, 1960).

For example, having set forth his conservative principles in *The Conscience of a Conservative*, Goldwater applied them, stating that "the only solution to the farm problem is the prompt and final termination of the Farm Subsidy Program." "Government has a right," he said, "to claim an equal percentage of each man's wealth, and no more." That is, he endorsed a flat tax. Because the welfare state transforms the individual from a dignified, industrious, self-reliant spiritual being, into a dependent animal creature without him knowing it, welfare-ism must first be a private concern, with public information primarily by local and state authorities rather than the federal government. The function of our schools, asserted Goldwater, is not to elevate society, but to educate individuals.

The last third of *The Conscience of a Conservative* was devoted to the Cold War, which, according to the senator, the enemy was determined to win, while the United States and the rest of the free world were playing for a tie. He proposed a seven-point program to achieve victory, including the maintenance of defensive alliances like NATO; the elimination of economic foreign aid; military superiority over the Soviet Union, and the encouragement of captive peoples to overthrow their captors.

While conceding that such a policy did involve the risk of war, Goldwater argued that any policy short of surrender carried such a risk. He predicted that the future world would unfold along one of two paths: Either the Communists would retain the offensive, ultimately forcing us to surrender, or to accept war under the most disadvantageous circumstances. Or Americans would summon the will and the means for taking the initiative and wage a war of attrition against the Communists, seeking to bring about, and I quote, "the internal disintegration of the Communist empire. For Americans who cherish their lives, but their freedom more," he concluded, "the choice cannot be difficult." And it was the latter course, a war of attrition, that President Reagan and the American people chose in the 1980s, leading the nation and the world to what Goldwater predicted in 1960: the disintegration of the Soviet empire, victory in the Cold War, both without firing a nuclear shot.

Now, let me say here, and Ken has already taken a little bit of my thunder away, that yes, it's true that Barry Goldwater did not write *The Conscience of a Conservative*. The actual words flowed from a red-haired Midwestern Roman Catholic convert named L. Brent Bozell, senior editor of *National Review* and brother-in-law of the famed William F. Buckley Jr. But theirs was a true collaboration, with the senator reviewing each chapter as it was written and approving the final draft. Everything in *The Conscience of a Conservative* is consistent with Goldwater's positions during the 1950s, when he was a senator from Arizona, and with what he said and proposed during his indispensable run for the presidency in 1964.

I say indispensable, for if Barry Goldwater had not been the GOP's presidential candidate in 1964, I believe there would have been no Reagan revolution in the 1980s and no historic Republican victory last November. Well, consider, if Goldwater had not won the Republican nomination for president, Reagan would certainly not have been asked by nominee Nelson Rockefeller, or William Scranton, or Richard Nixon, to deliver his brilliant TV address, "A Time for Choosing," in the closing days of the campaign. And if he had not given that speech, Reagan would not have become a national political star overnight, and gone on to become governor of California in 1966, and then president of these United States in 1980.

Goldwater's conservative conscience was not a sometime thing. In 1964, during the campaign, over the objections of most of his advisors, his conscience drove him, again and again, to say publicly what many in Congress would only admit privately; Social Security was in actuarial trouble and would be strengthened through a voluntary option; to suggest that parts of TVA, the Tennessee Valley Authority, ought to be sold to the private sector; to oppose the bussing of school children as an example of doctrinaire and misguided egalitarianism; to endorse a constitutional amendment allowing voluntary prayer in public schools.

He quoted Tom Jefferson, "God who gave us life, gave us liberty.

Can the liberties of a nation be secure when we have removed a conviction that these liberties are the gift of God." To seek to strengthen the nation's schools through tax credits to those who bear the cost of education, the parents. To state unequivocally that the rights of victims should always take precedence over the rights of criminals. Beyond question, Goldwater's bold articulation of private solutions to public problems laid the foundation for Nixon's appeal to the silent majority in 1968, Reagan's themes of less government and stronger national defense in 1980, and Newt Gingrich's Contract with America in 1994.

Although not really understood at the time, the 1964 campaign transformed the Republican Party into the conservative party, the anti-big-government party, and the Democratic Party into the liberal party, the pro-big-government party. And, most importantly, it broke the Democratic back of the solid South. The transformation of our two parties in American politics would not have occurred with the conservative conscience and the actions based on that conscience of Barry Goldwater.

In his famous soliloquy that begins, "To be or not to be ...," Hamlet says that conscience does make cowards of us all. But Hamlet is referring to those who don't have the courage of their convictions, who fail to take arms against a sea of troubles. There is no sickly pale cast of thought or irresolution about Barry Goldwater. He does not suffer quietly the slings and arrows of outrageous fortune, especially when launched from the Left.

Now, has Goldwater ever erred? Of course he has. As his former Senate colleague Sam Nunn has remarked, Barry's motto has always been the same: ready, fire, aim. No one hits the bull's eye every time. Goldwater's present-day views on abortion, gay rights, the Christian Right are far off the mark in the minds of most conservatives, most of us in this room. Conscience can mislead when it loses its moorings. If not grounded in the right principles, conscience is merely opinion.

But why does Goldwater attack Christian conservatives, asserting they shouldn't be involved in politics, defend gays in the military?

"You don't need to be straight to fight and die for your country," he says, "you just need to shoot straight." That's a good line, by the way. Why does he counsel Republicans to omit any reference to abortion in their national platform? Well, to begin, Goldwater is being what he's always been: provocative, unpredictable, in your face. As Bill Buckley says, Goldwater was born with an inclination to keep his listeners on their toes. Secondly, Goldwater is eighty-six, albeit a vigorous eighty-six. There are signs of what I call the Truman syndrome: when a man in his later years says anything he damn well pleases without regard for the consequences. Third, Goldwater is no longer an elected representative of the people of Arizona, or of the Republican Party. He has only a constituency of one: himself. Fourth, like all of us, Goldwater personalizes his positions. He has, in fact, a gay grandson and a lesbian niece. And there's a long history of abortion in his family. But there's another, and I think central, philosophical reason for his current positions. The traditionalist libertarian balance, the fusionism that prevailed within the Goldwater of the 1950s and 1960s, has been replaced by a strong libertarian tilt, an almost unbridled emphasis on the individual, regardless of the issue.

Goldwater has seemingly forgotten what he wrote in *The Conscience of a Conservative*—that the economic and spiritual aspects of man's nature are inextricably intertwined. He neglects that in 1964 he constantly called for morality in government, and asserted that those in public office must avoid scandal and corruption, and set a good example to help bring about a good society.

In 1964, Goldwater was a political fusionist. Today he is a fissionist. Still, for all his fulminations, most conservatives comment, as Phyllis Schlafly does, "Well, let him enjoy his retirement." His legacy is the way the twenty-seven million who braved the vitriol of big media in 1964 lived to grow into the fifty-four million that validated the Reagan revolution in 1980 and 1984.

Conservatives should not fall into the liberal trap of arguing that Goldwater is no longer a conservative. The main themes of his '64 campaign–repealing laws, reducing government, cutting taxes, eliminating subsidies and regulations, maintaining a strong defense–are the central themes of the Contract with America, which produced a Republican majority in the Congress last November, and which have the liberals on the run today.

Now, as to the topic of this panel—you thought I'd never get to it, maybe–it's really quite easy, I think, to say what the conscience of a conservative should be in the 1990s. It's the same as the conscience of a conservative in the 1960s or the 1860s or the 1760s. The conscience remains the same because the principles of conservatism that undergird the conscience remain the same.

Unlike the quickly-dated beliefs of liberalism, that government is best which governs most, the basic principles of conservatism are as valid today as they were at the time of the founding of the Republic. A committed Jeffersonian, Barry Goldwater would argue that these principles include: individualism, a belief in the ability of man to reason and, therefore, govern himself; Republicanism, government should be kept as close to the people as possible; anti-centralism, the rights of the states must be protected against the federal government; strict constructionism, the federal government can only exercise power delegated to it by the Constitution. And finally, the reality that man is not only an economic but a spiritual creature.

These conservative principles will never go out of date, any more than the Ten Commandments, or the Golden Rule, or the Constitution ever will.

The Conscience of a Conservative in the 1990s

By Morton Blackwell

Thank you, Ken. It's almost impossible for people who grew up in the Goldwater for President effort to be objective now about Senator Goldwater. We can't help loving him, no matter what he might do. We know he paid his lifetime dues more than thirty years ago.

Judging the long political career of Barry Goldwater, as most politicians are judged, one might say he was a failure. His 1964 presidential campaign set records for losing. Every traditional Republican state was swept by President Lyndon Johnson, whose popular vote victory margin was almost sixteen million votes. Republicans lost a staggering thirty-seven seats in the House of Representatives and two in the Senate. The next year, my friend Tom Pauken, then College Republican national chairman, and now state chairman of the Republican Party of Texas, told me the term conservative was so badly discredited,that we would have to think of some other word to describe our pro-freedom political philosophy.

Senator Goldwater's legislative record, measured by usual standards, didn't look much better. Rarely did he propose major bills or amendments which passed; rarely did his opposition prevent major bills or amendments from passing. Yet Barry Goldwater was an essential man for American conservatives. If America shakes off any of the increasingly heavy shackles of big government, it will be because of what Senator Goldwater did.

The presidential election landslides of the 1980s, the many special and off-year elections during the two years after the 1992 defeat of President George Bush, and the sweeping Republican landslide victory in November 1994 were all made possible by the earlier efforts of Barry Goldwater; not that he intended these specific political results. What Adam Smith called an invisible hand can work in a free political system, as well as in a free economic system. The new normal governing majority in American politics is composed of economic issue conservatives, and social issue conservatives. That was no part of Goldwater's intention, certainly not after his 1964 defeat.

Barry Goldwater campaigned for political power to implement his conservative philosophy. In that, he was unsuccessful. But he was a highly successful communicator of ideas, who challenged the reigning political orthodoxy and created a base of activists who went on to build our country's new normal governing majority. Those who cannot remember Goldwater in his prime, before his 1964 defeat, can have little idea of how powerfully he expressed pro-freedom ideas.

He was never given his due by the dominant news and opinion media. They did all they could to belittle and marginalize him. There have been few subsequent books, none of them of wide circulation, which would reveal even to serious students the significance of Barry Goldwater. That is why Dr. Lee Edwards' new book, *Goldwater*,[33] will be so valuable. The book's carefully-worded subtitle, *The Man Who Made a Revolution*, states its theme. Goldwater did not win the conservative revolution, but he made it, he created it.

Principled, articulate, handsome, tireless. In the later 1950s and early 1960s, he was an exciting personality. He spoke out for the historic ideas of America–limited government, free enterprise, strong national defense and, yes, traditional moral values. Goldwater's ringing proclamations struck responsive chords where these ideas were still cherished in the hearts of millions of Americans who had never accepted Franklin

---

33 Lee Edwards, *Goldwater: The Man Who Made a Revolution* (Washington, D.C.: Regnery Publishing, 1995).

Roosevelt's New Deal or its lineal descendants. Lee Edwards captures the authentic Goldwater for posterity.

Goldwater fearlessly spoke truths—truths about the dangers of big government, truths about the nature of Communism, and yes, truths about our culture. He spoke truths which those on the American political Left hoped had been buried and eliminated forever from political discourse. As he vigorously spoke out for endangered conservative principles, Goldwater was David against Goliath. He was Horatio at the bridge. He was Leonidas at Thermopylae. He was the honest boy who shouted that the emperor had no clothes. No wonder he became the hero of so many Americans.

For those who agreed with him, Barry Goldwater had charisma with a capital C. His pure message was unadulterated with the opportunism so commonly found in politicians. He said exactly what he thought, with almost no discernible concern about the political consequences. Long before his presidential campaign adopted its slogan, in our hearts, conservatives knew he was right.

Self-educated, he never pretended to be an intellectual. But for conservatives, there was no question of our intellectual respectability. Goldwater and those Americans who looked to him as our political spokesman, had a solid foundation of intellectual support–Milton Friedman, Russell Kirk, F.A. Hayek, William F. Buckley Jr., William A. Rusher, Frank Meyer, and dozens of other exceptionally bright people were, during these years, thinking, writing, teaching and speaking at the height of their powers. Most of them worked diligently and effectively to make converts to their views.

A conservative student admirer of Senator Goldwater might not be able to argue toe to toe with his local leftist professor. But that student had access to brilliant, inspiring books, articles, columns and speeches by conservative intellectuals whom he knew could debate circles around the most clever liberal academician. Confident that they were in the right in the sense of being correct, conservative students, intellectuals and just plain citizens jumped on the Goldwater bandwagon, many becoming political activists for the first time in their lives.

For a new political phenomenon, the conservative movement made remarkable strides. Before the 1963 assassination of President Kennedy, Goldwater was doing much better in the polls against Jack Kennedy than he ever did against Lyndon Johnson. Even facing an almost certainly hopeless race against President Johnson, the Goldwater forces soundly defeated the long dominant Republican, liberal eastern establishment in contests for delegates to the 1964 Republican National Convention, and captured about half of the state parties.

The crushing defeat of Goldwater in November 1964 demoralized many Goldwater activists. Some dropped out of politics. Many of us, however, had enjoyed the taste of success in our intra-party battles. We concluded that victory in 1964 had not been possible; that Lyndon Johnson's victory was not conservatives' fault, that our cause was ultimately winnable, and that our political prospects depended on our own future actions. We remained active and built on our experience.

The Republican Party's youth organizations stayed in explicitly Goldwaterite hands for more than a decade, recruiting a new generation of like mind. Eventually, many of us became organizational entrepreneurs, building political action committees, lobbies and foundations, which multiplied the number and effectiveness of conservative activists. Others became scholars, congressional staff or senior Republican Party leaders. All this is recounted in interesting detail in Lee Edwards' book.

Proof of participation in the Goldwater campaign became a badge of honor, sometimes a lifelong credential for many of us. In a political world teeming with opportunists, the battle for Goldwater was like Shakespeare's account of Agincourt; we happy few became a band of brothers. All this, Goldwater made possible, and more.

In 1965, a young man named Richard A. Viguerie showed up at the General Accounting Office in Washington D.C. and began to copy out from government records the names and addresses of donors who had contributed fifty dollars or more to the Goldwater for President Committee. That was legal in those days. Soon, his hands tired, so he hired Kelly Girls to come in and copy more of the names. Before the General Accounting Office staff threw them out, Viguerie had a list of 12,500 Goldwater donors. With that list, Viguerie built a new industry.

At that time, the donor lists of none of the existing conservative organizations [were] available for use or rental by others. At first, Viguerie's list was the only one on the market. The stunning new technology of direct mail in the public policy process, soon learned by many others, enabled conservatives to fund a staggering variety of independent organizations and election campaigns, to communicate personally with mass numbers of voters, and to lobby effectively for conservative causes. Conservative movement direct mail broke the back of the left-wing communications monopoly in America, and it began with the list of 1964 Goldwater donors.

After 1964, the conservative movement gradually went on the offensive; Barry Goldwater went on the defensive. Before 1964, Goldwater was everywhere available to help conservative candidates and organizations. After 1964, at best, Goldwater was like a defender under siege at his post on a wall. From time to time, he'd take a shot at some barbarian who rode by, but his days of advancing the conservative cause were over. He made news primarily on those occasions when he took potshots at fellow conservatives. Rather abruptly, he underwent a transformation from an inspiring hero to an endearing curmudgeon.

An anecdote: Congressman Sam Steiger of Arizona, cut from much the same cloth as Barry Goldwater, asked his old friend Barry to sign a fundraising letter for his 1974 reelection campaign; Goldwater agreed. Steiger asked Richard Viguerie to handle the mailing. Working for Viguerie at the time, I was assigned the job of drafting the letter and overseeing the production of the mailing, which we hoped would raise $40,000. There was no way the Viguerie company could make much money from such a mailing. Viguerie undertook the mailing as a favor to Congressman Steiger.

Drafting the letter, I poured myself into Barry Goldwater's persona. I tried to write a letter Barry might have personally written to an old friend from the 1964 campaign. Between 1958 and 1964, I had read every scrap I could find about and by Goldwater, and taken every opportunity to see and hear him in person. My autographed copy of *Conscience of a Conservative* was dated October 1960. I had been on the original eleven-member steering committee of National Youth for Goldwater, as well as his youngest delegate to the 1964 Republican National Convention. So, I was happy to try my hand at writing a letter for his signature.

Senator Goldwater approved my draft letter. We mailed it to a list, including the surviving Goldwater donors from a decade earlier, which we thought large enough to raise the $40,000 Congressman Steiger wanted. Far surpassing our expectations, the letter netted the Steiger campaign a total of $160,000. Viguerie had charged the Steiger campaign on a per-letter-mailed basis. He would have been paid the same if the letter had netted only the expected amount or even less. But when Senator Goldwater learned how much had been raised, he angrily concluded the direct mail company had made an outrageous profit. To this day, he still believes that.

And from that day, he virtually stopped signing letters for conservative organizations or for individual conservative candidates. Intransigent as always, he would not listen to the facts of the matter. His signature on that letter to that list simply did much better for his friend Sam Steiger than could reasonably have been expected. Goldwater was clearly uncomfortable with the growth of the conservative movement after he stopped being its standard bearer. Frank Meyer, senior editor of *National Review*, had persuaded most movement conservatives well before 1964 that our future success lay in the fusion of economic conservatives and traditional values conservatives. Before his defeat, Senator Goldwater acted as if he concurred. Later, he resented the new and essentially defensive activism of social issue conservatives who were outraged at attacks on their values. The federal courts, previously a target of Barry Goldwater's frequent criticism, overturned settled laws and social policy in every jurisdiction in America. To be fair, it must be admitted that Goldwater probably had never been asked in 1964 his position on legalizing abortion. It was illegal everywhere, like bank robbery.

Undoubtedly, Barry Goldwater also resented Ronald Reagan, as Lee Edwards's excellent new book amply documents. Reagan was an even better communicator. Reagan knew how to say unpleasant things pleasantly. Reagan shared Goldwater's conservative principles, but unlike Goldwater, Reagan obviously cared what others thought of him. Most aggravating of all, Ronald Reagan was successful where Goldwater had failed. Like Moses, Barry Goldwater was not destined to lead his people into the promised land. Unfortunately, also like Moses, Barry was unhappy about that fate. But we must always be grateful for what he did for us and for America.

The Conscience of a Conservative in the 1990s

By Ronald E. Robinson

[Recording begins with the talk in progress]

Previously been stated. And I tried to keep those aspects, in terms of the general philosophy of Barry Goldwater, to a minimum. Nevertheless, I cited the exact same passage that Lee did, because it moved me when I first read it, and it has moved me ever since. And when I look for what should be the defining purpose of a senator or a House member, or even a candidate, that passage that Lee read comes back to us, as the passages of so much of *The Conscience of a Conservative* do to us conservatives.

It was a book that captured the attention of every conservative at the time. It was an enormous success. But we should not forget that it was not published by a major publisher, not even by the two major conservative publishers at the time. It took the Manion family and the individual effort of Barry Goldwater to get the book actually published. But part of Goldwater's central message was that conservatism, once articulated, and once presented to the American people, would be enormously popular. In his later work, Goldwater, the senator, wrote, "Sales of the book soared beyond our wildest dreams. The book became a symbol of the new political consciousness."

Goldwater took a special delight at the reception it had among young Americans. He wrote, "*The Conscience of the Conservative* was the college student underground book of the times." It was virtually ignored by the media, most college professors, and other liberals that held a monopoly on the information flowing to the American people. When Goldwater made an indelible print on young people at that time, he ensured that his ideas would define the conservative movement for decades to come. But it was also the clarity of Goldwater's message that ensured that it would echo down through the years. *The Conscience of a Conservative* made a compelling case for limiting the powers of government. Goldwater later wrote that it reflected his central tenet: that people are responsible for their own spiritual and material development, and that these should not be dictated by outside forces such as the government.

At this particular point, I would have echoed the passage that Lee read, because I think it is the most concise statement of conservative philosophy that an elected official has ever made, at least in my times. Goldwater stated his philosophy clearly, and he sought out new audiences, whether it be the former yellow dog Democrats of the South, or the young audience at the time. In the foreword of *The Conscience of the Conservative*, he wrote, "The challenge for conservatives today is quite simply to demonstrate the bearing of a proven philosophy on the problems of our time. I find that America is fundamentally a conservative nation. The preponderant judgment of the American people, especially among young people, is that the radical or liberal approach has not worked and is not working. They yearn for a return to conservative principles."

Goldwater recognized the need for additional voices to articulate that conservative philosophy. That, in fact, was a central part of his message. He wrote at the time, in *The Conscience of a Conservative*, "My hope is that one more conservative, one more conservative voice will be helpful in meeting this challenge." Goldwater recognized that it was a comparatively small number of individuals that spoke out on behalf of the principles that we believe in. And to me, that is still one of the most surprising observations about the conservative movement today, how dependent we are on a few relatively unpredictable individuals who champion our cause with unprecedented success.

Our success comes, I believe, as Goldwater believed, from the underlying correctness, its common sense. That was an essential part of Goldwater's theses. The American people respond with unbelievable relief when a conservative steps forward and articulates conservative principles. That was the secret of Ronald Reagan's popularity, despite the disdain with which he was held by the media and academia during both his terms as governor of California, and both terms as president of the United States. The American people simply shared his beliefs.

The small number of individuals who stepped forward to present the conservative ideas is especially surprising. Then again, I suspect most conservatives are conservative for the reasons Goldwater cited: they like to be left alone, to live their own lives, to raise their own families and to save their own souls. They're not looking for a crusade, and they are not looking to use the coercive power of the federal government to reorder the lives of others. The conservative minded individuals often go into law, into business, or focus their attention on raising their families, rather than going into the opinion forming sector on a full time basis.

The few conservatives that are left to go into general education, or in the public policy organizations, are numerically overwhelmed by the leftists, whose mission in life is to coerce the masses to live their lives as they see fit. That's part of the reason why so many modern-day conservative leaders come from surprising backgrounds. Ronald Reagan was a mildly successful movie actor. Jack Kemp was the Buffalo Bills' quarterback. Rush Limbaugh was the Kansas City Royals' promoter. Peggy Noonan, I think the greatest speechwriter of our times, was a coed at Fairleigh Dickinson, who was appalled by how little was left in her grocery store generated paycheck after she paid her taxes and her union dues. And Newt Gingrich and Dick Armey were happy to be college professors until their liberal colleagues made their academic life a day-to-day hell. And Barry Goldwater would cite college students, also an unpredictable force, in propelling conservatism forward in the public arena, into its political success.

So, it's little wonder, when you look at these cast of characters, the Left often ask themselves, where do these people come from? Surely, they're not the trained leaders like the Clintons or the Gores who have spent all their lives preparing to serve in government; or even the Donna Shalalas or the Jocelyn Elders or the Sheldon Hackneys or the Robert Reichs, who came directly out of academia. No, my friends, we rely on a relatively few number of individuals, usually from an unpredictable occupation, to step forward and make the case for conservatism.

Goldwater knew that the conservative activist was crucial. That's why he repeatedly cited the importance of young people. And that's why we must be concerned, to this day, about our ability to reach young people with our message. Within eight weeks of the national election, *Time* magazine ran two cover stories attacking Newt Gingrich. Now, to be sure, the national media ran similar stories attacking Ronald Reagan in 1981. And I think that Gingrich can overcome those, just as Reagan did. But I think we need to recall what Goldwater felt was his essential reason for writing *The Conscience of a Conservative*, and that is our need to articulate our viewpoint and to express it in the public arena as much as we possibly can.

An important part for Goldwater was that you get an, essentially, a solid education. Now that may be self-evident to members of the Philadelphia Society, but it was not as clearly defined at that particular time. But Goldwater's ninth chapter in *The Conscience of a Conservative* dealt with the current and future problems in education. Barry warned that the liberal solution was simply going to be to just spend more money. "Their solution is to spend more money. Mine is to raise standards. Their recourse is to the federal government, mine is to the local school board, the private school, and individual citizens, as far away from the federal government as you possibly could go." Goldwater knew that the liberal position would inevitably lead to an attack on Western civilization and he said it: "I suspect that if we knew which of these two views of education will eventually prevail, we would also know whether Western civilization is due to survive or to pass away."

Goldwater, at that time, didn't address the Left's desire to monopolize our educational institutions. But it is no surprise to me that *The Conscience of a Conservative* was a victim of that attempt to monopolize it. I was generally shocked in the mid 1980s when I looked to have *The Conscience of a Conservative* be used as a textbook, or as a book for a Young America's Foundation essay contest. And I started to look around at some of the courses around the country and found that I couldn't find a single course in the country that offered this classic work, this great bestseller in the post-World War II era, on any course, in any campus in the country, including those purported courses on conservatism, and including those schools that we consider to be our conservative schools. And I also found in the course, of course, that it was no surprise, then, that the book, in fact, was out of print. And that was what led to the effort of Regnery Publishing, Senator Goldwater, and Young America's Foundation to reprint that particular issue.

Conservative students today must be urged to read *The Conscience of a Conservative*, just as they should read the other great classics of our time—those by Nobel Laureates Solzhenitsyn, Friedman, and Hayek. We know that students will not be assigned this book, or those other books as well. So, I think, once again, we have to do our part in urging students to read this book, and keeping it alive as the defining book, for the future of the conservative movement.

The second, I think that Goldwater understood, is that you ultimately had to express your ideas to those people around you. Again, it comes back to the preface of *The Conscience*. Many are surprised, as Barry Goldwater was, how quickly people share the conservative ideas that he articulated. I think that the success of *The Conscience of a Conservative*, the most successful political tract of its time, is an indication that the country was anxious to hear the conservative message, and I believe it is today. Reaching out to a wider audience became a central part of that.

In writing on welfare, Goldwater cited our biggest challenge would be communication. He wrote in *The Conscience of a Conservative*,

"We're through unless conservatives can demonstrate and communicate their message." Goldwater also understood the importance of approaching the audiences with great enthusiasm. I think that one of the aspects of Goldwater that initially scared the American people was that he was so enthusiastic about his ideas. But I think that it's true that our generation and his generation would not have considered conservative ideas unless he approached it with a degree of enthusiasm that he did. Part of the reason the 1964 campaign was not successful was the degree that he was so enthusiastic about his ideas, that it was easy to scare the American people and say that this man was not fit to be president. But that enthusiasm allowed the ideas that he embedded in an American discussion to become the cornerstone of building the conservative successes in the 1970s and the 1980s and the 1990s.

Finally, I think Goldwater learned a message that–the hard way, if you will–that we conservatives still should underscore, and that is to surround yourself with people that reinforce your work. Later in his book, Goldwater said he regretted dismissing the F. Clifton Whites and the Bill Rushes and the Bill Buckleys from his inner circle, because he felt that those individuals who more closely shared his ideas would have [done] a much better job of selling those ideas to the American people. Goldwater's book was published because Goldwater was not willing to simply say, "I tried, through the existing institutions, the opportunities were foreclosed to me and I was going to go back to just being a United States senator." He was prepared to publish his book completely independent of a major publisher, underscoring to me one other message that the conservative movement and conservatives should never forget. And that is, if existing institutions are thwarting our advancement, we should never hesitate to create our own institutions.

Rush Limbaugh would have never risen to the top if he simply tried to get along in a newsroom at CBS News. Thank God Bill Buckley began and struggled with *National Review*, rather than just trying to publish in *The New Yorker*, or *Atlantic Monthly*, or the *New Republic*. And thank God that Henry Regnery decided to publish writers such as Russell Kirk and Bill Buckley. And yes, thankful too, that Gingrich and Armey said the heck with the petty academic games that their liberal counterparts were trying to tie them down with, and went off and ran for Congress.

This is the type of spirit that Barry Goldwater had in publishing *The Conscience of a Conservative* in the first place. I have seen our conservative ideas applied by a very unpredictable group: Ronald Reagan, the movie actor; Jack Kemp, the Bills' quarterback; the disgruntled grocery store employee, Peggy Noonan; the Royals' promoter, Rush Limbaugh: and indeed, the frustrated politician, Barry Goldwater. Goldwater said we basically have it within our hands to have our movement succeed, because the principles have been defined; we know the American people support them. Goldwater said in *The Conscience of a Conservative*, "Our future, like our past, will be determined by what we, individually, make of it." Thank you very much.

The Conscience of a Conservative in the 1990s

By Donald Devine

It's rather presumptuous, and assumes I'm going to stick to my time limit. But we know that this is a conservative organization because we don't follow the progressive line, but we go from youth to age, and follow tradition.

It's a pleasure to be here. One of the good things about age—and those up near my age know there aren't a lot—is that you can serve to correct some of your younger fellows. Morton Blackwell mentioned a story about Richard Viguerie going to the General Accounting Office and copying the contributors to the Goldwater campaign. Morton is young enough not to know is, of course, Richard Viguerie was the first who started the list business, mainly with Young Americans for Freedom in 1960. He was there just getting his list back from Goldwater.

And I thought it was interesting that Ron Robinson mentioned his interview with a PBS show, about them not knowing much about history. Ron, you'll be pleased to know that things haven't changed very much. Yesterday, I read a Knight Ridder article on people getting angry with government. And the reporter said in this article that, you know, people have been getting sick of government in the United States all the way back to Watergate.

So, we've still got a lot of work to do. You can tell I'm not a progressive. I started in politics in 1960. Barry Goldwater just set a fire in me. Then, of course, I was with Ronald Reagan in 1976; 1980 was pleased to serve in his administration. And now, I don't follow progress; now I'm Bob Dole's senior consultant. I wanted to mention that because Stan Evans took a shot at him the other day.

But you know, it's an interesting thing about Barry Goldwater's life. It shows how tough the role of politician is, because Barry Goldwater was most successful when he stepped out of the role of being a politician, and stepped into the role of being a movement leader. And of course, that's what he did with *The Conscience of a Conservative* in 1960. You can't be a movement leader and a political leader at the same time, because times and circumstances change. Some of the previous speakers mentioned some of the disappointments most of us had with Barry Goldwater over the years. But you know, we're dealing with people.

Again, one of the benefits of age is going through all this. And being in Washington as much as my good friends around the country make fun of me being part of the inside the beltway—one thing you do learn there is the terrible human toll that that terrible system takes on people. But Barry Goldwater, for me, will always be the Barry Goldwater of *Conscience of a Conservative*. And what does it have to say to us today?

Several speakers, Morton primarily, talked about the social conservative and the economic conservative. Lee mentioned the fusionist. It's important to remember what did inflame and start this movement. And it's right in *Conscience of a Conservative*—as an old professor, if you kind of forgive me for that. I kind of went back and read it very seriously before this meeting. Incredible wisdom. It would take a great intellectual like Brent Bozell to write it down. But as Lee correctly said, it was Barry Goldwater looking over his shoulder; it's both of them. But it really did take somebody with the touch. What a wonderful book.

I'm going to quote some things that aren't inspiring in the same way that have been quoted, but they're more important, at least in my opinion. Goldwater directly says, "Conservatism is not an economic theory, although it has economic implications. It is socialism that subordinates all to man's material wellbeing." And it seems to me that's very important in this economic and social conservative debate. What Barry Goldwater is saying, and what created the conservative movement, was this fusion of both.

Goldwater goes on, that's what it's not about. He says, "What is it about? The first thing about conservatism is that each member is unique, and that his most sacred possession is his individual soul." This isn't some anarchist libertarian talking. This is somebody who's in what I consider the true libertarian tradition, that looks first at the sacredness of man as why we allow him to, or why he must be free.

Secondly, quote, "The economic and spiritual aspects of man's nature are inextricably interwound," unquote. Now, to me that's about as good a definition of conservatism, of this fusionist conservatism, that they're bound together as one thing. Third, he says, "Nothing happens from abstract forces. It happens from real things, real people, real institutions created by people." And then, only fourth, then comes the conclusion that the government is to allow the maximum freedom for individuals that is consistent with the maintenance of social order.

To me, that is very profound, and done in a way–very journalistic language, not philosophical language, but language of inspiration and conversation and common sense. He says that conservatism has to be appropriate for its time. It's very interesting, he says, he talks about the maximum freedom consistent with social order. He says the order question today "is taken care of." And, therefore, our primary obligation is to emphasize the need for freedom.

That isn't the same case today, is it? I mean, freedom is still the preeminent social value to me, but order is not taken care of anymore, is it, as it was in 1960 when this was written. And that's why without changing our philosophy, the conservative–and we're supposed to be talking about *The Conscience* for the future–us conservatives, as we look to the future, have to be more concerned with the order and social side of this equation in 1995 than we were in 1960. It's not that the principles have changed. It's not that we become social conservatives.

It's that that social side of the conservative equation is now much more under stress.

I'll take the liberty, because this is a Philadelphia Society, one of the first forums that I spoke at as a young academic then, to raise an issue that I've mentioned here many times, about the strange nature of this conservative philosophy that we hold. You know, Leo Strauss, the great professor of political philosophy, wrote voluminously; taught among many of us here. But he said that our philosophy was what he called "dualistic"–confused because it wasn't truly philosophical in the sense of having one single ultimate focus and thrust.

He mentioned this about St. Thomas, about Locke, about Burke. In lectures, he mentioned it about some of the founders, some of his other students were very explicit about it. They talked about this conservative philosophy as being confused. And why confused? Because we look at this inextricable connection between freedom and tradition–and tradition in its broader senses, reaching back to its creator–that we look at both sides of this equation, this confusion that we have that we want both sides of this; that we insist on both freedom and order; that we insist on both values and a subjectively-driven market.

This confusion goes back to its roots, goes back to St. Paul, that John Locke wrote so much about. It goes back to Jesus. It goes back to Aristotle. It goes back to the prophets, to Moses. Really the center of our civilization has always been "confused" when compared to abstract philosophy, not connected to ultimate things, or even connected, I would argue, to reality.

What ignited the modern conservative movement in *Conscience of a Conservative* was this extraordinary coincidence of a great writer and a great man of courage, to write in *Conscience of a Conservative*, the fundamental truths of our Western civilization, in language everyone could understand. That was what made this such a great piece of work. In fact, in the preface, Goldwater/Bozell said this is not a book about philosophy. Now, think of how profound this is. And they mean it in the sense that I've tried to talk about. "The ancient and tested truths that guided our republic through its early days will do equally well for us," unquote. It's not philosophy, it's those fundamental truths.

This was a great work to reignite that tradition, a tradition that almost died in the United States of America. Someone mentioned yesterday Hayek's *Road to Serfdom*, during the war, is perhaps the first flicker. But of course, it wasn't published here originally. It did come here and had success here. But it was by—it needed somebody in the soil of America to make that flame ignite, and to ignite the hearts of everyone up here, most of those–everyone here got our start around that time–a little younger, but around that time. We can't underestimate this great work because it's not sixteen volumes. Its beauty is its ability to say so much that's so profound, in such simple words of common sense that reaches the hearts and minds of the tradition of America.

It's a great time to be alive. Two or three days ago the Supreme Court of the United States, in the *Lopez* decision, said the Commerce Clause has limits. In his first substantive chapter on limited government, Barry Goldwater said that's where we have to start. His second substantive chapter was on states' rights. Now, whatever you may think politically, Bob Dole goes around the country, the Senate majority leader, and pulls out of his pocket and reads at every speech—at least as much as I can get him to do it—the Tenth Amendment of our Constitution; the document that sums up the whole of what limited government is. We've gone a long, long way since *Conscience of a Conservative* in 1960. Let's complete the revolution.

CHAPTER 7

Conservatism Then and Now

April 28-30, 2000
Chicago, Illinois

Friday, April 28
7:00-9:00

Conservatism Then and Now

George Nash, Chairman

M Stanton Evans, "Conservatism Then and Now"

Conservatism Then and Now

By M. Stanton Evans

Thank you, George, for that fine introduction and thank all of you for the welcome, it is great to be here. I did—I'm sorry, I misunderstood the topic. I thought it was to be "Conservativism, now and then." And so, I was going to give a talk about Orrin Hatch, about, so—and then Jon told me I had it wrong, so. I am—I'm deeply honored to be here.

As my vita suggests, I'm a journalist, not a scholar or not an academic. And as a journalist, I wanted to share a couple of items out of the news. Some of you may be ahead of me on this. Today–it's an incredible coincidence–today is National Hairball Awareness Day, so declared. And Jon thought it was next week, but it's today and so declared. And I'm sure some of the cat fans here, you're way ahead of me on this. That's true, this is Hairball Awareness Day, and this leads, naturally, to the topic of Fidel Castro.

And certainly one of the great constants in my adult life has been Fidel Castro. And he was around when I was coming up, and he's still around. And the other constant is American presidents and administrations knuckling under to Fidel Castro, and that, certainly, continues to this day. And the other is the treatment of Fidel Castro by the media. And I brought with me a clipping from *The Washington Post*, this is one of many such that could be cited, but this was the story from last Thursday's *Post*. It was right after the 11th Circuit Court of Appeals had issued the order basically saying that Elian should not be turned over to his father right away or to the Cubans right away. And as so there is reporter of *The Washington Post* in Cardenas, Cuba, which is the hometown of Elian, a fellow named Jon Ward Anderson. And he wrote this story about the outrage of the citizens of this town about this interference of our courts with President Clinton's action. And they did not understand this. How could a court—so, ask these randomly selected Cuban citizens, how can a court interfere with the order of the president? And so, this *Washington Post* reporter writes this, "Cubans in general who are accustomed to swift and forceful justice under Castro." Rewrite that sentence, "Germans in general"—one could say a lot more about that, but I won't.

The other thing that struck me, I am a Methodist, I don't know how many of you knew that, I don't brag about it. But my church, the Methodist church or some spin-off thereof, is involved with this, it's either Craig Greg, or Greg Craig, I can't get it straight and the National Council of Churches, they're all kind of intertwined with this guy and he's representing the father, and he's representing Clinton, and he's representing Castro, I guess. And so some conservatives said the National Council of Churches is involved in this, and isn't that mixing religion and politics? And I say, well you know, that's really not fair because the National Council of Churches has nothing to do with religion, so they're very consistent about that. And in any event, that's the news items of the day, the Elian story goes on.

That is not my assignment, I will now go ahead and try to perform my assignment. I don't think I have any great words of wisdom to impart on this, I'm sure I don't. But I can kind of recap the history of it as I saw it and to some degree took part in it. And this is kind of necessary, many people here know quite as much about this as I do and did also take part in it. But the public at large, perhaps, doesn't know this, and so we should all try to get it down and get it communicated.

And the problem we have in the historical profession today is we have two kinds of history, basically. There's liberal history and then there's no history. And the liberal history is tendentious to put it mildly, and the spiritual father of this was Rousseau, who in his *Discourse on*

Inequality says very early, let us begin by putting aside all the facts, for they do not affect the question. Well, that's kind of the way the liberal history books are written. The facts are secondary to the thesis and to the predetermined conclusion and then you kind of hustle up stuff to support that.

And then, the no history, which perhaps is equally prevalent, is just the fact that people don't know any history at all. And the classic case of this was reported to me by Pat Korten, who is, I think, known to many in this room, as a member of our board at the National Journalism Center. He told me a story, a true story, that he was watching in some city, somewhere in the country, back in 1994, which was the fiftieth anniversary of D-Day, programming about the Normandy invasion and so on. And he was watching this young lady, could have been a guy now, it just happened to be a young lady, reading the teleprompter about these events. And in so reading she referred to World War Eleven. And so we've got this kind of mix of the liberal history and then you have World War Eleven type history.

And so, the history that we get about the conservative movement and about Ronald Reagan and so on is kind of a mix of these two things. The classic study of this is the book by Edmund Morris that came out last year called *Dutch*,[34] which as far as I know none of Reagan's friends ever called him. But Morris decided to make that the title, and everybody kind of got after him for having introduced himself as a fictional character in Ronald Reagan's life and that became, sort of, the big story about that book. But the bigger story to me was the abysmal ignorance of the book about the policies of Ronald Reagan and the politics that brought Ronald Reagan to the presidency. And there was sort of–it was amalgam of the liberal history and the World War Eleven type history. And he had the whole package there.

So basically, what Morris tells us, and you can read in Lou Cannon's

---

34 Lee Edwards, *Goldwater: The Man Who Made a Revolution* (Washington, D.C.: Regnery Publishing, 1995).

books about Reagan or any of Bob Schieffer's—any book about Reagan. You can read that one morning in 1980, or I'm sorry, one morning in 1966, Ronald Reagan woke up and had been elected governor of California. And then fourteen years later, he woke up one morning and he had been elected president of the United States. And then he did a whole bunch of illegal things and bad—you know, cut the budget, and threw people out in the snow, and helped the Contras illegally and so forth and so on. And all that policy stuff is just totally wrong.

But what I want to focus on is the political stuff, because to hear them tell it, to read Edmond Morris's treatment, Ronald Reagan just came from nowhere and all of the sudden here's this actor whose president of the United States and he was the Teflon president, or he was a good communicator. And even though people didn't like his views, he got elected because of that. I mean, that's what these books say over and over again. And all this is just totally erroneous, it has no connection to fact.

And so, what I would like to do in the three and a half hours that I have here is slowly, slowly, to walk through all of this step by step. And so, let me begin with—I go back to the period that George mentioned, well, about the time I got out of college because if you go back before that, you really have to go to carbon dating and so, we'll start there. And there was a period of about ten years from 1950, mid '50s to mid '60s, when a lot of things were going on that Edmond Morris and Lou Cannon and lots of other folks weren't paying attention to and still don't know about. So, maybe we can put this story together for them to read somewhere.

First of all, if you look at what happened in that era, a number of things, I think, should be said. One is that the conservative movement was an embryo, it was just barely getting going. But there was one great advantage that we had then that we don't have today. And that was that the country generally was strong. The traditional values that undergirded America were still pretty much in place. And so, you had a kind of matrix of potential support out there which was ready to be energized if we could reach it and articulate a case to it of what needed to be done from the standpoint of those traditional values.

We also, in that period, were uniquely blessed—and in looking back at it, we didn't really fully appreciate it at the time–in the first rank scholars who appeared in that period, [and] had appeared earlier, and continued to write in that period, and I don't want to start listing all the names but Russell Kirk, Frank Meyer, Milton Friedman, Voegelin [were] very productive in that period. Of course, Mises, Hayek, Richard Weaver, we had all of that going for us at that time and bit by bit we found our way to these writers and scholars and others like them.

And so, there was a very strong underpinning at that level for the entire enterprise. And we had publishers who brought out marvelous books. George and I have talked about this, the quote that I heard, the statement I heard Richard Weaver make here in Chicago—I'm sorry, it was Indianapolis, you tracked it down, it was an ISI event in Indianapolis. And I remember asking him and I was a young neophyte there and he was speaking. I said, what is needed to redeem the times, what do we need? And Professor Weaver said without any hesitation, "what we need are unshakable books." And he wrote unshakable books himself and so did these other folks. And we had those unshakable books and we have them to this day. So, this was a tremendous advantage to us at that era to have such intellectual leadership as we did.

We, in addition, began to develop—we meaning generically conservatives at large—circuits of communication. We'd had *Human Events* and *The Freeman* magazine dating back to the '40s and '50s. In 1955, added to this, Bill Buckley founded *National Review*, and then in 1957, Russell and Henry Regnery founded *Modern Age*. So, we developed a method of communicating among ourselves with these publications and also of writing and publishing scholarly articles that could not otherwise find a venue.

This was a period in which the Intercollegiate Studies Institute, then called the Intercollegiate Society of Individualists, was building its cadres on the campuses and our dear good friend Don Lipsett,

Vic Milione, and others were very active in that enterprise. In 1960, Young Americans for Freedom was founded from which today's Young America's Foundation is descended. And these organizations were very active on the campuses in the early 1960s. And all of this began to percolate into the political community. And the College Republicans, the Young Republicans, and thereafter in the senior party.

And finally, I would add at this very narrow period of time from 1960 to 1964, there was a lot of spontaneous conservative activity all over the country—rallies and meetings and whatnot, speeches. And all of this converged in 1962, '63, '64, into the Goldwater movement. All of these streams of activity came together in that movement and that really is the way the process worked. It started with the ideas, it started with the philosophy, it started with the books, it started with the scholars and then in sequence made its way into the political arena. And this intellectual activity that preceded the political activity, in my view, cannot be stressed too much. It was important intrinsically because we need good scholarship. But in these terms, it was important because, first, it gave us–conservatives, traditionalist, libertarians, and we debated those issues a lot as some of you know back then—a common ground. We began to see the commonalities, as opposed to the superficial conflicts, we began to see how traditional values were needed to undergird a free society and so that was important. But in addition, it gave us a core of principle that made the movement rock solid. It was rock solid. I mean, you could not shake these people.

And so, that was of the utmost significance because we all knew as soon as John Kennedy was killed in November of 1963, there wasn't anybody that thought Barry Goldwater could be elected president in 1964. He didn't think he was going to be elected president and I don't know anybody else who thought it. But that did not stop the Goldwater movement and that long march–that really began here in the Cow Palace in 1960. And I won't go to that, I don't have time—that long march continued. And we knew that we were going to take a tough defeat in November of '64 and we had everything against us.

Every medium of communication, all the magazines, all the television networks, everything just pounding Goldwater day after day after day. We knew it was going to be tough, and it was. It was a tough morning after.

And the thing for some of you young people may not understand in those days we had no grief counselors. And so, it made it—I mean, I could tell you stories, we did not even have remotes for the TV, so if you were you in a mall—I mean, these kids need to hear this stuff. You were in a mall, you went out of the Circuit City, into the Gap, you were outdoors, those malls were not, there was no cover. So, we were tough people is what I'm saying and so as a result of being so tough, we—after the defeat, you know, *The New York Times* exalted, that's it, they had their ideological, you know, excursion, went down in defeat, that's the end of it. Goodbye Barry Goldwater, goodbye conservative movement, we won't be hearing from you anymore. But they did.

We picked ourselves up, all of us. We got up the next day, literally, as soon as, you know, we dug out from under the rubble, and started over. Or more accurately, kept going. And it's interesting that part of that activity to keep going was the founding of this group, which was really founded in a sequence of meetings in 1964, then came into being after the election and the first national meeting—Ed Feulner was reminding me—was in this very hotel in 1965. So, the Philadelphia Society was, itself, a product of this resolution of this core principle: we would not be stopped, we would keep going.

American Conservative Union was, again, founded in the immediate aftermath of the 1964 election. And of course, the main thing that caught people's attention was that in 1965, Henry Salvatori and some other folks out in California said, "we need to get Ronald Reagan to run for Governor of California." And they did–he did and got elected. And that's the way this thing unfolded, and I won't bore you with the more recent history but basically Reagan went on the run in '76, and the run in 1976 was fueled by exactly the same kind of people that worked for Goldwater candidacy in 1964.

They were going against the establishment, state after state after state after state. They were driven by the ideas, they were driven by their principles, they weren't looking for jobs, they weren't pragmatically testing the wind. They knew that if they went against the governor, the sitting governor in state after state after state, or the party chairman, there was no political future for them in doing that, but they did it. And that run in '76 in turn set the table for the run in 1980 and Reagan's election as president.

There are two lessons there from my standpoint. The first is, I've said already, the primacy of ideas, the primacy of principles, convictions. The second is that the action was at the grassroots. The two most important elections in my view, which were involved in this sequence, were the 1964 Republican presidential primary in California when Goldwater and Rockefeller went head-to-head, and the 1976 North Carolina primary between Reagan and Gerald Ford. And if either of those primaries had gone the other way. If Goldwater had lost to Rocky in California, I think they could have denied him the nomination in '64. And if Reagan had lost to Ford in Carolina in '76 that would have been the end of Ronald Reagan as a presidential candidate. In fact, some of the people in his entourage were negotiating the surrender of his sword with Rogers Morton at the very time that primary was being won. The distinctive aspect of those two primaries is that they had nothing to do with anybody in Washington, D.C. There was nobody in Washington, D.C., that was doing any of that, it was all done by the grassroots people in the states who had the principles, who had the beliefs, and who had the toughness to battle it out. Okay. So, that's my version of where it all came from.

We come forward to more recent times. You can see that some of what I'm talking about kind of got lost along the way in the 1980s. And some of that loss was inevitable because it was the consequence of the success of Ronald Reagan. When Ronald Reagan got elected president lots of things changed. And the most obvious thing that changed was all these grassroots activists who had been out there in Texas or Indiana or wherever working for Reagan as insurgents came to Washington to help staff the administration. And as well they should have, however, that took them out of the grassroots and brought them to the government.

Something else that happened, which again was incident to the success and probably unavoidable, was that while a number of people, such as our good friend Ed Feulner and others, have struggled to maintain the primacy of ideas in the conservative political enterprise in Washington. Inevitably, what we saw coming to the floor was the primacy of politics and that had a lot of consequences.

For example, young people who two decades before would have come out of college and gone to work in the Goldwater campaign or gone onto become conservative activists or something, now wanted to come to Washington to get a job at HUD, you know. And so, it didn't exactly, you know, it wasn't quite the same thing. And then we picked up the inevitable, again the inevitable consequence of success: the courtiers, the zeitgeist surfers, and other folks, just job seekers, generally, that any successful political movement will pick up. And this, again, is the catch twenty-two, a large movement, a large successful movement, is going to be necessarily less focused than an insurgent movement. And that's kind of what happened. And I'm not even saying it could have been avoided, but the consequence was a lack of gravitas to put it—lack of ballast in some of our folks there who had not gone through the fiery furnace, who had not done the homework, and who kind of didn't know what it was all about and tended to get caught up in the game in Washington. And we've all seen a lot of that. And this becomes the more serious problem when one looks at the intractability of what is in Washington.

The entitlement machine and the built in, locked in advantage of the spending interest and the bureaucracy in the programs that have been so embedded in authorizations that they run almost automatically, irrespective of the appropriations process, and we've all seen too much of that. I heard someone once describe this process, the way the government works in the real world as opposed to the civics book, as a self-licking ice cream cone. And it just, you know, it just keeps going and one consequence of observing that is I have come to realize that our model, the model in which we were working all these years, I wouldn't say it was an inaccurate model, but it was an incomplete model. Our model was a model of electoral politics driven in the fashion I've described. And we assume that once we won the election, that we or people like us would actually control the government. Wrong. That's not the way it works. And so, you've got to have something–just winning the election, you got to win the elections. I'm not disparaging that, but that is not nearly adequate. And I see a lot of folks, Dan Oliver and others sitting around the room here that know what I'm talking about because you've worked in that environment, and you know what the intractabilities are.

Now, [there has been some backsliding and negatives on the balance sheet]. One is that the strength of the country, the general strength of moral capital based on traditional values has been seriously depleted, to put it charitably. Second, the colleges and universities as the ISI, Young America's Foundation, and other folks know all too well, are much, much worse than they were in the past. And third, the mainstream media are much worse also.

And all of these things converge, and I have just an anecdote that something I saw on TV a couple years ago just kind of summed it up for me. It was on CNBC, and this is supposed to be a financial network, right, and the explosion of cable is going to give us more options and it has. But also in my calculations, it's sort of given us more things that are not worth watching. And so, I'm surfing the channels and CNBC has an interview show where the very nice-looking anchor type couple, man, and woman, they're interviewing two crossdressers. And it was a very serious interview, and these two guys are sitting there, and they did not look like women. They look–have you ever seen these Bud Light commercials where the guy is, they're dressed up like women and they're trying to get the free drinks on ladies' night? They kind of look like that. And they wore wigs, and they had a purse and pearls and lipstick and so forth. And one thing I found out that crossdressing is not the same as transvestitism. I didn't know that, did you know that? Totally, totally, different thing and so anyways that was the first thing. But they talked about the, you know, benefits of this crossdressing and why they did it and, you know, it made them feel good and so on. So, it really sounded very, very positive and so at one point in this interview, the one interviewer says, well, I mean, you make it sound so good, is there like any downside? And so, this one guy says, yeah, he says sometimes if you're in a bar, weirdos will come on to you. Who does this guy think is a weirdo, so I—okay then—you got that, I mean, that's–why is this on my television set?

But then we go to what I call the politics of vapidity, and this is the world of shouting heads on TV. We don't have talking heads anymore, people are shouting at each other very, very informative and we also have perception management. There is actually a firm in Washington that sent a card to me, but I won't name it, and it says on it: perception management, that's what they do. We have focus groups. The Republican Party in Congress can't do anything unless it calls together a focus group and finds out what the focus group thinks about it, or reads the polls. Now, looking at all of that perception management, focus groups, there would never have been a Goldwater movement ever, if that's the way people had operated back then.

And the politics of vapidity is so pervasive that one could go on and on about it for a long time. Let me just—this is another true story I will cite. People question the fact that the election calendar has been pushed back earlier and earlier and earlier. And you remember the stuff about the Iowa caucuses and the New Hampshire primary, then it was straw polls back in '99 and it's getting very, very early. However, at the National Journalism Center, we date the election cycle in a different way, and we date it earlier than that. We date it at the sighting of the first lumberjack shirt, and it turned out that the first lumberjack shirt in this election cycle was spotted and it was photographed, it was on the front page, or not on the front page, on the pages of both *The*

Washington Post and *The Washington Times*, and it was actually prior to the 1998 by-elections. That's how early we spotted this shirt. And to no one's surprise it was on Al Gore, he was wearing it.

And the story was that Gore and Governor Glendening of Maryland were going to be with a group of farmers to tell the farmers why, for some reason that I can't remember, they couldn't do something with their land. That's what they always are always telling the farmers these days. And so, they were going to meet with the group of farmers in Maryland, and the pictures show Gore and Glendening looking very, very manly, alpha male type guys striding forth in their lumberjack shirts to meet these farmers. And then the other picture or the other papers showed them with the farmers.

Now, it so happened that none of the farmers [were] wearing a lumberjack shirt. All of the farmers were wearing coats and ties. And people say this is an anomaly, well, it really isn't. None of the farmers are running for public office. So, anyway that's some of the many, many such anecdotes that, anyway, it's worse than that though because when you get this sort of vapid politics, you end up rudderless to put it mildly at the national policy level and worse. And you can look at any, I mean, the Elian thing is just, you know, a case study in everything possible that could be wrong in Washington, D.C., but it isn't just that, Clinton has been giving the store away to Red China, transferring technology to Red China to improve their missiles and many, many other things of that nature.

And in that regard, I might say that the president actually joked about this on the side which was picked up by, I think, Jerry Seper of *The Washington Times*, and he said to one of his aides he said, you know the problem with appeasing Red China is that a couple hours later you want to do it again. And so, he did not really say that I–I made that up. So, I mean, and Bill Clinton is arguably the most, well he is, the most despicable president we've ever had in the history of the United States. He proves it every day and everybody knows he's a liar and, you know, there's really no contest in that. And yet, he's beating our brains out, it's like he's just beating the Republican Party to death. And so, it's kind of bad news for the Republicans.

However, I do have some good news for the Republican Party. I know there's some Republicans in this room and this good news is that the National Right to Life Committee voted, just last week, to endorse every Republican congressional candidate in the forthcoming November election. Every last one of them, which is unprecedented. And the reason for this is in recognition of the many months that the Republican leadership in Congress has spent in the fetal position. That joke was tested with a focus group, so I don't think we should be getting that kind of feedback here.

All right, that's—Jim Hines is going to get on my case, say I'm too negative, he's already done this once, so I'm going to talk about some positive stuff here, Jim. There are many things and I mention Ed Feulner, I was going to—I called up you were out of the city, but you had a very fine column in *The Washington Post* answering these various folks, saying the Conservative movement is dead and all of that and I thought you said it very well. It's not dead, no way is it dead.

There are many, many, many positive factors here. One is an observation that is now commonplace that everyone acknowledges that markets are superior to government intervention, at least in theory. Now getting that in practice is another matter. So, that's a huge, huge conceptual victory for the position we have taken for so many years. If you look at the infrastructure policy—the policy infrastructure, the intellectual transmission belts by which the intellectual stuff reaches the political arena, look at the Heritage Foundation, Cato, look at the state think tanks, these are tremendous assets. We have many, many good, new circuits of communication for our point of view. The ISI and Young America's Foundation are both vigorously working the campuses very hard. Things like the home-schooling movement, many, many other conservative groups, books, and great financial resources, there's a lot there, there's a lot there to work with. And the question is, can we take what's there and build further on what already has been accomplished intellectually and politically.

And I'm going to defer any political proposals in this forum, but just thinking about who we are, where we are, one principle I've always believed in is you know you can sit back and carp and complain about or suggest what other people should do, but we can't really control what other people do, but we can control what we do. So, that's where we really need to take inventory and decide what our agenda should be and what our priorities are, and there is so much which is in the domain of the Philadelphia Society. And I think of all the fine scholars such as the Forest McDonalds, the Stephen Tonsors and so many others I shouldn't start naming them, who have long been members of this Society and then looking at these new younger scholars coming online, that is a tremendous enterprise and tremendously encouraging. And we need that scholarship to recover our history, not just the history of the conservative movement, but the history of our country and the history of our civilization, which has, again, been warped and misstated repeatedly by the liberal historians.

We need to continue working with these youth groups. The ISI and Young America's Foundation groups on the campuses. We've got to have them out there. And again, they interact so strongly with the Philadelphia Society. And the colleges, again, [if I] start listing names it's trouble, but Hillsdale and Rose City and Aquinas and many, many, others that we all know of that are keeping the faith and are working to give a truly sound education to young people, which is not the case on so many other campuses.

But beyond this, I think we need an offense. I think we need—and there's still sporadic fighting on some of these fronts over political correctness and things of that nature—we need to go on the offense against what is happening in the so-called mainstream colleges and universities. The outrages that occur there are not just the speech codes, not just the burning of papers and all that, as bad as that is. It's what is taught day in and day out in those classrooms.

I know myself as an alumnus of Yale University, when I get my

Yale alumni magazine—and Lou, I'm sure you read yours just as I do mine—I'm looking to see our classmates and so on. What they will not tell you—they're talking about the Harvard game and the good days when you were at Yale and we're going to take a trip to the Mediterranean and all that stuff—but what they won't tell you is what they're teaching in the classrooms of New Haven. And that is true of every alumni operation in every major college university in the United States. That needs to be overcome and we need some kind of effort to communicate to taxpayers in the case of state universities, alumni in the case of all universities, parents, legislators in the case of the state schools, what is actually happening in the classrooms of these universities. And finally, I'm back around to my ballpark, the media. We need much more effort to reclaim the media. They are as bad as the universities in their way.

Now, so that's assets, liabilities, and a modest, for academics, scholarly agenda. And again, I want to end on a more positive note. Please don't get me wrong that I am immensely gratified by many, many, developments of the past four decades. I've lived quite a while now and there were two things I never thought I would live to see. One was Elton John singing in Westminster Abbey. I remember John Wilson and I were, in 1975, and I heard him singing "Yellow Brick Road" and I said to John, I said that guy's a terrific singer. Too bad he will never sing in Westminster Abbey, and yet that happened, that happened. And there was another thing, what was the other thing? I know, I know, the fall of Communism, that was the other thing, which, arguably, was even more important than Elton John singing in Westminster Abbey. So if those things can happen, anything can happen.

So, just to put it this way, in the past forty years, many good, allegedly impossible things have indeed been accomplished. If we remember and go back to and stick to the basics as members of this Society have always done, the next forty years can be better yet. My time is up, I thank you for yours.

CHAPTER 8

What Have We Learned from Conservative Governance?

April 28-30, 2000
Chicago, Illinois

Saturday, April 29

4:00-5:30

What Have We Learned from Conservative Governance?

T. Kenneth Crib, Chairman

Lee Edwards

Steven Calabrisi

What Have We Learned from Conservative Governance?

By Lee Edwards

Well, I'm going to speak from the basic proposition that conservatives can govern. Although there is some recent evidence, I freely admit to the contrary. Let me offer as proof of this assertion some accomplishments of conservatives in three quite different decades.

Let's go back to 1948. President Truman achieved an historic upset victory by running, not against his opponent, Thomas E. Dewey, but against what he called "the do nothing Eightieth Congress," "the do nothing." But what in fact did that Congress, with its Republican majority, accomplish? Number one, a reduction of 7.5 percent in federal spending. Now, that's not in the growth of spending, that's [an] outright cut in spending itself, 7.5 percent. Number two, a cut in personal income taxes with reduced rates by 10.5 percent at the top and removed 7.5 million people in the lower brackets from the rolls. Three, passage of the Taft-Hartley Act, which redressed a labor management imbalance that had been around for over a decade. And four, passage of the Truman Doctrine and the Marshall Plan, which were basic building blocks in the policy of containment against Communism. And yet, Truman convinced the people in his election campaign in the fall of 1948 that the Eightieth Republican Congress had done nothing.

Why? Because Republicans led by their presidential candidate, Mr. Dewey, did not bother to rebut Truman's false charges. Robert A. Taft, who was the leader of the Senate and of that wonderful Republican Eightieth Congress, was more concerned and he urged Dewey, who was the nominee, "hit Truman hard every time he opens his mouth." That was Taft's urgent advice and recommendation to Dewey. But a complacent Dewey responded that over the years, he had found that when he got into controversies, he lost votes. So, to avoid controversy he did not get into an argument with Mr. Truman, and as a result, lost that election. Keep those facts in mind; we'll come back to them in just a minute.

Let's go now to December of '81. President Reagan signed the Economic Recovery Act–which Ken has already made reference to–which cut all marginal tax rates by 25 percent [and] indexed tax rates to offset the impact of inflation. As we know, within a little more than a year, stagflation, created by President Carter and his policies, had disappeared and [an] unparalleled period of economic prosperity and growth began, which is still continuing today, some seventeen years later. In 1982, President Reagan told the British Parliament at Westminster that the march of freedom and democracy will lead Marxism-Leninism on the ash-heap of history. [He] was very skeptically received at the time in early of 1982, but he was right. Just seven years later, after challenging Mikhail Gorbachev to tear down the Berlin Wall, the Wall did fall, and Communism collapsed behind that once seemingly indestructible iron curtain.

Well, why was Reagan so successful? Ken's outlined, I think, four very good reasons why, but let me just suggest a couple of other things. Because he concentrated on doing a few things very well and let others worry about who was going to use the tennis court. And yet, he could focus when it counted. As you, I'm sure, will remember very well, Ken, in that very critical period there, the spring and summer of '81, to try to get through the Economic Recovery Act, Ronald Reagan was not disengaged, he was not sitting up there eating tuna fish sandwiches, he was making telephone calls, he was making personal calls. As a matter of fact, I've seen some figures where he was making two and three hundred personal visits and calls on members of Congress, members of the Senate, reinforcing and particularly going after the Boll Weevils, those Democrats, those Southern Democrats, those moderate conservative Democrats, whose votes were needed because the House was Democratic at that point. The Senate was Republican. And President Reagan got engaged when it counted.

He also succeeded because he was a genius at building and maintaining coalitions. Able to reach out, get people, work with people, try to get them to look at the bigger picture and not just at their own special interests. He's also a pretty fair speaker as we well remember. And, I think, very important and something that Bob Taft did not have back there in '47 and '48, he could call on a vital conservative movement for ideas, political muscle, and people to run his administration. People like Ken Cribb, Ed Meese, and others who are here in this room. Those kinds of people were certainly were not available to Mr. Eisenhower when he won the presidency and was looking around to staff his administration in 1953.

So, keep in mind '48, '81, '82, now let's look at '95 and '96. The 104th Republican Congress. It's much maligned and I think unfairly. If we step back, not only did it win, with the Contract with America, an out and out Republican majority, House, and Senate, what did it do in terms of specific accomplishments, historic accomplishments? A balanced budget, now we conservatives have been talking about a balanced budget for decades and it finally came about because of Newt Gingrich and other leaders of that particular Congress.

Welfare reform, there wouldn't have been any welfare reform and there would not be welfare reform today if it were not for that Republican Congress, which forced over two, as I recall, two Clinton vetoes finally to sign that welfare reform. Part of that was the elimination of the first welfare program, AFDC, since the New Deal. And beyond that the phasing out of farm subsidies. And yet, as we recall, President Bill Clinton won reelection by running against that Republican Congress in 1996. Harry Truman in '48, Bill Clinton in 1996. Taft and that Eightieth Congress, Gingrich and the 104th Congress, very interesting parallels between those two Congresses.

What were they? I'm going to suggest a few to you. Lessons for us to keep in mind for the future.

Both were ruled by hubris; I mean they just were cocky. They thought they were invincible. Both were more often ideological than prudential. The idea of shutting down the government, that was not a very prudential idea and they paid dearly for it. Both misjudged the political skills of the president they faced. Dewey sort of dismissing Harry Truman as this Missouri farmer and Newt Gingrich thinking, well, this is some Arkansas guy that he could take. The guy in the White House, he turned out to be a lot more clever than Newt Gingrich.

And both took the people for granted. And I think this is one of the things which—there's something intrinsic in the conservative character perhaps, that we just—we won those victories, but then we took the people for granted. Having won what they considered to be a mandate, Republicans did not think they had to bother communicating what they were doing and why to the public. Ronald Reagan certainly did not make those kinds of mistakes.

Let me give an example, an ancient example, way back in 1948. I made reference earlier to the Truman Doctrine and the Marshall Plan, which by the way Bob Taft supported. It's not true, as some people suggested, that Taft was some, you know, crazy isolationist. He was prudential and he saw both the Truman Doctrine and Marshall Plan as necessary measures to take against Communism in Europe and he backed both of those. He tried to cut the Truman Doctrine appropriations and also the Marshall Plan, but he voted for final passage, and he said, as a matter of fact, there must be a final vote and he made sure there was a final vote on the Marshall Plan. There was a prudential politician who understood practical politics.

But Harry Truman called Arthur Vandenberg into the White House, into the Oval Office in the fall of 1948, Arthur Vandenberg, the Republican senator from Michigan, someone who had been very much in support of these same measures. And he said, well, "Arthur you know it's wonderful," the president said, "we've been able to pass these measures, I certainly think we ought to keep this bipartisan, don't you? We certainly shouldn't get partisan about this, in this campaign. We should rise above it, should we not?" And Arthur Vandenberg said, "that's a wonderful idea, Mr. President, I agree with you, we should be bipartisan, and I certainly am not going to make a partisan issue out of these kinds of issues." And Harry Truman went out the very next day and just blasted the hell out of the Eightieth Congress as a do-nothing Congress, and Arthur Vandenberg was just, you know, caught too late to try to get the necessary time to rebut and respond to that kind of partisan attack.

Let me just finish up with sort of—what are the role of ideas, let me suggest a few things. What were the role of ideas for these three leaders, particularly, that we're talking about here, Taft, Reagan, and Gingrich? Now, Bob Taft was not an intellectual. He was a professional politician. But he was brilliant, he had a brilliant mind, the most brilliant mind of the Senate. Incisive, analytical, logical. But he was a reader of legislation, not of books. The one document he knew by heart was the U.S. Constitution, and he would not deviate from it. He was also a prudent politician, in the tradition of Edmund Burke. For example, when Fred Hartley, who was the House supporter of the Labor Reform Act, wanted to eliminate strikes from their famous Labor Reform Bill, Taft blocked the move, saying no, workers have a right to strike and besides such a provision went too far and would endanger passage of the bill.

Ronald Reagan, what about the ideas there? [He was] a great reader, a fantastic reader. Anne and I had the opportunity way back in 1965 to visit him in his house in Pacific Palisades before he ran for governor. And he went to the kitchen to get some iced tea and I admittedly went and began looking through his library and pulling out books and there were bookshelves filled with hundreds of books. I'm wondering, you know, are these fake, are they real? I began pulling them out and they were dog eared, and they were marked, and they were annotated, and they were filled with his inscriptions. And what were they? They were books of politics, books of economics, Henry Hazlitt, *Economics in One Lesson*,[35] was one of them I recall. *The Law* by Bastiat was another.[36] Not bad reading for a B family actor down there in Hollywood.

And there was one book in particular, two books in particular which I want to mention, which had an influence. And for our younger scholars here, if you haven't read these, there have been frequent references to one of them and I think to the other as well, you should go out and get paperback copies and read them tomorrow. *The Road to Serfdom* by Hayek and Whittaker Chambers' *Witness*.[37] Both of those had a profound impact on Ronald Reagan.

Now, I have to, in the interest of truth telling here, say that I never asked him specifically about this, but I do know that he read, not the original 1944 edition of the *The Road to Serfdom*, but the *Reader's Digest* version of it, which appeared here in 1945 or '46. I never asked him whether he had read the full version or not, but I did go back and read that *Reader's Digest* version, it's got all the elements in it. And that book stayed with him. It was one other very important conservative politician who also read that same *Reader's Digest* version and referred to for the rest of his life, and that was Barry Goldwater, who was then a young Arizona businessman. I might also mention that Ronald Reagan was an original subscriber to *National Review*, but, equal time, he also was reading *Human Events* even before he read *National Review*. He was also, by the way, a member of the Conservative Book Club and read voluminously those.

Finally, Newt Gingrich, well, Newt Gingrich's problem was he read too much. *The Federalist*, Peter Drucker, Toffler, et cetera, et cetera. There's a story of Newt and the role of ideas, which members

35 Henry Hazlitt, *Economics in One Lesson* (New York: Three Rivers Press, 1981).

36 Frederick Bastiat, The Law (Publication Location Unspecified: 2010, 1850).

37 F.A. Hayek, *The Road to Serfdom* (Chicago: University of Chicago Press, 1944).

of the Congressional Campaign Committee tell. When he first came to Washington in the early '80s, he would come over there with an idea, and idea, and an idea. He'd come bursting in, just this freshman congressman from Georgia talking about achieving a Republican majority in the House. People thought he was a little bit crazy back in 1980, but of course, it happened in 1994. But even so, ideas of how to come about wedge ideas, positive ideas, negative ideas. So, after a while they caught on and years later, they said they would take people over to a corner and there would be three gigantic metal drawer–filing cabinets, Newt ideas, Newt ideas, Newt ideas, Newt ideas, and then way down at the bottom of the third cabinet, this one drawer, good Newt ideas. A proper form, I'm not so sure. And yet, Newt Gingrich stood on the shoulders of those who had become him, and he's openly acknowledged this, Barry Goldwater, Ronald Reagan, and their influence is evident in the Contract with America and the other legislative accomplishments of the 104th Congress.

Well, given the size of Leviathan—we've been talking a lot about Leviathan today—conservatives [it] seems to me must take the long view, and I think that is what many here in this room have done, have taken the long view. The modern welfare state was not built in a day, and it's not going to be dismantled in a day. And to prevail in politics, it seems to me that you must be prepared to run not a hundred-yard dash, but a marathon. But amid all the inevitable ups and downs and the backs and forwards, and the advances, and retreats, conservatives can take solace from the fact, to paraphrase T.S. Eliot, that in politics, there are no permanent victories or defeats. Thank you.

What Have We Learned from Conservative Governance?

By Steven Calabresi

[Recording begins with the talk in progress]

Governance. I approach this topic, both as a former member of the Reagan and Bush administrations, and as a Northwestern law professor who teaches constitutional law. My experience, my academic writing, and my teaching all have been focused on the presidency and on the role of the federal courts. And I, therefore, want to discuss today three lessons we might learn from the Reagan/Bush years about conservative governance in the White House. And three that we might learn from those years about the federal courts.

The first lesson of the Reagan/Bush presidencies, I think, is the tremendous importance of the first two years of any administration that's in the White House. The modern presidency, for better or worse, is something of a lightning rod. Presidents have little constitutional power in peacetime, and they can advance a domestic agenda only with support in Congress. For decades now, presidents like Reagan have had the most supporting Congress in the first two years of their term, and have watched it dwindle with every election after the first. While Reagan did not lose the 1982 midterm elections as badly as Clinton lost the 1994 midterm elections, he did accomplish much less in the last six years of his term.

Since 1934, every first midterm election has turned out the presidents' opponents in higher numbers relative to his supporters than had occurred two years before. This is not only relevant to a president's support in the House and the Senate, but also to his support in state houses across the country. Well over thirty states, including all the major ones, elect their governors and state legislators during the off-year midterm cycle. It's no accident that Republicans picked up the majority of governorships in 1994 for the first time since the 1960s, precisely as Democrats had controlled a majority of governorships during the Reagan/Bush and Nixon/Ford years.

All this means, I think, two somewhat contradictory things. First, it's important to make the first two years of any conservative administration really count. In fact, there's not a moment to spare. Nor is there any time to develop an agenda if you were not elected with one. Successful presidents must have a successful first eight months, and there's just, simply, no time to lose at the start of his administration. At the same time, one also doesn't want to scare the public unnecessarily or make a presidency even more of a lightning rod than the office naturally seems to have become. President Clinton, obviously, made this mistake in many ways in his first two years in office.

President Reagan, of course, came in with a clear agenda. He executed it against formidable odds, and then he was able to stay the course for the next six years as his opponents tried, at every turn, to undo what he had largely already set in motion. We need to make sure that the next conservative president who's elected makes the same good use of his first two years in office.

A second aspect of the modern presidency, which I think challenges us as Conservatives, is the press' and the public's desire for constant action and entertainment. Journalists make their living by selling newspapers, articles, magazines, and TV shows. They have an insatiable appetite for news, gossip, and entertainment, both because of their need to satisfy the public and because of their competition with one another. The emergence of the intensely competitive twenty-four-hour news cycle and of many new media has made this phenomenon worse than ever. We seem, unfortunately, slated to go from news frenzy to news frenzy, from OJ to Princess Diana, to Monica, to Jon Benet, to Elián.

This sad aspect of modern life poses special challenges for a conservative president. Conservatives by temperament dislike flurries of proposals, action for its own sake, and government action in particular. And yet, the public today has very little tolerance for inaction. The key problem faced by George Bush Sr., and by Gerald Ford before him, was the feeling that they were not doing anything. While I personally preferred Bush/Ford inaction to what happened when Jimmy Carter and Bill Clinton started doing something, for much of the public there was, and still is, a great yearning to see a steady flow of proposals, speeches, programs, et cetera out of the White House. A conservative president who sits back, even briefly, as Bush and Ford did gets defined by the opposition and is forced to play defense. The president has to play offense and to lead. The public, rightly, expects that much. Reagan succeeded because he led with a vision of where the country and the world ought to go, and he always spoke and worked towards those ends of limited government.

A third and final lesson from the Reagan/Bush years, for the executive branch, is the critical importance of defending and using the institutional powers of the presidency. The president has substantial ability on his own to make at least some important policy changes. Through executive orders, regulations, and rule makings, and signing statements at the time a bill becomes law, the president can, importantly, affect many areas of public policy. Ronald Reagan's executive orders on OMB oversight of the regulatory agencies, and on federalism, and on takings of private property, and on abortion counseling, were all important uses of this power. This is made clear by President Clinton's repeal or rewriting of each of these Reagan initiatives, in one case, during his first twenty-four hours as president.

Of similar importance, was President Reagan's initiative on signing statements, which Reagan launched, and which President Bush continued. Under this initiative, detailed presidential history was added for the first time into the record every time Reagan or Bush signed a bill. A conservative president-elect will need immediately to assign staffers to figure out what can be done and should be done by the president unilaterally on his first day or days in office. This is an important opportunity to seize the honeymoon window and make the most of it and to lay out an agenda for others to follow.

I want now to turn from the presidency, which is my main area of expertise as a law professor, to the federal courts. And here, again, let me discuss a few lessons from the Reagan/Bush era. A first lesson is the importance of nominating justices and judges who are firmly committed to the enforcement of the Constitution and to judicial restraint. Both Presidents Reagan and Bush made an unprecedented effort to find prospective justices and judges who were originalists, who would follow the text of the Constitution and laws, who understood that court decisions were not to be a function of results or consequences, but that they were to be faithful to the law. Judges who understood, as Bush once said, that they should not be running around all over the front pages of the newspaper.

Reagan and Bush did much better on this score than had the three preceding Republican presidents, Ford, Nixon, and Eisenhower. In the wake of the Warren and Burger Court fiascos, heroic efforts to appoint judges who believed in the separation of powers were rewarded. Nonetheless, while the final results were better than those achieved by Nixon, Ford, and Eisenhower, some appointments were disappointing, especially David Souter, and to a lesser extent Sandra Day O'Conner and Anthony Kennedy.

The obvious question is how does the next conservative administration build and improve on this record? How do we make sure that the court is filled with Rehnquists, Scalias, and Thomases who follow the Constitution, rather than with Souters and Kennedys who either make it up or waffle at critical junctures? The answer to that query is as easy to state as it is hard to accomplish. Hold on to a solid majority in the US Senate. The key moment at which the Reagan/Bush drive to appoint restrained justices stalled was the Bork confirmation fight.

Imagine that Robert Bork or another comparable rule of law jurist had been confirmed by a Republican Senate to Lewis Powell's seat. Imagine now that incoming President Bush still had a Republican Senate and had not been bruised by the John Tower nomination defeat at the very outset of his presidency. At that point, Bush and his top aides would have been much less likely to throw the disastrous Hail Mary pass that was the David Souter nomination, and much more likely to appoint any of a number of able conservative jurists on the US Courts of Appeals.

Conservatives have to remember that even a popular president of the United States can do only so much without support in Congress and in this case in the Senate. From 1986 to '92, Reagan and Bush did not have that senatorial support and they faced well-funded opposition from groups financed by Hollywood and by big labor. The Left was, and remains, highly dependent on the Supreme Court to protect its agenda of legal abortion, legal pornography, and of keeping religion out of public life. Left wing groups will, again, fight viciously against pro-rule of law judicial nominees. And if there is a Democratic majority in the Senate, it will be very hard to win unless there are an extraordinary number of vacancies and appointments.

The first thing the Reagan/Bush experience suggests out of this, is that a conservative president must at all costs keep nominating one good justice or judge after another, after another, if need be. If the Left has a majority in the Senate, or if the Senate is closely divided, or if nominees are smeared, we will have, and have to expect, to take losses. The only solution is to keep coming back with more good nominees. As Reagan was once forced to grimly say, the Senate cannot defeat them all, and that is true. In fact, many senators hate judicial confirmation fights, and they may tend to have voted against a president on one nomination to be with him on the next, even if the two nominees are not all that different. The first key to success with judges, then, is for the president and his staff to have a long and good list of choices.

A second key lesson is the importance of fighting hard for a good nominee, like Robert Bork. Confirmation fights like the Bork or

Thomas fights are nothing less than mini presidential campaigns with national fundraising, polling, and mobilization. Finding a good lawyer who would make a good justice, who is also a compelling figure in such a fight is hard. Mobilizing the president's administration and supporters on behalf of that nominee is harder still. But it is critical that a president fight and fight hard for his nominees even if he loses. Reagan and Bush, by and large, did this and Clinton, as Zoe Baird and Kimba Wood quickly learned, does not. It's critical to a president's success that he fight hard for his judicial nominees.

Another lesson from the Reagan/Bush era that bears on the federal courts is the tremendous importance of the lower federal courts, both district courts and federal circuit courts of appeals. [The] U.S. Supreme Court today decides only eighty of the several 100,000 cases a year that are filed in the federal courts. This means that as a practical matter for the overwhelming majority of litigants and of cases, more than 99 percent, a district or circuit judge has the final word. Both Presidents Reagan and Bush made a determined effort to find lower court judicial nominees who were as qualified as Supreme Court justices.

Such an effort for the lower federal courts requires a large staff based in the Department of Justice, not the White House, if it is to be done thoroughly. Everything written or published by a nominee needs to be read carefully by several individuals with a great deal of training themselves to help identify the best candidates. Reading a prospective nominee's prior opinions, articles, briefs, or other writings is the best way to learn whether they have an understanding of what distinguishes the role of a judge. Had David Souter's New Hampshire Supreme Court opinions been read more carefully by more people under less time pressure, the indicia of his activism and lack of understanding of the proper judicial role would have been seen.

A final point of critical importance is the quality of the litigation effort presented by the Department of Justice in the U.S. Supreme Court and in the lower federal courts on key constitutional issues. This effort in turn depends greatly on the ability and jurisprudential philosophy of the solicitor general, of the key assistant attorneys general, and of the attorney general himself. The Reagan and Bush litigation efforts were continuously set back by recalcitrant career lawyers in the Solicitor General's Office and by the personalities of the men who served as solicitor general.

The briefs an administration files in the Supreme Court or in the lower courts on major constitutional issues are critically important. They provide much of the raw material and sometimes all too much of the reasoning that goes into the final opinions themselves. Those briefs must be first rate and *jurisprudentially* sound. A conservative administration cannot rely on pro-rule of law judges to save the country from the administration's own lawyers. Good constitutional decisions or opinions or, if need be, dissents are aided by hiring terrific lawyers who file terrific briefs. Twelve or twenty years ago it was hard to find enough good originalist lawyers to write such briefs; today it should be no problem at all.

In closing, I've tried to suggest a number of things the next conservative president might do, bearing on the executive and judicial branches, growing out of the experiences of past administrations, and relying upon what I've learned from studying, writing about, and teaching constitutional law. The task ahead will be challenging, but it's been made much easier, as have so many things, by Ronald Reagan, who showed us all how governance from the White House could be done right. Thank you.

CHAPTER 9

The Conservative Movement for Forty Years

April 30-May 2, 2004
Chicago, Illinois

Friday, April 30
7:00-9:00

Lee Edwards, Chairman

John A. Howard

George W. Bush

Edwin J. Feulner

Milton Friedman

Bill Campbell

Lee Edwards

William F. Buckley, Jr.

The Conservative Movement for Forty Years

By Lee Edwards

Well, good evening, ladies and gentlemen. My name is Lee Edwards, and I am the president of the Philadelphia Society. It's a beautiful morning in Chicago and a great day to be alive. Now, that's how one of the most popular DJs in Chicago used to begin his morning radio program. And I offer a slight variation. It's a beautiful evening in Chicago and a great day to be alive, especially if you're a member or a guest of the Philadelphia Society celebrating our 40th national meeting. I want to pay special tribute to all our generous benefactors, foundations, corporations, and individuals who have made this gala possible. They are listed on pages twenty-one and twenty-three of the official program before you. They all deserve a warm round of applause. Indeed, some really warrant a standing ovation for the unprecedented degree of their generosity.

I'm happy to announce this evening that we are halfway to raising \$400,000 in our capital funds campaign, just over \$200,000. And you will be hearing from us to help raise the remaining half. Once asked why we were called the Philadelphia Society, the irrepressible Ben Rogge responded, "Because our annual meetings are always held in Chicago." And that was the case, from our very first meeting in 1965 through 1986, although we have found other venues since then. But why Chicago? Well, its central geographical location is one obvious reason, and in previous years, one could get fairly decent rates at venerable establishments like the Drake, where the bathroom was often as big as your own living room.

But there's a more telling reason. Chicago has often served, if you think about it, as the center of the conservative movement for much of the last forty years and even longer. Chicago is, after all, the birthplace of *Modern Age*, still the most important journal of conservative thought in America. It was the long-time home of the Henry Regnery Company, which published, among others, seminal conservative works: *The China Story* by Freda Utley; *God and Man at Yale* by William F. Buckley Jr.; and *The Conservative Mind* by Russell Kirk. All three, by the way, were bestsellers.

Chicago counts among its institutions of higher learning the University of Chicago, whose faculty includes five Nobel Laureates in economics, all free-marketers, and whose press has published such conservative classics as *The Road to Serfdom* by Friedrich Hayek, *Ideas Have Consequences* by Richard Weaver, and *Capitalism and Freedom* by Milton Friedman. While Chicago, as we know, is a city of meetings: political, fraternal, medical, and conservative.

It was here at the 1960 Republican National Convention that Barry Goldwater told fellow Republicans that conservatives could take over the GOP if they worked hard enough. It was here at an ISI seminar that Richard Weaver discussed the common ground of conservatives and libertarians, a mutual respect for constitutional government with its list of "Thou shalt nots." It was here in our first national meeting that Milton Friedman, Stanley Perry, Frank Meyer, Russell Kirk, George Stigler, Eliseo Vivas, Robert Strausz-Hupe, L. Brent Bozell, and Warren Nutter discussed the future of freedom, problems and prospects, concluding that ideology and fanaticism are always to be feared and that conservatives must rely on reason to combat liberal ideology. It was at a Society meeting that Irving Kristol, one-time Trotskyite, first gave public notice that he was no longer one of them, but one of us. And it was here in Chicago at our 22nd national meeting that Stephen Tonsor explained why he was not a neoconservative.

It was here at our 30th national meeting in 1994 that Milton

Friedman, ever the optimist, suggested that "There is a tendency to underestimate the power of ideas because of the length of time it takes for them to work." The question should be why not Chicago as the locus of our meetings. So let us give thanks for this great American city, the home of Richard Daley, Saul Bellow, Al Capone. Where the hamburger, Crackerjack, and deep-dish pizza were first served. The place that Billy Sunday couldn't shut down. Site of the first mail-order house, the first controlled atomic reaction, and the world's tallest building. And most important of all, the place where Don Lipsett compiled his list of important laws, including John Ryan's law of public oratory, "Everybody except me speaks too long." William Rusher's other law: "When you find a good thing, run it into the ground." The Harris law of nugatory achievement: "If a thing isn't worth doing, it isn't worth doing well." Think about it. And Mike Mooney's law: "You can't always count on your friends, but you can always count on your enemies."

Well, that's why we're here tonight in Chicago. And now to our program. I call on Dr. John Howard, a distinguished member and former president of the Philadelphia Society, to give the invocation.

The Conservative Movement for Forty Years

By George W. Bush

Bill Campbell and so many good and distinguished friends at the fortieth anniversary of the Philadelphia Society, Laura and I send our best wishes for a memorable event. Through its gatherings and in its writings of its members, the Philadelphia Society has made valuable contributions to the intellectual and cultural life of our nation. The Society has benefitted from having as its members some of the great economic and political thinkers of our time, including Russell Kirk, Milton Friedman, William F. Buckley, and many others. Named for the birthplace of our freedom, the Philadelphia Society has always been guided by a commitment to spreading liberty. That work is as important today as it's ever been, and recent history gives us cause for great hope. In a little over a generation, we have witnessed the swiftest advance of freedom in the history of democracy. In just the past two years, fifty million people in Afghanistan and Iraq, who once lived under tyranny, now live in freedom. Working for the spread of liberty is hard, yet we're not alone. Freedom has its allies in every country and in every culture. And as we meet the terror and violence of the world, we can be certain the author of freedom is not indifferent to the fate of freedom. For forty years, the Philadelphia Society has been an ally and protector of freedom. I want to thank you for your good work and for letting me join you on this special occasion. May God bless you all, and may God continue to bless America.

The Conservative Movement for Forty Years

By Edwin Feulner

Thanks very much, Lee Edwards. Ladies and gentlemen, what a thrill it is to be here at the fortieth anniversary of the Philadelphia Society. And my first assignment this evening is much more a labor of love than an assignment. That is to recognize a very special person, a dear lady who for more than a quarter century was truly the First Lady of the Philadelphia Society.

Necktie designer extraordinaire, she took the Adam Smith cravat, rather a dowdy black thing with a gold version of the Towsey medallion from the UK, spiced it up and made it respectable for such leaders as Ed Meese and many others to wear in subsequent years. Artiste in residence, not only in residence in Michigan and Indiana, but in residence in her works in various places around the country and indeed around the world; letterhead supplier to all, the Invisible Hand Society, the Stephen Decatur Society and its subsidiary, the Stephen Decatur Shop, and other organizations–some too secret to mention. The spouse of our late friend, counselor, and adviser, Don. Ladies and gentlemen, it's a great pleasure to welcome Norma Lipsett back to the Philadelphia Society.

Bill Campbell's instructions in the timeline say, "Ed Feulner makes brief remarks about Philadelphia Society and introduces Milton Friedman video." Well, Campbell, at the moment, it's my microphone. I bought it, and I'm going to use it, so...

You have in front of you, ladies and gentlemen, the fortieth anniversary book commemorating the Philadelphia Society, and it tells a very interesting story about the founding of the Society as recounted by our current president, Dr. Lee Edwards. It's interesting as far as it goes, but in many ways, a careful reading can only give you clues as to the real story. So as Peter Sellers in *The Pink Panther* would say, "Let me give you some facts, and then we can go from there." There are two of them, anyway.

Dr. Edwards does point out that it was that November Tuesday after the defeat of Barry Goldwater in 1964 at the Sheraton Atlantic Hotel across the street from Penn Station in Manhattan that William F. Buckley first met Milton Friedman at the founding get-together of five individuals of the Philadelphia Society. Quoting a movie, "this could be the start of a beautiful friendship." Buckley and Friedman went on to be skiing buddies and intellectual comrades over future years. Continuing that story, Dr. Edwards points out that on that occasion, Mr. Buckley wrote a personal check in the amount of $100 payable to the Philadelphia Society and turned it over to Lipsett and Feulner. What he does not note is that Buckley first assured himself that we had return tickets to Philadelphia later that afternoon. Well, there's one of two explanations for that. Either he wanted us out of Manhattan before sundown or he wanted to make sure we didn't endorse the check over to the Pennsylvania Railroad to buy our return tickets. But in any event, the check made it back to Philadelphia. It was deposited, and an account was opened at the Philadelphia National Bank.

Now, what happened over the next fourteen years, again, is an unstated fact in the history of the Philadelphia Society. The bank account was opened at the Philadelphia National, but in the subsequent fourteen years when the account was held there, on three separate occasions, the Philadelphia National Bank changed its name. And every time, that coincided with a cash crisis of the Philadelphia Society. Since then, however, Dave Stuart had found a bank called Bank One that is not located in the deer rendering plant in Jerome, Michigan, but rather located in Fort Wayne, Indiana, and there have been no subsequent financial crises since.

A final secret that might interest some of you would be to look at this book, and on an early page, you will see the Philadelphia Society and its roster of presidents. In its forty year history, there have in fact been twenty-eight separate presidents, and if you count Liggio twice, because he did not serve consecutively, there were twenty-nine. But twenty-eight in forty years is almost as good as Italy has done with prime ministers in the postwar period.

The question might be asked, "Why such short terms of presidents?" I'm going to violate my oath of secrecy as a former president and tell you the truth, that one of the very few perks of office of the presidency of the Philadelphia Society is that wherever the meeting is held, usually here in Chicago, the president occupies appropriately the presidential suite, which comes to the Society on a complimentary basis usually because of the number of rooms that the Society books in the hotel. What you are not informed of beforehand is that on both Friday and Saturday nights, you are sharing said suite with Karl Ziebarth and his several cases of booze and Jameson Campaigne, Dave Keene, and eight other cigar smokers, and about seventy-eight other booze drinkers who will stay in your suite until about three a.m. And that, ladies and gentlemen, is the reason why over those forty years there have only been four individuals who served more than one term. All four of those incidentally were academics: Glenn Campbell, John Howard, Leonard Liggio, and Forrest McDonald. And they all managed to survive more than one term, and I'll leave it to your imagination as to why that happened.

So much for an unofficial version of some early parts of the history of the Philadelphia Society. Now, Bill, may we have the Friedman video?

The Conservative Movement for Forty Years

By Milton Friedman

Two score and no years ago, Don Lipsett brought forward in this land a new society, conceived in liberty and dedicated to sponsoring, and I quote, "the interchange of ideas through discussion and writing in the interest of deepening the intellectual foundation of a free and ordered society and of broadening the understanding of its basic principles and traditions."

You are meant to celebrate that event, and the celebration is very much in order. The Society has flourished and is continuing to provide a gathering place for believers in a free society, thanks in large measure to the loving care that Don and Norma Lipsett lavished upon the Society.

Conditions were very different forty years ago than they are today. Intellectual opinion at that time was overwhelmingly socialist. Those of us who were true believers in a free society, believers in classical liberalism and libertarian, were regarded as strange creatures. We were a beleaguered minority, regarded by our fellow intellectuals as a bunch of nuts. Today, the situation is almost reversed. The true believers in socialism are now a small, beleaguered minority, and we regard them as a bunch of nuts. Intellectual opinion is overwhelmingly in favor of free private markets, which doesn't seem to prevent it from also being in favor of big government.

Intellectual argument, including that provided by our society, has undoubtedly played a part in this change in public opinion. But much more important undoubtedly was experience, culminating in the fall of the Berlin Wall and the collapse of the Soviet Union. Given this change in opinion, we may ask the question, "Is there still a role for our Society?"

To answer that question, we have to go beyond opinion and look at what has happened in practice. Here, the situation is much more complex. Deregulation has led to a decline in detailed government control of industry prices and output, leading to intensified competition in transportation, telecommunications, and other areas. On the other hand, there has been a great expansion of the welfare state, beginning with LBJ's Great Society, enactment of Medicare and Medicaid in 1965, and followed by Nixon's Environmental Protection Agency, Occupational Health and Safety Administration, Consumer Products Safety Commission, Legal Services Commission, Economic Employment Opportunity Commission, and the Department of Energy, and followed also by George H.W. Bush's Americans with Disabilities Act (ADA). All in all, government is both bigger and more intrusive today than it was forty years ago when the Society was founded.

Two statistics will summarize. On bigger: In 1964, government spending, federal, state, and local, was thirty-two percent of national income. Today, it is close to forty percent. On intrusive: In 1964, the number of pages in the federal register was less than 20,000. Currently, it is close to 80,000, nearly four times as large. What this illustrates is a long lag between changes in opinion and changes in practice, but it also indicates how shallow is the public understanding of the basic principles of a free society and how much there remains for us to do. Freedom today is threatened less by classical socialism than by modern welfarism. That situation offers a new challenge to our society. Do classical liberal principles apply to these new circumstances? Do they need to be changed? And if so, how? Long live the Philadelphia Society.

The Conservative Movement for Forty Years

By William F. Buckley

I keep wondering when Lee Edwards will receive the critical attention he has earned from his continuing work as historian of our movement. His most recent book, *Educating for Liberty: The First Half-Century of the Intercollegiate Studies Institute*, is wise, penetrating, and readable. His "Brief History of the Philadelphia Society," published in the program we have, is a remarkable feat of research and organization. I am pleased to be reminded, as I was earlier by Ed Feulner, that I put up $100 to launch the Philadelphia Society's bank account and forever ruptured my relations with the bank that used to be friendly to me, but went on to spend most of its time coping with the Society's overdrafts. Indeed, my concern for the Society's financial distresses is more regular than my irregular attendance at its proceedings. That concern is a bit, at one level, steadfast, another absolutely reckless.

I remember trying anxiously to reach Senator Goldwater on the phone years ago because I needed his vote before the end of a trustees' meeting at noon the next day in order to effect a grant to the Philadelphia Society. I couldn't locate him. He was off somewhere flying his airplane. In desperation, I sent a telegram to all ten of our fellow trustees, registering approval of the proposed grant to the Philadelphia Society. I signed it, "Best regards, Barry M. Goldwater." I was enormously relieved, when his airplane finally landed and I was able to tell him what I had done, to hear him say, "Fine, okay." He added, "when I'm not at the Senate, you can just send a telegram registering my vote." It was an enormous relief to me that he approved retroactively my use of his name, which also lightened the prosecutorial obligations of the FBI.

You think you can stop me naming names? Well, you can't.

The most economical way to put it is, what would our movement have done if Ed Feulner had never been born? There is, of course, the popular fiction that he has wandered about all these years with three identical twin brothers, attending to our needs, introducing our meetings, writing our books, congratulating us on our good deeds, lamenting the causes of our misfortunes, and arranging for mass when we die. But enough of that. He is the most remarkable biological phenomenon since pithecanthropus erectus. And I hope that before too long they will name a tower, a city, or a state after him. When that happens, I hope to be alive and to be there, as I know all of you Philadelphians will be including Stanton Evans if he has finished his book on McCarthy.

There are others bound to this Society whom I admire and am indebted to, but I tax my reserves on your time and on my own patience, and so I'll close with a full-fledged note about the Commodore. Consider only the mentions of Don Lipsett already made in the program by Bill Campbell. I know of nobody anywhere whose personality so suffused the organization he represented. And this, in his case, meant not only the Philadelphia Society. His affiliations with light and truth had stretched back to the Foundation of Economic Freedom. He went from there to *National Review*, where, in his eighteen months, he created absolute chaos in the circulation department. When he left, he left us tearful at the prospect of life without his inattentions. And without him in the office every day, his illustrious career with Vice-Commodore Norma is annotated in Lee Edwards's essay. And I have to add only that his character truly affected this organization.

It was a benignity there—a benignity of which seemed to detoxify any malign culture that was stirring. The puffs from his pipe didn't exactly dissipate ideological, historical, or philosophical differences, but they managed to convey to us that life would go on, heartening the one impulse dormant in all of us. Namely, that you could never permit anything that would disappoint Don Lipsett. His powers of persuasion, quietly, sweetly exercised with a smile and a little self-effacement, could wring manna from desert soil. It was, I think, his ability to produce a corporate jet at just the right moment to address just this or that emergency, which, untended, would keep a desperately desired guest speaker from coming or going, that brought on his designation as the Commodore. He went along with the act to the point of emblazoning an admiral's insignia on his stationery.

Don Lipsett never asked too much, which is why when he did ask for something, it was greeted as the only alternative to lifelong self-hatred to credit to him. Commodore, of course, did not tell his friends, not even Ed Feulner, that leukemia had been detected. No one had any advanced notice when the news came that he had gone, the most attractive and selfless American to figure prominently in the revival of the American conservative spirit.

Am I done? Well, yes. I have nothing left over for Milton Friedman or Russell Kirk or Adam Smith or Ibn Khaldun. You hardly want, let alone need, a catalog of unfinished national business, but one thing: that which is unfinished will remain so. One reason for it is that the reduction in the size of the state is an asymptotic enterprise. Eliminate the state, and one has only ugly anarchy and the absolute predictable loss of liberty so that exercises in the limitation of the state have to be done on finer canvasses than some even members of this Society have enjoyed drawing on for a substitute constitutional blueprint.

Here is a focus I find both useful and elusive and touched on by Milton in his remarks a few moments ago. It begins by asking how we objectify privations that are traceable to state activity. I have in the past recommended that conservatives take advantage of the popular acceptance of the theory of the slippery slope. We should adopt the metaphor for our purposes. The critical intelligentsia have argued since the initial prohibition of the novel *Ulysses* by the censors that if you set out to censor "Deep Throat," the next thing you know, you will be censoring James Joyce.

I have pondered skeptically this teleological enormity as something that we can't define a difference between the two, but I grant the usefulness of that line of argument, the perils of the slippery slope. An attempt to appropriate it wholesale is the–in the matter of taxation introduces correlative questions. The corresponding position on zero censorship would be zero taxation. Since we cannot have that in any earthly enterprise, we have played with variations of this ideal. One of us in a lovely fantasy proposed that taxes should be paid voluntarily. The proposal, as will not surprise, proved to have no legs. The alternative of the flat tax incorporates as its dynamic engine the assumption that no tax can ever be enacted in a democratic society, which imposes inordinate taxation on anyone. Anyone under the flat-tax code is of course everyone. It is impossible to victimize anybody or any class under strict flat-tax dispensations. That of course is the primary reason why flat tax has not been written into law. That, plus the sociological point made by Milton Friedman, which is that the great national lobbying enterprise, in which are engaged not only individual lobbyists but also federal agencies, corporate agents, and state legislatures, would have suddenly to face disenfranchisement if there were no tax code on which to practice their pressures and seductions.

But there is no reason not to get on with deciphering a tax index which would convey location by location the fiscal status in positions of life in that state, which is to say a number that informs the resident of every state what is the level of taxation where he lives. Adding together federal and state income taxes, payroll taxes, property and sales taxes, it is likely that the whole hypnotic process of tax assimilation is at work, even as the withholding taxes, including the payroll tax, succeeded in concealing to the point of near-invisibility what it is that is actually being extracted at the source.

The tax allotment in America is the easiest to rectify, but much more difficult, as Milton has suggested, are the regulatory impositions. They can't be weighed, often cannot be seen, and sometimes not even suspected, that fly paper that attracts impediments to your catching a flight, building a house, mowing your lawn, or educating your child. The relatively scant popular reaction to those impositions on us by taxation and regulation calls up thought on why there is this insensibility. The most obvious reason is that people get used to these things.

Those of you who ever saw the play *My Sister Eileen* will remember how she and her roommate suspended unquestioningly all conversation every four minutes to let the subway overhead pass by. But there is another perspective at hand, which we need to consider, not merely to criticize, but to deliberate, I think, deeply, is that an affluent society can afford extravagances ill suited to poorer nations. I noticed some months ago the remark of a cosmopolitan Englishman who had been asked about persistent British unemployment. It has sat there for many years at about ten percent. He says that all that those figures revealed was that some of his fellow citizens preferred not to work. I think he said that unemployment is something we can simply afford. Well, of course it is, and we in America can afford subsidies of various kinds, which is different from saying that in detached judgment we approve exactions from the public purse, extrinsic to safety and justice.

Adam Smith did teach us that we correctly impose upon the state the burdens of paying for public monuments. The image sneaks its way up on the imagination. Are the unemployed, in an expanded focus, entitled to pass as a monument to what an affluent society can sustain as a kind of testimonial to its latitude of varying impulses? The easiest answer to that question, almost certainly the correct one, is no, such extensions of what Adam Smith acknowledged as social embellishments of the business, not of the state, but the YMCA. Still, a fugitive thought to take to bed tonight or another night–tonight's thought is being reserved for gratification, having spent time in one another's company.

So we must sleep well, even though there are always grounds for discouragement. But those who are staring at the data hard in the face, are driven to inconsolability, would do well to guard against that temptation. Richard Posner observed in a column in *The Wall Street*

Journal on Wednesday, "Conservatives have a duty to be cheerful because they have no right to be disappointed by their failures, which failures can't surprise us, knowing as we do about the limitations of the state and the weaknesses of human beings." Mr. Posner is surely correct, and surely that counsel of his shone always through the face and the attitude towards the life of Don Lipsett.

We have many forebears. Albert Jay Nock is but one, and his investment in pessimism is once again not, I think, for us. In many years, I have come to admire Mr. Nock more for how he said what he had to say than for what he had to say. We are devoted here to the proposition that what we do and say and write does matter, does have an effect. Mr. Nock wrote in the closing pages of his book on the state, "I would be the first to acknowledge that no results of the kind, which we agree to call 'practical,' could accrue to the credit of a book of this order." He spoke of his book *Our Enemy, the State*. Were it a hundred times as cogent as this one, no results—that is, that would in the least retard the state's progress in self aggrandizement and thus modify the consequences of the state's force—manifest that there has been a slowing down of statist impositions, even if not on the scale that the Philadelphia Society seeks.

Mr. Nock was the total Platonist in respect of what can be achieved on Earth. Efforts to do such as all of us here would try to do might indeed, in his language, be thought ourselves to be bound to this enterprise as a matter of abstract duties, then. He says of the remnant that they, we, do indeed have an intellectual curiosity sometimes touched with emotion concerning the august order of nature. Never mind that. What we do is of no purpose. But, of course, it does have purpose. It could even be held with utmost seriousness that the work of the Philadelphia Society—and this is testimony primarily to our meetings here with one another—are themselves proofs of our substantiality. I have been with you from the beginning, and my investment of $100 in your society, I insist, and I tell this to our cherished bankers, has surely yielded a historic harvest. I am in your debt, and so is the republic.

CHAPTER 10

Black History and Conservative Principles

October 1-2, 2004
Philadelphia, Pennsylvania

Friday, October 1

7:00-9:00

Black History and Conservative Principles

Midge Decter, Chairman

Bill Campbell, “Welcome to Philadelphia”

Shelby Steele, “Black History and Conservative Principles”

Black History and Conservative Principles

By Shelby Steele

I'm just going to use that on the dustjacket of my next book. That was a beautiful introduction. Thank you so much for that. Well, when Midge invited me to speak, she mentioned that once again you were this weekend going to be wrestling with the whole matter of where we went wrong in race relations since the '60s certainly, and so I thought that's what I would try to focus on. I'm just finishing a book on white guilt, so we're going to talk about white guilt tonight one way or another. I don't think my talk answers entirely the question of where America went wrong in the '60s, but I hope a small part of it might be relevant.

I began to sort of think about this problem back not long ago when President Clinton was going through the Monica Lewinsky affair and the whole national crisis that this sexual indiscretion put us through. And I remember hearing on the radio, when I was a kid, that President Eisenhower back in the '50s was heard to have used the N word on the golf course. I don't know whether this is true or urban legend. In the black community where I grew up, it hardly made a ripple. We didn't really assume otherwise. And if there were reporters around, again, they did nothing about it.

It sort of made me wonder: If Eisenhower, back in the '50s, had had a sexual affair with a young, twenty-one-year-old intern, and we knew all of those details, he probably would've been out of office in a week or two, and America simply would not have tolerated that kind of an indiscretion. On the other hand, he could say the N word, and

America really wouldn't care. It wouldn't make the newspapers. Then, conversely, if for some reason we had a tape of President Clinton when he was with Monica or not with Monica, and President Clinton used the N word, and we had it on tape, and it played on 24-hour channel cable news shows, my guess is that he would not have lasted a week or two at the very most. On the other hand, he did survive a flagrant, salacious sexual indiscretion, and though he was impeached, he stayed in office.

So the point is that we have moral tests in any society that we apply to people who want to hold power and will say, "If you meet these moral tests, then you have legitimacy, and you have the authority to remain in power and hold the public trust." And it seems to me that in the times that we live in that we've seen a real reversal so that today, social morality—what you think about other groups, racism, bigotries of all kinds—is vastly more important. And in this area of morality, we are absolutely puritanical.

We are more puritanical, and certainly as puritanical as we have ever been, in enforcing this moral code, and if you violate it, you are banished. Trent Lott is a relatively recent example of someone who was at one moment at the pinnacle of power and sort of reduced instantly to being a backbencher because of an indiscretion that crossed social morality. And so America in effect said, "You don't have the kind of legitimacy, moral legitimacy, that we expect of someone in your position. And so you will be banished, and not only will you be banished, but there will be no redemption for you, and nobody wants to be near you, and no one wants to be in a photograph with you, and you are now on the periphery. We're not going to kick you out entirely, but you no longer will have much say in national affairs."

On the other hand, we say that the president of the United States, who has an affair with a 21-year-old intern, is just fine. We are now sophisticated and tolerant and open-minded and maybe even a little European about characterological virtue, but again, we are puritanical about social morality. Freud talks about this in *Civilization and Its*

Discontents. You can judge societies by where they apply repression, where they repress people and where they don't. And certainly we've had a kind of reversal of oppression where we now repress people in the area of social morality but not in the area of character-based morality.

How did we get here? How did we get from the Eisenhower era to the Clinton era? How did this reversal of our focus happen? I think it goes back to the civil rights movement. I think it has to do with race, which is the deepest schism in our history as a society. By no means is that the only area that contributed to this change, but I think it did begin there, and I would locate it actually beginning at around 1963, '64, '65, that sort of March on Washington through the '64 Civil Rights Bill and '65 Voting Rights Act. I think there was an event that occurred there at that time in our history that has been interestingly unexplained. It seems to me we've not spent much time on it at all, and I think that's where we went wrong.

What happened in those years was that the United States of America acknowledged almost four centuries of slavery and segregation, practiced in a country that was explicitly a model of democracy to the world, so that everyone in that country had democratic values, had an idea of individual freedom, individual rights. The United States of America acknowledged that these extraordinary wrongs were committed century in and century out. I call this, for lack of a better term, "The Great Acknowledgment." I think it's one of the seminal events in late 20th century American life, if not in all of our history. The Civil Rights Bill and Voting Rights Acts are formal pieces of legislation that in fact acknowledge that America has practiced what by its own principles constitutes a human evil, and that many, many millions of people had suffered because of it, and America now was owning up to it and wanted to change.

So, on the one hand, this may have been America's greatest moment. Certainly no other society in human history that I'm aware of has in a time of peace confronted itself in this way and acknowledged on this scale its history and its betrayal of its own principles for no good reason, really. Only a great society would be capable of doing what America did in the early and mid-'60s. I think it was a great moment. I am proud of America for what it did then for this self-confrontation and this determination really to change, to be a different kind of society, to move beyond this old embedded habitual evil of segregating people, and limiting human opportunity, and so forth and so on purely on the basis of skin color. It was a moment of real greatness. And personally, I'm thankful for it.

Growing up, I didn't know if it would ever come, and I was rather surprised to see it did come, but it did. On the other hand, when you acknowledge a wrong—this is where I think we understandably did not have as much foresight as we might've had—and a wrong that's serious and has injured many people and contradicted your values for so long, a wrong on that kind of almost unimaginable scale, the price it seems to me that you pay, and that Americans have paid, is losing your moral authority around race, around anything having to do with race. The most powerful result of this great acknowledgment has been this loss of moral authority and in many ways also—which the two terms are almost interchangeable—legitimacy. This particularly has affected our institutions.

What America did not foresee is that all of a sudden it had no moral authority. The people who ran the country, who were still of course whites, had no moral authority. This lack of moral authority, this disappearance, vanishing of it overnight, is what I call white guilt. It's not remotely a guilt having to do with any sort of guilt of conscience or any feeling of anguish or anything over the suffering of others—no. If that was white guilt, I don't think it would be a very big thing because I don't think people feel white guilt—very often at any rate—on a personal level. "I can't get up in the morning because I'm so guilty about our history." I don't think that's realistic. But I think all white people in America today do live with a vacuum of moral authority, with a timidity around racial issues, with a fear, with an anxiety that if they speak, they're going to put their foot in their mouth. They're going to make a mistake. They're going to be somehow identified with that racist past, and they're going to be stigmatized and called "racist."

This anxiety, again, is a part of white guilt and how it works. This guilt works, I think, in exactly the same way that racism itself worked. Racism worked by stigma. If you were black, you were stigmatized, and you had to live the life that blacks were allowed to live, and you had to follow the patterns, restrictions, and so forth no matter who you were because the stigma was indifferent to your individuality. It had no interest in your individuality whatsoever, so the stigma was "you're black and you're inferior"—that's it. You can't eat here, you can't buy a house there, and you can't so forth and so on.

I always think it poignant that Duke Ellington, to eat, had to sit in the kitchen of the hotels that his band and orchestra played in because he was unable to go into the restaurant. Probably the greatest American composer of the 20th century had to do that for the majority of his career. Why? Because the stigma was indifferent to the fact that this was a great man. It didn't care. He was a black man, and that was the end of it.

White guilt works exactly the same way. It doesn't care who you are. It doesn't care what your feelings are about blacks or if you knew one when you were young. It doesn't care. You're white, and you have no authority out of which to speak, and you may have never had the slightest sort of impulse towards racism, but it doesn't matter. A white child, I think, born today in the United States of America, will live with white guilt because, again, it functions irrationally by stigma. When a child gets to be old enough to know anything at all about American history, that child will be lumped among the whites, who in some way or the other we will probably wrongly presume benefited from racism. Now this child who was born today will be on the defensive and will learn to speak in a politically correct way so that he or she never jeopardizes his or her good name.

My point is that this reality of white guilt, the fact that it can be invoked so instantly and so universally with all people who have white skin and live inside of America, or immigrants who came last week—it doesn't matter—constitutes an enormous social power in American life. It makes things happen. It determines the way our institutions function. It determines the way we live together with each other, the kind of language we use with each other, because it's a relentless pressure. It seems to me to be one that has interestingly been unexamined. I won't go into everything about it, but an offshoot of an aspect of white guilt is what I call "white blindness."

It's interesting that blindness is one of the great themes in black American literature. You see it in the work of Richard Wright, James Baldwin, and certainly I think the greatest articulator of white blindness was Ralph Ellison. But there is, again, this preoccupation that minorities have with the blindness of whites, the invisibility of blacks, and so forth. There is one incident in Ellison's *Invisible Man* that I think is the best sort of fictional dramatization of white blindness ever written. If you've read the novel, you'll know the Mr. Norton section.

Mr. Norton is a very well-to-do northern philanthropist who comes to this small black college in the south which is sort of a takeoff on Tuskegee. And he is being driven around the campus and gets into all sorts of adventures, which I won't go into, by the invisible man, by the young black protagonist in the novel. And the invisible man doesn't get this guy because he's got all sorts of weird things he talks about, one of which is he keeps telling him that, "You are my destiny. You are my destiny, young man." And the invisible man of course has absolutely no idea what that means and is perturbed by it. And it's something that even, in all the criticism about Ellison, I don't see very much written about, but it is an example of white blindness, and it works like this. Whites are in this one down position of forever having to prove the negative, to prove that they are not racist, that the stigma does not apply to them. What that means in effect is that white guilt has placed a contingency on the exercise of white power. It has placed a contingency on moral authority and legitimacy. By that, I mean it says that you cannot have moral authority. You cannot be a decent American. Your institution cannot have legitimacy. You cannot exercise power until you meet a contingency that proves that you are not racist. In other words, until you somehow, symbolically, at the very least, dissociate from racism. You have to dissociate from it. If you do conspicuously dissociate from it, then we'll let you go about your business.

I call this white blindness because whites, whenever the racial issue comes up or whenever they meet a black, are under threat. And the thing that they become preoccupied with—I think quite naturally—is not the black person or the racial issue but their stake in it. How can they make it clear that they're not racist? How can they meet this contingency? What do they have to do, in other words, to dissociate from racism? So there's the race issue. There's the black person, but the white has got to be primarily focused around this problem. His problem is how in the hell do I dissociate and make it clear that I'm not racist and therefore be able to go on about my business, and run my institution, or whatever?

This, I think, is one of the things that Norton in this character means when he keeps saying to the invisible man, "You are my destiny." He's saying this: "I have to do something for you to dissociate myself from the past in order to have legitimacy. In order to have moral authority, I need you. You are my destiny. I cannot function." And he is a symbol of northern white America. I cannot function. I will not have legitimacy except that which I get through you by in some way dissociating from America's racist past. My feeling is that all race-related public policy since the mid-'60s, since the beginning of the Great Society, is defined by white blindness, which is to say that its purpose has nothing on earth to do with the development or advancement of the minorities who in some way suffered all those centuries of slavery and segregation. It has instead to do solely with the dissociation of whites from the stigma of racism in the past. It is entirely consumed, I think, and defined by white blindness.

Most recently, we had the Michigan affirmative action case. I think it makes this point fairly well. Over one hundred American institutions submitted briefs to the Supreme Court in favor of racial preferences. One hundred. More than one hundred. More than, I think, there were in the entire history of the court. Well, did they do that because they were just absolutely racked with guilt and anguish over the poor academic performance of black American schoolchildren? Obviously they were not. Obviously I don't think that the academic performance difficulties that blacks are having in the United States today in assimilating into the academic and intellectual part of our culture, and they're having profound problems there, crossed the mind of a single one of those people.

I don't think it's mentioned in any one of those one hundred briefs that were submitted to the court. What they said simply was, "Listen, Supreme Court. We've got to have those damn preferences because it's the only way we can dissociate ourselves from American history and have the legitimacy to function in American society. It's the only thing that will make the University of Michigan, a state university, legitimate. I don't know whether it's going to help the blacks or not. Who cares? It's going to make us a legitimate institution. If, on the other hand, we don't have them and we have to let blacks in here on the basis of their ability to compete, we won't have enough for legitimacy. We won't have enough to dissociate, and so we have to have it for that reason."

Well, you can go through again the kind of welfare that came into being in the late '60s and all the way up to welfare reform in the late '90s. We'll give you a subsidy to live on, and we will ask absolutely nothing of you. We don't care what you do. We don't care whether you raise your children or not, whether you prepare to get a job. Nothing. You just get the money. And then your children, when they have their first baby, will get their money. They don't have to do anything either.

When in human history has a government ever given to people basically a subsistence living, a little better, and asked absolutely nothing? Because then white America would have crossed that line and confirmed the fact that they're racist, and no such policy would dissociate them from racism. They would in fact seem to be agreeing with the policy, and so again, a form of welfare devoted entirely to this—the need of white Americans to dissociate from racism.

Of course, I don't think there was any worse policy in American history than that of welfare. I think it created the black underclass, destroyed the black family in ways that segregation was never able to, took every incentive away from people to be decent human beings in any way. There was no degree of failure beneath which you could go to cut your money off. The incentive basically was to fail. It was obviously a cruel and thoughtless policy that conforms perfectly to white blindness because it made minorities invisible. They were never thought about. No one saw them. And what again invisibility is, is a failure to see the human problems of people across racial lines. The failure to see them as human beings.

Could President Johnson, when he's coming out with this Great Society, stand there and say, "Look. You're behind. You can't read as well. You can't write as well. You haven't been taught. You've got a lot of work to do. If you get busy, you'll see it's not that difficult. You'll be fine, and you'll be competitive as human beings. And what you need most of all is to feel that you are competitive with the other citizens in your society. And so we're going to ask that. We're going to demand that of you. And, above all, human life sometimes is ironic. Yes, it's too bad you got oppressed and that now you've got to work harder, but the fact is you were oppressed, and now you have to work harder, and you have to learn things that you didn't know before, and so forth and so on."

Well, again, rather than do that, what America said is, "We'll throw things at them. We'll give them racial preferences and ask nothing. When they get the racial preference and they get on the college campus, we don't even say you have to have a certain grade point average to keep the preference. We don't even say that. We don't ask anything of the welfare mother and so forth. Diversity is really a fascinating example because there hasn't been any discrimination in American universities for over 50 years, so you can't justify a racial preference on the basis of actual discrimination. You're hurting these people. You're keeping them out and so forth. There's got to be redress. There's no redress here because there's been no discrimination. The only discrimination has been in favor of minorities. So then how do you justify the preference? So they invented diversity.

Wave discovered that if you don't have a critical mass of black students, the intellectual quality of the discussion goes down. There's absolutely no evidence to support that, but the point is that the institution is saying, "Dammit, we're going to have our preferences because we need them to dissociate from the past and to claim our moral authority and our legitimacy. And so if there's no discrimination, we'll invent something, and we'll call it diversity, and we'll do it that way." And that's what we're now at.

Now you have redress for no wrong. You have policies that are supposed to remedy something that hasn't been there in 50 years, so you're remedying nothing. But, again, the institution needs it for dissociation.

I think white blindness has given us this new social virtue that I called a virtue of dissociation. And it is very different from the kind of virtue we cared about back before this great divide between these two periods, the age of racism and the age of white guilt. The acknowledgement is the dividing point. We live now in the age of white guilt. Our society needs a new idea of virtue that will enable people and institutions in society to dissociate and reclaim their legitimacy. The old kind of virtue where you're just a good person is based on the individual, and individual responsibility, and self restraint, initiative, and that sort of thing. Those virtues are of secondary importance now because they don't reclaim moral authority. They don't dissociate.

So, if you're good now, you stay married to your wife and raise your kids, so what? It doesn't make a contribution to this dissociation, to this moral authority that we now must have, and so we don't really care. What we care about again is that you're able to dissociate. This virtue has—I'll just mention four quickly—certain characteristics. The first one is, you're all familiar with it, social engineering. One of the things that is now deemed to be a social good in and of itself is social engineering. It's creating diversity. If you support that, again, you earn your dissociation and your moral authority, and you're a good person. You can go about your business. If you don't support social engineering, then—boom. The stigma comes down on you. You are now identified with racist America, and that's that.

The second quality is also, I think, familiar: moral relativism. Everybody's culture is just as good as everybody else's culture. Everything is just as good. And when you see minority groups involved in oftentimes pathological behavior, that's okay because that's their culture, and there's this tolerance of virtually everything, any kind of behavior. The illegitimacy rate today in black America is still hovering around 70 percent. Boy, isn't that a scandal? Isn't that horrible? But you can't say that because, again, it's moral relativism. That's just a mark of the tragic history of slavery and segregation and so forth.

Of course, the illegitimacy rates in segregation and even slavery were nowhere near that high. But, again, your tolerance, your moral relativism around minority issues, your loosey goosey sort of attitude wins you moral authority, makes a virtuous person, a good American. "I support affirmative action. I'm a good American." If you say you don't support it, then of course you're a bad one.

A third feature is called deference and license toward minorities. You defer to their greater moral authority, and you offer them a license not to meet the same requirements and standards as other people, as whites. Preferences are the perfect means of that. You lower the standards. You offer them a license not to have to struggle and work as hard as others because, again, this shows that you're sensitive to the tragedy of their past, and it dissociates you from the past.

A last feature of this new virtue, I think, is anti-Americanism as a source of virtue for white Americans. If you don't like America, if you say America has at its core an impulse to evil, to oppression, to imperialism, et cetera, et cetera, then you are a good person. You are a better person than someone who works hard, raises a family, and so forth because what better way to dissociate from America's racist past than to say America is, at its very core, evil. Interestingly, in this sense, anti-Americanism becomes a means of political power in our society because the people who espouse it have an irrefutable virtue. They are above America's past. They dissociate from America's racism, bigotry, sexism, and so forth. They hate all of that, and they hate even the country that did that, and they are the future of this country, and they deserve to be elected to office and so forth and so on because they hate America. That's a virtue in and of itself because it's so dissociational. It cleans them of America's past.

So that, too, is a part of this new virtue that we live with. At least a mild nodding anti-Americanism is helpful to you in American society, particularly if you run institutions in American society, corporations even, universities certainly, government agencies, a sort of. Anti-Americanism enables a person to seem more virtuous, to dissociate from all that past evil and earn the moral authority and legitimacy to rightfully claim power. You see people like Michael Moore and others who made a high art out of tapping this dissociational virtue. And you don't have to think or anything. You just hate America and so forth.

Just a couple little quick points, and then I'll shut up and we can talk. To some degree, this whole problem, this particular kind of virtue that is just based on a dissociation from the evils of the past, has now spread throughout the Western world almost entirely. Certainly all of the great European powers of the past have colonialism behind them, Nazism behind them, and so forth. Now they too have seemed to me to have found a source of real power in anti-Americanism. They projected the last four or five centuries of white evil onto America, and they now dissociate and dislike us, and see our president as a cowboy and us as unilateralist imperialists who want to rape and pillage the world.

And it has, I think, transformed into a real power in many European societies today. Anti-Americanism in itself is a virtue. It makes you a good person and more suitable to hold power.

Another kind of example in the current presidential race is when you try to look at the difference between John Kerry and George W. Bush's policy on Iraq. What you basically see is that John Kerry is saying, "I'm going to do about the same thing, but I'm going to live within the parameters of white guilt. I'm going to be nuanced, and I'm going to be sensitive. I'm going to be sensitive, especially sensitive." In other words, "I'm going to dissociate. I'm going to dissociate from the ugliness of Western life, and I'm going to do it in a new multilateral bureaucratic way." His rationale for taking power is that he would be a good white person who will not be that ugly, foaming-at-the mouth racist that his opponent clearly is. He hopes that'll work. I don't know. It's certainly gotten him fairly far. How far this will work and how long this will go on, I don't know. But I do think that this is at least one of the ways we have gone wrong because we've again not paid attention.

There's another whole side of this in terms of how minorities have reacted, how we have formed our identity around protesting and protesting and protesting and protesting because we keep trying to get whites to dissociate, to throw us little crumbs like preferences and so forth. We then create a whole identity around what we think will get us those crumbs. And, of course, in the process, we just keep ourselves in this posture of victimization, weakness, and inferiority: the very stigma that we ought to be overcoming. So there is this, again, a symbiosis that both sides have gotten hooked into.

CHAPTER 11

The Civil Rights Movement and Black Political Economy

October 1-2, 2004
Philadelphia, Pennsylvania

Saturday, October 2

2:00-3:30

Political Economy and Black History

Richard W. Rahn, Chairman

David M. Levy, "Black History and Conservative Principles"

Walter E. Williams, "The False Civil Rights Vision"

BLACK HISTORY AND CONSERVATIVE PRINCIPLES

By David Levy

I'm going to talk about the larger context in which classical British political economy becomes intertwined with black history. The larger picture is one of whether people are all the same or all different.

There are two sides in the debate. And one side of the debate are the political economists and the evangelicals, who hold that everybody is more or less the same. On the other side of the debate are literary folks, anthropologists, and biostatisticians who say that people are different.

What this is, is a preview of another book that's coming out from Michigan. Yeah, that's the same place that we heard about yesterday, but this book passed faculty review at the University of Michigan Press. And its pictures are going to be on the literary side because the biostatistics don't make nice pictures. So the picture. That's a real picture. It comes from tobacco public relations in the 1870s. That's John Ruskin on the horse, trampling an evangelical who has a little pamphlet that says "political economy." And on the tag of the evangelical is a word that says "can't." And "can't" is a term for evangelicals. In one of the chapters in the book, we do the linguistics of that phrase.

So that's a visualization of the pictures and the debate. On one side, you've got evangelical economists on the bottom getting crunched by Ruskin and Carlyle, one of the greatest literary figures in that era of Britain.

Dismal science is an old term for economics or political economy. It came into the language in 1849 in an article Thomas Carlyle wrote called "Occasional Discourse of the Negro Question." Now, there are two colors. What's in the yellow is what's in the *Oxford English Dictionary*.

What's in the white is what's not in the *Oxford English Dictionary*. So the *Oxford English Dictionary* has the reference. It's got the name wrong, but that's an understandable mistake. The article is supposed to be a talk in Exeter Hall, the political center of the anti-slavery movement in Britain. This is 1849. It's between British emancipation and American emancipation. The Brits have gotten rid of slavery in the empire. Now the attention is focused on America.

So, this talk at Exeter Hall starts off, "Truly, my philanthropic friends, Exeter Hall philanthropy is wonderful," and he kicks in, "the social science is not a gay science but a rueful which finds the secret of the universe in supply and demand." Then he stops. "And reduces the duty of human governors to that of letting men alone is also wonderful. Not a gay science, I should say, like some we have heard of; no, a dreary, desolate, indeed quite an object and distressing one, on what we might call by way of eminence the dismal science."

Then the *OED* goes off again. "These two, Exeter Hall Philanthropy and the Dismal Science, led by any sacred cause of Black Emancipation or the like to fall in love, and make wedding of it, will give birth to progenies and prodigies, dark extensive mooncalves, unnamable abortions, wide-coiled monstrosities, such as the world has not seen hitherto." This paragraph I could put on the board without getting in trouble. A friend of mine in Michigan in the philosophy department said this is the ur-text of racial politics. It is not. A lot of our stuff is up on the Liberty Fund website, Econlib. The text is not up there because it is too ghastly. So this is where the dismal science got its name.

Carlyle is completely clear, completely candid, completely honest that because of its conjunction, the political association with evangelicals is for black emancipation. If you go to the *Oxford English Dictionary* to find out where the word came from, what the word meant, you will find nothing whatsoever about Exeter Hall or black emancipation. You will find something about supply and demand. That's right. That's good. That's there. The *OED* is not making up words. It's just slicing them. So that's where the word comes from.

Carlyle was an incredibly famous person once upon a time, not so anymore. Probably more important, you can still read him in college with Charles Dickens. I want to show some pictures that either have references to one of Dickens's best-known pieces, *Bleak House*, or on the cover of *Bleak House*.

Bleak House came out serially. That's how Dickens usually wrote. There's a cover illustration. Look at that cover illustration. One of the plots of *Bleak House* involves a lady, Mrs. Jellyby, who is much more concerned about the fate of Africans than she is about her kids. And the chapter introducing Mrs. Jellyby is called "Telescopic Philanthropy." She's interested in distant people, not the people at home.

Let's see some pictures. This one says, "Ain't we black enough to care for?" This is from Punch, 1865. It's about four or five months before the massacre in Jamaica. It's hard to see what's going on in the picture, so look here. Everybody here is black except the white minister. You've got this picture that Dickens referenced in a racial context. You say, "Oh, that's distortion. Misrepresentation." Okay. This is a slice from the front cover of *Bleak House*, and there's a lady—presumably Mrs. Jellyby—holding a couple of African kids right next to a sign that says "Exeter Hall." That's the anti-slavery movement.

If you look on the top, you'll see, apparently, that somebody scribbled and vandalized it there. No, no, no. That's how the Library of Congress marked it. The Library of Congress marks photographs of anything you want, so this comes from the Library of Congress's holdings. Now one of the things we have to do is preserve the generality of the debate. The issue is whether people are the same or different. There are lots of different people in the world. There are black people. There are Irish people. There are Jewish people. There are lots and lots of different people. So the debates go in many directions.

One of the most striking images in *Punch*, where the telescopic philanthropy came from, are the Irish images. And one of the most interesting pictures shows John Bright, who was a Quaker, member of Parliament, free trader, and abolitionist. There's got to be more offensive things, but that'll do. And he's proposing, God help us, democracy for Ireland. And *Punch* thinks that, I guess, the Irish aren't up to it. Now there's a reference in the image which I missed, which actually just proves that I'm a real economist, but David Laidler got it. That's an operatic reference. David told us that he now got a rate of return for his operatic investment. You see here John Bright hawking democracy, radical reform, and that the Irish men are apelike. There's a term in the literature for this. It's called simianized paddy. Nice term. If you look at the simianized paddies, they're all the same. That's sort of where the white guilt comes from: all white people have the same belief structures, they're all the same. This is what that sort of stuff looks like.

So here we've got Bright, a minor league economist in the history of the discipline. He's important politically. Free trade came because of Bright and Cobden. But from a theoretical point of view, he's a nonstarter. There are many cartoons in *Punch* that link John Bright to John Stuart Mill, a heavy hitter. It would take my full 20 minutes or whatever to list his theoretical contributions. Mill was a Parliament man. Here the image says Mill's *On Liberty*. There's this linkage between Bright and Mill in the *Punch* version, so these are the economists.

Bright's a Quaker. You can always tell Bright because he's got the Quaker hat. Broad-brimmed philanthropy was a phrase at the time. This is *Punch*'s idea about how you treat the Irish because they're not fully human. This is right after the massacre in Jamaica. This is, you know, how you treat the Irish who don't behave. This next one, it says, "What do we do with these troublesome people? Try isolation first, my dear."

You've got a picture about what you do with troublesome subhumans. Three guesses. Now there are other pictures, and we'll get some more. Now the structure of the day works like this. Is human nature a policy variable? Can we change human beings by policy? The phrase "the new man" ought to resonate. It's got a context. And one of the leaders on this side, which is why Ruskin is always pictured in opposition in some images: because of his chemical political economy, the idea that people can be remade in deep structure.

Economists think that if you change relative prices, people's behavior changes. Ruskin thinks you can remake people. This is Mr. Ruskin's condemnation of modern social conditions, that we manufacture everything except men. We blanch cotton, strengthen steel, refine sugar, shape pottery. But to brighten, strengthen, refine, or form a single living spirit never enters into our estimation of advantages. The idea that human beings are policy can be remade by the betters is the trope. Then, of course, the question is what happens when people don't want to be remade. Well, it also has the consequence that race–and this is why it gets difficult for modern people to read–becomes a choice.

You can decline to listen to your betters and by so doing devolve. I actually put this on a t-shirt and dared my students to wear it. The idea seems to be that a lady goes into the household, leads the magnificent hierarchy of home and husband, goes to work as a maid, and then what happens? She changes in deep structure.

We're in a world where we think race is fixed. Some people don't think race exists. But what if we believe race is fixed? These guys didn't. Race is a policy variable. You can make people better or worse by policies. Free trade makes people worse. On the other hand, there are more Irish. They don't look like the *Punch* Irish because they're human. Obedience makes you human in this view of the world. Those are the loyal Irish, and they're obviously drawn naturalistically. And then, closing slide, the reaction of people who don't like this sort of stuff is to say, "Okay. You guys are focusing on Mill or maybe Adam Smith." Mill's a nice guy. He married a very liberal lady, so it's really not economists. It's Harriet Taylor and John Stuart Mill, the hand puppet.

Okay. We'll play it that way. Okay. Here is a statement, which is very famous in the period, from the one great mathematician in classical political economy, Charles Babbage. This is the guy who designed the computer. He was Newton's successor at Cambridge. This is his take, his linking of religion and anti-slavery, and this is the second full paragraph: "The soul of the Negro whose fettered body surviving the living charnel-house of this infected prison"—it's obviously the middle passage—"was thrown into the sea to lighten the ship that his Christian master might escape the limited justice at length assigned by civilized man to crimes whose profit had long gilded their atrocity will need at the last great day of human account no living witness of this earth the agon. When man and all his race have disappeared from the face of our planet, ask every particle of air still floating over the unpeopled earth, and it will record the cruel mandate of the tyrant, interrogate every wave which breaks unimpeded on 10,000 desolate shores, and it will give evidence to this last gurgle of the waters which closed over the head of the dying victim, confront the murder with every corporeal atom of his immobilized slave, and in still quivering moments, he will read the prophets' denunciation of the prophet king. Thou art the man."

So this is Charles Babbage, the greatest mathematician in the classical tradition that envisions a cosmic war, an active universe where God as a physical law will remember terrible things. Thank you.

The False Civil Rights Visioin

By Walter Williams

Thanks particularly to Midge Decter and Mr. Campbell for arranging this conference. I think it's very important. I'm glad to be here to participate. The title of my talk is "The False Civil Rights Vision." Whether there's agreement with my general ideas on racial issues or not, I think we all can agree that for too large a segment of the black community, things are getting progressively worse. I think that those of us—many of us in this room—who fought or participated in the civil rights battles in the '40s, and '50s, and '60s, and that yielded the *Brown vs. Board of Education* decision culminating in the Civil Rights Act of 1964, had every reasonable expectation that our racial problems would have been solved some four decades later. Indeed, there has been unprecedented progress, and I think that a lot of times we don't pay attention to the progress.

Now, if I'm not being too chauvinistic, I think it's fair to say that black Americans as a group have made the greatest progress over some of the highest hurdles in the shortest span of time than any other racial group in the history of mankind. Let's look at a little bit of evidence for such a bold assertion. If we were to think of black Americans just as a nation within our nation and add up the income that black Americans earn each year, and consider ourselves having a GNP, we would be the 13th or 14th richest nation in the world.

Black Americans have been chief executives of some of the world's largest and richest cities. It was a black American in the person of Colin

Powell who was the chief officer of the world's mightiest military and later secretary of state. Black Americans rank among the world's most famous personalities, and a few black Americans are among the world's richest people. Now, some of the significance of this is that in 1865, neither a slave nor a slave owner would have believed that such an achievement would've been possible in the mere space of a century or so, if ever.

These achievements speak well of the moral character and the intentional fortitude of a people, but just as significantly—and we should not forget—the achievements also speak well of a nation in which these achievements were possible. That is, they would've been impossible anywhere else in the world.

Now, despite these monumental gains, there's a large segment of the black community for whom these gains remain elusive. Moreover, given the status quo and the conventional wisdom, there's little prospect for progress. A large part of the problem is that of vision. Today's devastating problems among a large segment of the black community are either ignored or dealt with ineffectively as we focus too much attention and expend energies and resources on what were yesteryear's big problems.

Let me be clear about what I'm saying. For all intents and purposes, the civil rights struggle in the United States is over and it's won. At one time, black Americans did not have the constitutional guarantees afforded other Americans. Today, that is not true. We have the same constitutional guarantees that every other American has. For the most part, if we have money, we can buy what we want and live where we want.

Now, let me again be clear. I am not saying that every vestige of racial discrimination has been eliminated. Blacks, like other ethnic minorities, still encounter residual discrimination. But today's discrimination is insignificant compared to that of yesteryear. And it's irrelevant compared to other problems that black Americans face.

Let me just spend a few minutes talking about these other problems. One major problem—a devastating problem—is family breakdown. We've all heard that term used. I don't quite use it all the time. What's often called family breakdown is not the proper description. It's families not forming in the first place.

Today, less than 40 percent of black children have the benefit of growing up in a home with both parents. There's an illegitimacy rate of almost 75 percent—somewhere between 70 and 75 percent. Now, you don't have to morally condemn single parenthood in order to acknowledge that it's better for children to be reared in a two-parent family. Not only are children who are raised by single parents five times more likely to be poor. They're more likely to do poorly in school, become dropouts, engage in antisocial behavior, and become single parents themselves.

It is difficult to lay the breakdown of the black family at the feet of racial discrimination in light of the fact that as early as the 1800s—let's say around 1875 to 1880—75 to 90 percent, depending on what city you're looking at, of black children lived in two-parent families. Even during slavery, more black children were raised in two-parent households. Whether the parents could legally marry was another question, but more black children were raised in two-parent families during slavery than now.

Another devastating problem that has little or nothing to do with racial discrimination is the high rate of crime in the black community. The high rate of crime takes a devastating toll on black neighborhoods. It has the full effect of the law mandating that there shall be little or no economic development in black neighborhoods. It acts as a massive tax on those least able to pay. Because of high crime, because of the costs associated with high crime, businesses such as supermarkets and banks are reluctant to locate in high-crime neighborhoods. That means that poor people in those neighborhoods must bear the additional cost of transportation to downtown shopping centers or to suburban malls, or settle for the high prices charged at mom-and-pop shops.

You might recall that after the Los Angeles riots, we saw interviews with people, interviews of black people, and they were complaining about the absence of supermarkets in their neighborhoods and the necessity to use check cashing stands and pay a high premium to cash their paycheck. They were wrong in blaming banks and supermarket owners for not coming to their neighborhoods. They should blame the thugs that made banking and supermarket operations a more costly proposition in black neighborhoods.

I had a friend in Philadelphia. He's since died, Al Mars, who was the vice president of a major Philadelphia bank, and he told me that he had to pay workers the equivalent of combat pay to work in some neighborhoods. Now, you're going to have to sit me down for a long time to convince me that white supermarket owners and white bank owners don't like green dollars coming out of black hands.

Go a few blocks up to where I used to live, and that is the way that businesses are done in black neighborhoods. By the way, I wouldn't suggest that you go up there. My daughter has sometimes asked me would I take her where I grew up, and I told her as soon as I can rent an armored personnel carrier, preferably with a periscope. But if you see the ways businesses are conducted in some black neighborhoods, you'll see guards in supermarkets. You'll see restricted access to products, higher prices, less convenient hours, and lower quality merchandise. These are all methods of the store owner to respond to the higher cost of doing business, and all these costs must be passed on to the consumer.

Another devastating problem that has nothing to do with racial discrimination is education. The devastating—I call it fraudulent—education that most black Americans, most black children receive, has strong socioeconomic implications. They can hardly be laid at the feet of racial discrimination. In fact, to bring this point home a little bit better, some of the worst education that black Americans receive is delivered in the very cities where a black is the mayor, a black is the superintendent of the schools, most of the principals and teachers are black. I'm talking about cities like Washington, D.C., and Philadelphia, and Detroit. I'm not stating a causal relationship between race and this poor-quality education. I'm saying that you cannot lay it at the feet of discrimination.

More money is not the answer. In fact, there's nearly a perfect negative correlation between the amount of money spent and the quality of education delivered. If you look at cities in New Jersey or New York, or at D.C, they spend more education dollars than any other jurisdiction in the country. Washington, D.C., spends—depending on whose calculations you're looking at—anywhere between $13,000 and $15,000 per kid. And where do you think Washington shows up nationally on academic achievement? Well, I tell you probably the people in Washington, D.C., are hoping that Mississippi does not secede from the union. Otherwise, they'd be dead last.

Fraudulent education has made many black youngsters virtually useless for the increasingly high-tech world of the 21st century. Most black youngsters who in fact graduate from high school, as Abigail Thernstrom and her husband have documented, have an academic achievement level around that of a white youngster who's in the seventh or eighth grade. Black politicians along with the educational establishment call for everything from more money, bussing, or Afrocentrism to improve education. Their vision of what needs to be done has failed.

I think part of the solution is to examine those islands of success in poor black neighborhoods, those islands of success where there is academic achievement. Go to places like Marcus Garvey School in Los Angeles, Marva Collins Preparatory School in Cincinnati, or Ivy Leaf right up on North Broad Street in Philadelphia. At each of these schools, 90 to 95 percent of the kids score at sometimes three and four years above grade level. And if you visit these schools, you'll see no magic. You'll see nothing that the educational establishment says is necessary for the academic achievement of black kids.

What you would see is that kids come to school in the morning ready for education. They've left their knives and guns at home. They come to school sober, and the parents reinforce the teachers. And, by the way, their annual tuition ranges anywhere between $3,000 to $4,000, a fraction of what the government schools charge.

One final area that we need to look at has to do with entry restriction.

Those of you who are familiar with some of my research know I've written a lot on the artificial barriers to entry in jobs and businesses that have devastating effects. One that I've paid particular attention to is occupational licensing. The taxi business is one that lends itself to people with a relatively poor education, but in New York, and in most places, you have to have a license for that. In New York, the license—they call it a medallion in New York—to own and operate one taxi is $275,000. Now you say, "What is the effect of that?" Well, it tends to discriminate against those getting in the taxi business who don't have $275,000 or bank credit to get such a loan for that, and it tends to be people with a little change.

I'll tell you one thing. I'm very pleased when I go to New York that the number of gypsy cabs—illegally operating cabs—exceeds the number of licensed cabs. As a matter of fact, I think the medallion cabs in New York are 11,787, and some of the estimates about the gypsy cabs run as high as 14,000. And when I was doing research for my book on occupational licensing, I used to go up to New York, to places like the Bronx and Harlem, and the side of some of those gypsy cabs used to have a little banner saying, "We're not yellow. We go anywhere." Probably they had some kind of anticrime technique available to them.

Let me close by saying that most of what needs to be done to solve the problems of a large segment of the black community can't be done by the government. Ask yourself questions like, "What's necessary for a kid to get in school, to do well in school?" Well, somebody has to make sure he goes to bed on time. Somebody has to wake him up in the morning. Somebody has to make him do his homework. Which one of those things can the United States Congress do? It can't do any.

What the general society can do to help is not make matters worse. That is to insist on high standards as opposed to lowered standards through affirmative action or guilty responses, as Shelby Steele was talking about last night.

Speaking of guilt, on my website, under GIFs, I have a proclamation for amnesty and pardon to all white Americans for both their own grievances and those of their forebears against my people. And if you read it carefully, it says, "Now that you have this pardon, you can stop feeling guilty."

Insist on high standards. Remove subsidies and other incentives for slovenly behavior. Society has made it cheap to have kids out of wedlock. Society has made it cheap to—or less costly—to not get a job, to be a bum. So what general society can do is to remove subsidies and other incentives for slovenly behavior. We also need to stigmatize drugs and crime instead of trying to explain them away, or instead of trying to say, "Oh, well, that's just the way they act." I think we need to stigmatize bizarre behavior.

I know I don't look like it, but I'm 68 years old. Probably most of you think I'm in my early 30s or something like that. If I could resurrect my grandmother and tell her some of the things that go on today, she would not believe me: people are using foul language, even girls using foul language, and people are just accepting it. Or people are looking like bums, wearing those long t-shirts and showing their bum. If I were an employer, I wouldn't even talk to somebody interviewing for a job if they looked like that. We need to stigmatize such behavior because accepting lower standards doesn't do anybody any good, whether it's lower standards in employment or in education.

As a matter of fact, I tell people one of the most fortunate things that happened to me is that I got all of my education before it became fashionable for white people to like black people. Which means that the C that I got in college was an honest-to-God, hard-earned C. Many black Americans don't have that opportunity.

At UCLA, where I got my doctorate in economics, when the PhD exam was given, 16 people took it and 13 flunked it. I was among the ones who flunked it, and one of my advisors told me, "Williams, your test was among the worst." Can you imagine? Not that many white teachers would tell a black kid that nowadays, and that doesn't help.

Let me stop there.

CHAPTER 12

Immigration and America

April 29-May 1, 2005
Miami, FLorida

Saturday, April 30

2:00-3:30

Immigrationi and America

Nicholas Capaldi, Chairman

Peter Brimelow

Benjamin Powell

Andrew Yuengert

Immigration and America

By Peter Brimelow

Thank you, Nick. Thank you, ladies and gentlemen. As will be immediately apparent to you, I'm an immigrant myself. Immigrants do the dirty jobs that Americans won't do, and here I am.

To begin at the end, we're talking about what an American is. My answer to that is that Americans just are. They are Americans. We're told that this is a nation of immigrants. I say it's a nation. Immigration is not as central to the American experience as a lot of romantic intellectuals would like you to think. It is true, as Nick just said, that the book I wrote, *Alien Nation*, exactly ten years ago, although it wasn't the first book on immigration, was perhaps the most noticed up to that point, which is to say, denounced.

The only useful thing I learned at the Stanford Graduate School of Business is the definition of a pioneer, a man on a covered wagon with an arrow in his back. Since then, of course, there have been, after prudent intervals, a number of books on the subject: by Michelle Malkin, Pat Buchanan, Sam Huntington, and of course Gordon H. Hanson. I can't say I've received an enormous amount of credit for this, which is sort of mildly irritating. My late wife, who some of you may remember, found it extremely irritating. But it is typical of the way that ideas slowly enter mainstream discourse.

In 1981 or 1982, I wrote an editorial for *Barron's* called "The Man in the Iron Mask," which is what I jokingly said the Reagan administration had done to one of its White House staffers, Peter Ferrara, who had dared to mention the idea of privatizing Social Security. That was twenty-odd years ago. By my count, we should see serious immigration reform in this country, by which I mean an immigration moratorium, sometime around the beginning of the next decade.

Now, to show you that I have assimilated culturally, I'm going to quote Will Rogers, who nobody in Britain has ever heard of. Do you all know who Will Rogers is? Oh, good. You never know nowadays. Will Rogers once said that it's not what people don't know that hurts them, it's what they know that ain't true. And this is preeminently the case with the immigration debate.

Although it preoccupies me as a financial journalist, when I came to look into the technical literature on the economics of immigration, it was in the early 1990s to right when I was researching *Alien Nation*. I was amazed to find that the consensus among labor economists was that this great inflow, which was triggered by the 1965 Act and the parallel breakdown of the southern border, in the aggregate is not beneficial. It brings no benefit to native-born Americans. It does increase GDP. But virtually all of that is captured by the immigrants themselves. The native-born Americans are simply no better off.

Since *Alien Nation* came out, my reading of the consensus was confirmed by the National Research Council's 1997 report called *The New Americans*. It estimated that the immigration surplus was something like $10 billion, utterly trivial in a $5 or $6 trillion economy and wiped out by the transfer costs, which are very substantial, that is to say the cost of schools and emergency room hospital care and that sort of thing, which are very substantial. In a microstudy, the NRC found the cost to every native-born family in California to the immigrant presence, as of 1996, was something like a thousand dollars a year. Every native born family is subsidizing the immigrant presence by about a thousand dollars a year. Essentially, Americans are subsidizing their own displacement.

Actually, I would say something similar may be true, although we don't know because it's not been properly researched. It's not clear that the last great wave of immigration between 1880 and 1920 raised the income of the native-born. Economists are extremely flexible in their use of labor. Essentially we were always told, particularly by the descendants of the great wave of immigration, that immigrants built America. But actually it's more like they got on a rolling bandwagon. The thing was already underway before they arrived.

Although immigration doesn't raise the wealth, or the per capita income, of the native-born, it does cause immense redistribution between the different native-born communities, amounting at that point to something like 2 percent of GDP shifted from labor to capital. That explains the class base of this debate. It is extremely beneficial to have immigration to people who go to country clubs and vote Republican. It is extremely non-beneficial if you're a blue-collar worker. It's particularly non-beneficial for the Blacks, for African Americans.

I am about to publish an article that shows that Black unemployment has actually risen since this recovery started thirteen quarters ago. This is exactly what happened with the first great wave. The movement of Blacks into the northern cities and northern industries stopped when immigration began. Booker T. Washington was highly aware of this. His famous Atlanta Exposition speech, half of it, was about how Blacks had to cast down their buckets where they were and acquire technical skills and so on. The other half was a passionate appeal. It's one of the great speeches in the language, a passionate appeal to whites and particularly to Southerners to stop mass immigration, people of strange habits and foreign tongues, he said, because they were displacing Blacks.

There's a second thing that people think they know about immigration, which isn't true. I guess Professor Hanson illustrated it last night. He referred at one point to America being a multiracial nation. Well, there are certainly a lot of races in America. But that's not how the Founding Fathers saw it. They actually forbade the naturalization of Blacks. They limited citizenship to free whites. Asians couldn't become citizens until well into this century. There was no substantial non-European immigration until 1965. Maybe it shouldn't have been that way, but it was. It was that way. In other words, the U.S. remained a substantially homogenous nation well into living memory.

John Jay, in Federalist No. 2, wrote this famous passage. He said we can make federalism work in this country because we are one united people, a people descended from the same ancestors, speaking the same language, professing the same religion, and he didn't mean Christianity. He meant Protestantism—attached to the same principles of government, very similar in their manners and customs.

This isn't a theoretical point. It goes to the very roots of American order. If you think America is an organic nation that's evolved like every other nation, then you have to be careful about how you introduce people into it, about immigration policy, whereas if you think it's like a credit agreement, just signing on the bottom line, then it's a proposition nation. You can be much more relaxed about it. The historical evidence shows to a much larger extent than people realize that the U.S. is a traditional nation.

The third thing that people think they know, which isn't true, is that the U.S. is a nation of immigrants. Of course all nations are nations of immigrants. There is no known case where people grew out of the ground. What happened in the U.S. was faster than elsewhere. But the U.S. was put together faster. It did in two hundred years what it took in England over a thousand years to do. But that raises the prospect that it can be undone just as fast as it was done, that the union may not hold together if really discordant elements are introduced.

There are two specific qualifications to this "nation of immigrants" idea that I recommend to you. One is that people think that immigration has existed throughout American history. But if you actually look at the data, it's highly discontinuous. There are floods of immigration followed by long periods when there's no immigration. There are pauses. The most recent pause, of course, was in the middle of the 20th century as a result of the cutoff in the 1920s. But there are many other pauses, stretching right back into American history.

There was a long period of time after the Revolution when there was very little immigration. When the Irish arrived in New England in the 1840s after the potato famine, they were coming into an area, which is where I now live by the way, where there had been no immigration for two hundred years of any significance. Yet New England had developed enormously through that period through natural increase. That's why it was such a shock to everybody. These pauses were essential to assimilation.

One of the things thrown at you if you're an immigration reformer is this argument: Ben Franklin was worried about the Germans. He said the Germans wouldn't assimilate, and look what happened to them. Of course, in fact, there are German-speaking enclaves in Pennsylvania. But the important thing that happened to the Germans was immigration stopped as a result of the Seven Years' War, which is here called the French and Indian War. It stopped, and it never resumed until the 1840s. So, there was a seventy-year period where there was no significant German immigration, and that allowed assimilation to take place.

We think America was built by immigrants because we live in New York or Los Angeles or somewhere like that, which are heavily immigrant cities, if not entirely immigrant cities. But the last estimate I've seen, when I was researching *Alien Nation*, was that if there had been no immigration at all after 1790, none at all, the population of the U.S. would still have been about half of what it is now through natural increase. It's what you call the founder's effect. In other words, because people who are there first start multiplying, you get compound interest in it. Obviously this is very hard to believe in New York or Miami or somewhere like that. But I live in the foothills of the Berkshires, in the Litchfield hills. And in my area there's a substantial number of blue collar workers who are colonial stock.

My son, Alexander, used to go up Tanner Hill on the school bus, and stop at Tanner Farm, and a kid would come out called Tanner, whose family bought the land from the Indians. There is a lot more of this out there than people think. I may say, by the way, that in the public schools of Litchfield County, my children have learned a great deal about Martin Luther King, and how awful whites were to Blacks. That area of Connecticut was a hotbed of abolitionism. These Connecticut farm boys joined up in vast numbers and died in vast numbers, fighting to free the slaves.

There was one particular regiment in Litchfield called the Litchfield County's 2nd Connecticut Heavy Artillery, which, despite its name, was an infantry regiment and was shot to pieces at Cold Harbor. The woman who cuts my hair, the man who delivers my mail, had relatives who died in that battle. They're aware of it, but I have never heard any mention of it in the public schools. I've asked teachers about it. I've asked the principals about it. None of them have ever heard of it. This goes to what we mean by a proposition nation. You know, maybe these kids are being taught some kind of a creed in the public schools. But what is it? Is it something we approve of? What is a nation?

It seems to me the only rational definition is that it has to be an ethnocultural unit. It is not entirely ethnic. Anybody, individuals of any race, can usually assimilate. But it's not entirely cultural either, as we are currently led to believe. There is a substantial ethnic component of it that has consequences about which we're not really clear, but we know they exist.

What we face now, with the post-1965 wave of immigration, is an unprecedented act of social engineering being performed by the government. The government is second-guessing the population on size because Americans of all races have got their population down to just a replacement level now. The population would stabilize, absent immigration. But in fact it's projected to go up to 400, maybe 500 million by 2050. Also, of course, we're rapidly shifting the racial balance. In 1960, the U.S. was 90 percent white. In 2050—by around 2050—whites will be about to be in the minority.

It seems to me that it's up to those who favor this transformation of America to explain why. What do they have against the America that existed in 1965? Why don't they explain it to the American people and let's have a democratic debate about it? Why does America have to be transformed? The conservative point of view, it seems to me, although you don't find it reflected in The *Wall Street Journal* or much else, is that if it's not necessary to change, it is necessary not to change.

I don't think it's necessary to change the U.S., certainly by as much as it's being changed right now. Solzhenitsyn said in his Nobel Prize speech that "the disappearance of nations would impoverish us no less than if all men had become alike with one personality, one face. Nations are the wealth of mankind, its collective personalities. The very least of them wears its own special colors, and bears within itself a special facet of God's design." A remarkable statement for somebody who was brought up a Marxist. It seems to me that the U.S., as it evolved in 1965, did reflect a special facet of God's design. And I want to know why the government wants to monkey around with it. Thank you very much.

Immigration and America

By Benjamin Powell

I am honored to speak to you today about immigration. You just heard an argument to restrict immigration and even close our borders from Peter Brimelow, a man with strong free-market credentials. Unfortunately, Peter's proposals will fail to save American culture and values and may serve to undermine them. His problems stem not only from faulty economic estimates but also from a failure to address the underlying problems that America faces.

The problems we observe with immigration are only symptoms of our perverse institutional environment, not the underlying problems themselves. I want to be clear from the outset that I do not support America's present immigration policy. Our current immigration problems stem from both our mixed interventionist economy and our current system of immigration rules. I agree with Peter that the 1965 law and subsequent acts create problems and should be eliminated. However, instead of restricting immigration completely, I favor opening the borders to all immigrants, in any quantity, from any location, so long as they are free of disease and demonstrated criminal activity, and that some private party is willing to provide a place for them to stay.

I do not advocate this because I believe in any special "right" to immigration. For that matter, I don't believe that "multiculturalism," "diversity," and other politically correct buzzwords that liberals use are necessarily good. I favor open immigration because it is the right policy for Americans who live here today.

Let me begin with some economic reasons. Peter bases his economic consequences of immigration on the work of George Borjas. Borjas uses what economists call a Harberger triangle to estimate the gains from immigration. His latest estimates in David Henderson's *Concise Encyclopedia of Economics* find that immigration increases GDP growth by about .2 percent, or $22 billion per year. While .2 percent sounds small, compounded over time this is still a significant gain for our economy. Anti-immigration advocates try to trivialize the size of the gain, but there are hundreds of government regulations in our economy that conservatives and classical liberals oppose that have much smaller effects. I doubt anyone in attendance would be against abolishing rent controls in Berkeley, California, even though the economic gains would be far smaller than those from immigration.

Virtually every estimate agrees that immigration has some positive economic impact. Even if the gain is $22 billion, a gain is a gain, and it's a heck of a lot better than a loss. Borjas and Brimelow, however, grossly underestimate the size of the gain. The Harberger triangle method they use is also used by economists to measure the net loss to society from monopolies. In the 1960s, some economists estimated these losses and found that the triangles were relatively small and began to conclude that government sanctioned monopolies do not introduce too big of an inefficiency into the economy. It took the public choice economist, Gordon Tullock, in a 1967 article that he is still awaiting his Nobel Prize for, to point out that it was not just the triangle that could be lost but the area economists previously considered a transfer.

Since a grant of monopoly privilege is a political favor bestowed upon a producer, producers have an incentive to engage in economically unproductive activities such as lobbying to try to obtain the transfer. Some of the value of what economists previously considered a transfer from consumers to producers would also be a net loss to society. Since that article was published, a large literature in public choice has emerged that describes the various conditions under which the rectangle (transfer) will be exactly dissipated into loss, over dissipated and under dissipated. The one conclusive result is that under all of their plausible models, there will be very significant deadweight costs in addition to the triangle.

Brimelow completely leaves this out of his estimates of the benefits of immigration. He assumes all that will be lost is the triangle and that the rectangle you see would be transferred from U.S. workers to U.S. owners of capital and land. For this to be even partially accurate, immigration would have to move from current policy to his vision of complete restriction with essentially no political fight. How likely is that? Quoting from his book *Alien Nation*, "It will be resisted hysterically. It will be sabotaged in every possible way. It will probably require repeated legislation. It could quite easily destroy the present political party system." That's going to be a big cost.

An article in the *Journal of Political Economy* estimated that once you count the political lobbying costs of trade restrictions, the losses to the economy increase by a factor of ten compared to just the triangle. That would make the $22 billion loss from immigration into $220 billion. This is not at all unreasonable given the passion of the fight that will likely ensue.

This is not to claim some workers won't lose. Some who compete for the same jobs as the immigrants could lose at least in the short run. A survey of the economics literature published in the J*ournal of Economic Perspectives* concluded, "Despite the popular belief that immigrants have a large adverse impact on the wages and employment opportunities of the native-born population, the literature on this question does not provide much support for the conclusion." However, even if it could be shown that wages of some groups of native-born workers decrease, I don't think conservative and classical liberal supporters of markets should abandon support of immigration. Virtually any policy that restricts competition benefits some workers at the expense of the vast majority and overall efficiency. Unless we can conclusively argue that these displaced workers had some special positive "right" to a job or particular wage that no one else does, a classical liberal should not advocate restricting competition.

Although immigration has overall economic benefits, it also has costs that current taxpayers bear. The most obvious occurs when an immigrant receives welfare. Critics of immigration point out that immigrants are more likely to go on welfare than is the general population. Some even claim that this trend is increasing, although research by Vedder, Gallaway, and Moore shows that these claims are grossly overstated. Once they control for other factors, they find little change in the proportion of people on welfare who are immigrants since 1970. Despite this finding, there clearly should be concern about people migrating here to receive welfare.

A two-child family in California is eligible for a $7,200 welfare cash benefit, an additional $3,000 in food stamps, and up to $6,500 in Medicaid for a total benefit of over $16,000. These benefits exceed the average per capita incomes in many countries around the world by a substantial margin. Milton Friedman has said, "It's just obvious that you can't have free immigration and a welfare state." Conservatives and classical liberals should agree with a resounding "here, here," and it's time to abolish the welfare state. I doubt there are many supporters of the welfare state in this room. But it is a mistake to take the welfare state's existence for granted and use it as an excuse to condone government interventions in immigration.

This is the problem Ludwig von Mises famously pointed out in his book *The Dynamics of Interventionism*. One government intervention in the economy produces undesirable and unintended results and planners are confronted with the choice of making further interventions or repealing prior ones. All too often, the government chooses the former. Mises points out that we must fight to roll back existing interventions so that the economy will not keep tending down what Hayek famously called "the road to serfdom."

Almost everybody in this room is opposed to rent control. But if rent control exists, landlords have an incentive to turn apartments into condos and sell them off at higher prices, leaving the poor with even fewer apartments available. Clearly this is an undesirable result. But almost no one here would advocate restricting the ability of landlords to convert their property to condos as a solution. We would instead focus our efforts repealing the first intervention, rent control, that caused our problem in the first place. The same should be true of the welfare state and immigration.

Conservatives and classical liberals should focus energy on rolling back the welfare state instead of trying to limit immigration. If a case to eliminate immigration is to be made, it must be independent of the existence of the welfare state. Some may reply that it's not politically likely that we can eliminate the welfare state right now. Well, it's also not politically likely that immigration can be completely restricted right now. If we are going to have a political fight, it might as well be for real conservative and classical liberal values, not a marginal step away from classical liberalism by restricting immigration.

Even if the political situation were different, I don't think we should advocate restricting immigration. In *The Intellectuals and Socialism*, Hayek wrote, "The main lesson which the true liberal must learn from the success of the socialists is that it was their courage to be Utopian which gained them support. We need intellectual leaders who are willing to work for an ideal, however small may be the prospects of its early realization." This is the position we should be fighting for on immigration, not one that assumes a welfare state.

Of course, there are other spillover costs of immigration in our economy. Public schooling, especially with bilingual education, is one example; crowding on public roads is another. But here, too, we have features of our economy that are not consistent with free markets. Our fight should be to eliminate public schooling and to privatize roads by allowing owners to charge for their use directly, not to stop immigration.

Virtually every economic cost of immigration is a product of an interventionist government and a welfare state, or a tragedy of the commons. In either case, the solution to the problems is private property reform and free markets. In fact, immigration restrictions not only create a new intervention, they fail to reform these underlying problems at all. Restricting immigration doesn't change all of the spillover costs that current native citizens place on each other. Immigration puts pressure on us to reform underlying problems and therefore should be welcomed. In the correct institutional setting, immigration is an unambiguous economic gain for existing citizens. Reform towards those institutions [is] what we need to agitate for.

Moving beyond economics: What about our culture? Our American values, self reliance, hard work, individual initiative? Couldn't bringing in people from other cultures undermine those values, or—even worse—pervert our politics?

American values have changed over the last two hundred years. Most of the public has moved away from these traditional values and come to believe that our nanny state is necessary. People have learned that instead of serving consumers to get ahead, they can lobby the government for transfers, use the court system for fraudulent lawsuits, beg the antitrust regulators to limit their more efficient competitors, take government handouts between jobs, or, even worse, take handouts nearly permanently. Values have changed as our institutional environment has changed.

As acts of Congress and court decisions have eroded our original constitutional environment, they have distorted the incentives facing people in our economy. As the benefits to unproductive entrepreneurship—what economists call rent seeking, or basically seeking transfers of wealth—have increased, more people engage in transfer seeking. This has eroded our culture. The costs and benefits people face have influenced our cultural values over time. This is true of both immigrants and natives.

The post-1965 immigrant wave is different from prior immigration waves. It is partly distorted by government policy that prevents Europeans and others from coming, but it's also different, not because the immigrants are fundamentally different, but because our culture is different than it was. Before, immigrants assimilated into a culture of hard work and self reliance. Those who failed here often had to go home. Few go home today because of failure. Instead, they are taught to assimilate into a system of government reliance where failure and laziness are not punished. The post-1965 immigration wave is the first that has come once we had a welfare state in place. Unfortunately, that welfare state not only makes them less productive; it also teaches them to undermine our old culture that made America successful.

This problem is not unique to immigrants though. All American culture is being perverted by the welfare state. Culture is influenced by the economic incentives facing actors; it is not something wholly determined by place of origin or ethnicity. Look at the many natural experiments: China, Taiwan, and Hong Kong; North and South Korea; Ireland and Northern Ireland—places with essentially the same geography and ethnicity where the political and economic cultures are completely different. In each case, one group was able to adopt a system of free market principles like those of the U.S. Their economy flourished and their culture grew to support it, while an otherwise similar group of people adopted different institutions and stagnated. In both cases, the cultures have carried on. Ethnicity alone doesn't determine what values a group will support. Culture evolves to respond to costs and benefits over time.

We need to focus on creating the right institutional environment in the U.S. so that the immigrants who come here will assimilate into the old American values, not our new perverted ones created by the nanny state.

Another concern is security. What about a wave of terrorists trying to immigrate? Just because we should have an open immigration policy doesn't mean we can't exclude criminals and known terrorists. People with criminal records should not be free to roam our streets—immigrant, native, or otherwise. By moving to a system of open immigration, we would slow the flow of the current illegal border crossings. As long as it was predictable that we would let anyone immigrate who enters through legal checkpoints and who does not have a criminal record, most immigrants would come through these channels. This would free up our resources devoted to monitoring illegal crossings so that they were concentrating on a smaller group, most likely criminals and terrorists, so they could better prevent them from entering.

Right now we do a horrible job of preventing illegal crossings because there are just too many attempts relative to enforcement resources. If we completely cut off immigration, there would likely be even more illegal attempts. By opening our borders and concentrating resources on the fewer attempts that occur, we would actually be more safe, not less.

Finally, I think there is an important ethical argument that needs to be considered in immigration policy: the rights of current American citizens to freedom of association. Our fundamental American cultural values were a right to life, liberty, and property. Those rights imply a freedom to sell or rent your property, to associate in business with, or to have as a guest on your property, anyone you desire. Immigrants have no special "right" to come here just as I have no special "right" to walk on your private property. The right is with our property owners in the U.S. to associate with whomever they please, be they an American citizen or not.

Current immigration policy unjustly filters our own right of freedom of association. The government has no just reason to place a blanket filter on whom we associate with. The only people who should be filtered out are those who have demonstrated that they have no respect for our rights of life, liberty, and property—namely criminals. And these people should be filtered out whether they are natives or immigrants. Any filter beyond that is an unjust restriction on our very American freedoms that we used to hold so dear.

Immigration and America

By Andrew Yuengert

I want to make three points about immigration in the U.S. One, there is a right to migrate, but it's not an absolute right. Two, the economic stakes of immigration policy are relatively small; if there are any real stakes, they are cultural. Three, illegal immigration, with special emphasis on the qualifier "illegal" as opposed to "undocumented," is the source of our most severe immigration problems, and is our most urgent challenge. Let's begin with rights.

My dissertation research was narrowly focused on the economics of immigration and assimilation. Several years ago I was asked to write a paper on Catholic Social Teaching and immigration, so for the first time I read what the popes have said about it. I was shocked to find in Catholic Social Teaching a very clearly enunciated right to migration.

Now, in my research on this topic I had never come across this term, "rights," in the context of immigration. Since I am a product of American rights culture, the claim of a right to migrate was bracing; rights language is fighting words in America; rights are employed as rhetorical trumps, or clubs, in the U.S., and often indicate an unwillingness to compromise. Appeals to rights are conversation stoppers.

You don't have to look far beyond the narrow boundaries of economic research to discover the important rights context of U.S. immigration policy. The 1965 Immigration Reform Act, which made possible the mass migration of the last forty years, should be understood as part of the civil rights movement of the sixties. It was an international counterpart to the Civil Rights Act and the Voting Rights Act: just as all citizens were to be treated as equals before the law, regardless of race or creed, all those seeking to become citizens should be treated equally.

Today, rights language is as out of control in immigration policy discussions as it is everywhere else in American life: we hear about the right to driver's licenses for illegals, even the right to citizenship. So what do the *popes* mean when they assert a right to migrate? It turns out, they are speaking from a tradition in which rights claims need not be absolute—which is more comfortable with tradeoffs among rights. In this tradition, the right to migrate is not absolute; the purpose of rights-language is not to end public policy debates and disagreements, but to orient them toward the common good of all persons, natives of the host country and immigrants alike.

In this tradition, rights are simply the flip side of justice: to have a right means that someone else has an obligation toward you in justice. To claim that someone has a right is to claim that something is due to him. The value of looking at rights from the side of justice is that it allows us to talk more naturally about the necessary balance among our obligations. We can't determine what is just towards one person without considering our obligations towards others and our scarce resources. In fact, because rights language is so unhelpful in U.S. discourse, it is more helpful to approach this topic from the direction of justice.

In the U.S., when we say immigrants have a right to migrate, it becomes difficult to consider abridging those rights in favor of the rights of natives. We speak of clashes of rights. But translate rights-talk into justice-talk, and we can more naturally speak of the balance between our just regard for immigrants and our just regard for common goods of economy, culture, and security. Our just obligations toward others arise from their dignity as human persons made in the image of God, placed in the world according to his purposes. It is in this sense that we are all created equal: we have a common destiny. Anything that bears on a person's development as a human person deserves our just respect, even solicitude.

When seen from the perspective of justice, the right to migrate is not absolute. An absolute right, like the right to life, involves access to a human good that has no substitute. When we abridge someone's right to life, we can't expect that he will be able to pursue his happiness through other means. Without life, there can be no human development.

When we abridge someone's right to migrate, however, we are foreclosing only one avenue for his development. Many immigrants can feed their families and find fulfillment without migrating to America. Those for whom migration is a crucial avenue of development—refugees and those trapped in grinding poverty in dysfunctional economies—have a stronger claim on us and a correspondingly stronger right. If our obligations in justice toward migrants put at risk our common goods as a society—our economic order, our culture, our security—then our just obligations to our own citizens and ourselves may force us to curtail the right to migrate.

It is important to note that restrictions on migration need not imply a denigration of the migrants themselves or of the value of migration to them. The benefits of immigration to immigrants themselves—the economic benefits of higher pay, remittances, and the potential benefits to dysfunctional nations of having an overseas community experienced in the benefits of a free society—should figure into our policy deliberations. If we self-protectively curtail immigration, it is fitting that we do so with a sense of regret and reluctance. We should not do so lightly, without consideration for those who stand to benefit from our generosity. A healthy rights perspective allows us to balance our generous welcome of immigrants against the burdens of immigration.

It is to these purported burdens of immigration that I now want to turn. These fall under three headings: economic, cultural, and security concerns.

In the economic realm, both the estimated costs and benefits of immigration are small. The National Academy of Sciences estimated that immigration increases the incomes of natives by $10 billion a year, which seems like a lot of money until you compare it to an $11 trillion economy. Immigration is neither destroying nor enriching our economy. Its continuation does not make us particularly richer, and its curtailment will not ruin our economy, no matter what it does to farming in California, to chicken processing in Arkansas, or to the nanny market in New York. The numbers are simply too small to matter much.

The supposedly alarming estimates of the net cost of immigration to government at all levels are similarly small, although they are trumpeted as if they are outrageously high. Careful estimates of the net fiscal cost of illegal immigration to the federal budget (not counting the modest benefits of immigration to Social Security) suggest that illegals impose $5 billion more in costs than they pay in federal taxes. Again, this seems like a large number, especially when the "b" in billion is pronounced with explosive emphasis: "*Billion!*"

This number must be put in perspective, however. Five billion is .2 percent of the $2.1 trillion federal budget. It is 1 percent of the federal deficit. The federal government loses five times that amount annually. The item in the federal budget for unreconciled transactions was $25 billion in 2003. Employees at the agriculture department were tallying up $5 billion a year in credit card fraud until recently. The federal government gives $80 billion a year away in corporate welfare, $30 billion to agriculture. Farmers in the Central Valley in California alone receive as much as $400 million a year in water subsidies. Waste and fraud in Medicare eat up $20-$30 billion annually. The $5 billion cost of illegals to the federal budget is simply not a terribly large number. It is not on the face of it too large a cost to bear; there are other, more alarming costs to illegal immigration than its effect on the federal budget.

The only economic numbers that come close to being significant are the fiscal burden of immigration in California and the effect of immigration on the wages of uneducated native workers. The $5 billion fiscal burden on state and local government in California—the Medicaid and education costs—is large when compared to the state's structural deficit of $6 billion. But even this can be put into perspective when compared to state and local spending in the U.S., which total one and a half trillion dollars a year. Because the fiscal burden of illegals is concentrated in a handful of states, those states where the burden is heaviest have a strong case for federal help.

Perhaps the most troubling economic impact of immigration is its modest effect on the wages of unskilled workers. Immigration has decreased unskilled wages by at most 3-4 percent over the last thirty years. This is a small effect over three decades, but it falls on the most vulnerable workers—those adversely affected by trade and information technology—so it should be troubling to those who place native interests above immigrant interest. However, compared to the gains to immigrants from immigration—a quintupling of wages for unskilled workers from Mexico, tens of billions of dollars sent back to poor Latin Americans each year—the losses to unskilled natives are small. Moreover, a reduction in immigration will not protect native unskilled workers from the effects of free trade and information technology, which have combined to account for much of the stagnation in the wages of the unskilled.

It should also be noted that the stakes are small in the debate over choosing skilled versus unskilled immigrants. Native workers do not benefit as much from skilled worker immigration as they do from unskilled worker immigration, and the gains from unskilled workers are small. Even the gains to GDP per capita are dubious. Canada, whose skilled-based immigration system is cited as a model for the U.S., has experienced growth rates in GDP per capita that are significantly smaller than U.S. rates during the last two decades when the U.S. inflow of unskilled workers was greatest.

After catching up to developed-nation living standards in the '70s, no-immigration Japan has suffered stagnation, not increased growth. Skilled immigration may boost living standards but does not appear to be the most important factor in economic growth. So, the economic stakes in immigration are small. The cultural stakes, whether they are large or small, generate the strong emotions that overshadow immigration debates.

There seem to be two major cultural concerns: First, are immigrants from non-European cultures in some way less suited for healthy democracy? Do they lack the habits of compromise, self-reliance, and association that support U.S. institutions? Second, is a multiethnic society necessarily prone to division? Is immigration a threat to national unity?

My expertise is in the economic aspects of this issue, so I do not have as much confidence addressing the cultural aspects. Nevertheless, I have several observations to make on culture. First, it seems strange to me that we should favor immigrants from white Europe on cultural grounds. Should we really prefer, say, 100,000 devoutly secular, globalist French over 100,000 religiously devout Mexicans? Perhaps we should, but I need to hear more discussion about what habits Europeans can bring to our democracy. The answer is not obvious. Perhaps devout Mexicans carry more healthy Western traditions into the U.S. than do Germans, Brits, and Italians.

Second, an important piece of data on assimilation, economic and cultural, is intermarriage rates. Intermarriage has always been an important route for assimilation as well as an indicator of assimilation. High rates of intermarriage played an important role in assimilating the unassimilable Irish, for example. These rates are generally high for Hispanics (45%), which bodes well for their assimilation.

Third, the English language is obviously crucial to assimilation. A basic knowledge of English should be a requirement of immigration.

Fourth, this is not the first time a non-white immigration has occurred in the U.S. Southern Europeans were not identified as whites in the 1920s. They hailed from alien cultures, alien religions, and were thought to be unsuited for the American experiment. The fact that we lump Italians, Greeks, and Hungarians together with Germans and English into a category we call "white" is a testimony to the assimilation of the inassimilable.

To discuss the security stakes in immigration brings to the fore the most troubling aspect of our immigration problems: the large numbers of illegal immigrants who live among us in plain sight. There is a long tradition in Western political thought that demands that laws be enforced, even to the point of recommending against the passage of laws that either are not enforced or are unenforceable. Laws which are universally ignored tend to undermine all respect for law and corrupt the culture. We should either enforce our immigration quotas or repeal them.

The presence of twelve million or so illegals in the U.S. is corrupting our law enforcement, our politics, our economy, and undermines our ability to protect ourselves from terrorists. This corruption is the biggest threat from illegal immigration. It begins with the consciences of the illegals themselves. Millions of otherwise good people are living a lie, pretending that they belong here, have rights here, and denying that there is anything wrong with their being here. Their illegal status undermines their ability to bargain for better wages, to resist abuses by employers, and their incentive to learn English and assimilate into U.S. culture.

Illegals are more likely to remain in immigrant enclaves, seeking safety in numbers. Illegal immigration corrupts our politics, since it forces us to pretend that laws we have passed democratically are not worth enforcing. Illegal immigrants even have their own lobbying groups; some illegals vote, no doubt. The advocates for illegal immigration insist not only that we tolerate their illegal presence but that we pretend that the breaking of our laws is a trivial matter, not to be brought up in polite company.

We are even forced to pretend that the biggest problem caused by illegal immigration is the lack of documentation, not illegal status. It is not politically correct to call illegal immigrants "illegal immigrants." We must instead call them "undocumented" workers. Instead of deporting illegals, we must develop new forms of ID for them: matricula consular IDs instead of passports, or driver's licenses just for them. We must treat them as if they are legal, granting them in-state tuition to our public schools.

Our lack of desire to enforce immigration laws corrupts the immigration service. One often hears complaints about how awful the INS used to be and how it would not be possible to enforce immigration laws without a complete overhaul of the immigration service. Much of the dysfunction at the INS was due to the impossible task it was given: to pretend to enforce the immigration law while not really enforcing it, to catch and release illegals, to go through the farce of informing illegal immigrants of their right to make bogus asylum claims. The immigration services are demoralized not because they are incompetent but because they are not allowed to do their jobs, although they must pretend they are being vigilant. The desire to appear to enforce immigration law while not really enforcing it has led to our policy of building fences at the border but not looking for illegals internally.

This lopsided enforcement has been counterproductive. Before the era of vigorous border enforcement, the typical illegal immigrant stayed in the U.S. for about a year and did not bring his family with him. Illegals cycled into and out of the U.S. After the border became more difficult to cross, the average stay in the U.S. lengthened considerably to about three to four years. Immigrants who got across the border were less likely to go home and and more likely to bring their families, to settle down, and demand driver's licenses and schools for their kids.

Most importantly, the presence of an underground market for smuggling and fake IDs undermines our security. Drug smuggling and human smuggling go hand in hand. Terrorists may use the well-worn illegal entryways and take advantage of the false ID infrastructure already in place. I suspect that addressing the problem of illegal immigrants will solve most of our immigration problems. To the extent that immigration depresses wages, it is most often the wages of legal immigrants. The ability to actually enforce that law would reinvigorate the immigration service.

Legal immigrants are more likely to assimilate than illegal immigrants. If there are fewer illegals, and we are not bashful about searching for them, there will be fewer ways for terrorists to hide in plain sight. Of course, one can accept that illegal immigration is a big problem and suggest different ways of dealing with it. One might eliminate all illegal immigration by opening the borders and giving out free green cards, or one might actually enforce the laws on the books.

I favor the second option. I am not concerned about the large volume of legal immigration, although I would make some changes in our current legal system, putting more emphasis on English language proficiency, but I believe the illegal immigration burden is much more urgent.

Let me end by reiterating my points. One, there is a right to migrate, but it does not mean open borders; instead, it means that the dignity and welfare of immigrants should figure into our policy debates. Second, the economic stakes in the immigration debate are relatively small; restrictions on immigration should not turn on the economic costs or benefits. Third, the most important trend is the large increase in illegal immigration. Illegal immigration is a systematic flouting of the rule of law; it corrupts our politics, our culture, and threatens to undermine our national security.

Photographs

William F. Buckley was a founding and distinguished member of the Philadelphia Society and provided an early loan to enable the organization to get started.

Nobel Prize-winning libertarian economist Milton Friedman is seen here at the mint. He was a distinguished member and provided an essential perspective for the society in its early years.

Don "The Commodore" Lipsett founded the Philadelphia Society and served as its permanent secretary from 1964 until his death in 1995.

Frank Meyer was an influential member of the Philadelphia Society who promoted the idea of fusionism and did a great deal to establish the culture of the Society as one where those interested in ordered liberty could come and discuss and often disagree.

Pictured here is a young M. Stanton Evans. Evans was a founder of the conservative movement. He worked with William F. Buckley in the early days of *National Review* and dedicated his life to the promotion of ordered liberty. Evans was a distinguished member of the Philadelphia Society.

Pictured here from left to right distinguished member of the society Al Campbell and Richard Weaver are in discussion. Through his scholarship, Weaver fought to defend and preserve southern values and tradition.

NOBEL PRIZE–WINNING LIBERTARIAN ECONOMIST F.A. HAYEK PROVIDED MANY IN THE FLEDGLING CONSERVATIVE MOVEMENT WITH A CRITIQUE OF CENTRALIZATION. HIS WORKS *THE ROAD TO SERFDOM* AND *THE CONSTITUTION OF LIBERTY* ARE STILL WIDELY READ, AND HIS ARTICLE "THE USE OF KNOWLEDGE IN SOCIETY" IS DEBATABLY THE MOST IMPORTANT ARTICLE IN ECONOMICS IN THE TWENTIETH CENTURY. HAYEK WAS A DISTINGUISHED MEMBER OF THE PHILADELPHIA SOCIETY.

RUSSELL KIRK WAS A MEMBER AND FREQUENT SPEAKER AT THE PHILADELPHIA SOCIETY, AND HIS BOOK *THE CONSERVATIVE MIND* WAS ONE OF THE MOST IMPORTANT WORKS IN GIVING SHAPE TO THE EARLY CONSERVATIVE MOVEMENT.

Annette Kirk is a distinguished member and still attends Philadelphia Society meetings. She has spent the last twenty-five years as president of the Russell Kirk Center for Cultural Renewal, which continues the legacy of Kirk by promoting traditional conservatism.

Forrest McDonald was one of the most prominent conservative historians in the United States and a distinguished member of the Philadelphia Society. His work on the early national period, the Constitution, republicanism, the South, and the American presidency are still read in history graduate programs today.

Eliseo Vivas was a conservative philosopher and literary theorist who was a distinguished member and regularly attended and spoke at Philadelphia Society meetings.

Here, left to right, Eric Voegelin and Ellis Sandoz are speaking. Voegelin was an influential political philosopher, and Sandoz was the director of the Eric Voegelin Institute for American Renaissance Studies at LSU. Both men have been honored as distinguished members of the Philadelphia Society.

From left to right, Henry Regnery is shaking hands with Russell Kirk while Louis Dehmlow looks on. Regnery, through his publishing company, played an essential role in the advent of the conservative movement. He financed *Human Events* and published Buckley's *God and Man at Yale* as well as Kirk's *The Conservative Mind*. Regnery was a distinguished member of the Philadelphia Society.

Harry Jaffa was a political philosopher, historian, and distinguished member of the Philadelphia Society. In addition to his works of history—most notably *Crisis of the House Divided: An Interpretation of the Issues in the Lincoln-Douglas Debates*—Jaffa developed an American application of Leo Strauss's philosophy.

Left to right, Edwin Feulner and Antonio Marino pose for a photograph. Feulner dedicated his life to the conservative movement and is best known for establishing the conservative think tank the Heritage Foundation and serving as its president for thirty-seven years. Feulner is a distinguished member of the Philadelphia Society.

Pictured left to right, Henry Regnery speaks with Nobel Prize–winning economist Ronald Coase. Coase is best best known for his articles "The Nature of the Firm" and "The Problem of Social Cost."

Don Devine is a political scientist who promoted fusionism and has published numerous books on American politics. He served in the Reagan administration as director of the US Office of Personnel Management. Devine is a distinguished member and frequent attendee and contributor at the Philadelphia Society.

George Nash is best known for his influential book *The Conservative Intellectual Movement in America since 1945*. He is also a biographer of Herbert Hoover and has worked tirelessly to understand the ever-evolving conservative movement. He is a distinguished member and regular attendee of the Philadelphia Society.

Pictured left to right, Richard Rahn and George Gilder. Rahn is an economist who served as the vice president and chief economist of the United States Chamber of Commerce during the Reagan administration, where he was a staunch advocate of supply-side economics. Gilder is an investor and co-founder of the Discovery Institute. In 1981 he authored *Wealth and Poverty*, which advocated for supply-side economics while Reagan was pushing his economic agenda. Gilder is a distinguished member of the Philadelphia Society.

Stephen Tonsor was a historian who wrote frequently in conservative publications. He was an ardent defender of conservatism, a distinguished member of the Philadelphia Society, and a frequent contributor at meetings.

Pictured left to right, Bill Campbell and Paul Kengor participate in a panel session. Campbell served as the secretary of the Philadelphia Society from 1995 to 2004 and is a distinguished member. Kengor is a political scientist at Grove City College and the executive director of the Institute for Faith and Freedom. He has authored numerous books on American politics.

Pictured left to right, Helen Campbell, Anne Edwards and Lee Edwards. Lee Edwards helped found Young Americans for Freedom and has spent his entire life chronicling the history of American conservatism. He is also a distinguished member of the Society.

Pictured left to right, David Meiselman and Lenore Ealy. Meiselman was an economist who worked with Milton Friedman on monetary policy and its effect on economic performance and interest rates. Ealy became the third secretary of the Society in 2004 and has been tireless in her efforts to bring young conservatives, libertarians, and classical liberals into the organization.

Pictured here left to right, back to front are many of the former presidents of the Philadelphia Society. Back Row: Edwin J. Feulner, George Nash, Claes Ryn, Daniel B. Hales, Leonard P. Liggio. Middle Row: Edwin Meese III, Ellis Sandoz, Forrest McDonald, John Wilson, William C. Dennis. Front Row: Midge Decter, Lee Edwards, T. Kenneth Cribb, John Howard, William F. Campbell, Lowell C. Smith, Victoria Hughes.

In recent years the Philadelphia Society along with partners—including Hillsdale College—have provided fellowships to attend meetings. In the back row, fifth from the left is Chris Malagisi, who is the executive director of outreach at Hillsdale in DC. On the far right is Allen Mendenhall, who is a trustee of the Philadelphia Society and has worked to bring more young conservatives, libertarians, and classical liberals into the organization.

Speaker Biographies

Martin Anderson (1936-2015): Anderson earned a bachelor's degree in engineering and a double master's in business and engineering from Dartmouth College. He earned his PhD in industrial management from the Massachusetts Institute of Technology. Anderson converted his dissertation into a book and *The Federal Bulldozer: A Critical Analysis of Urban Renewal, 1949-1962* was published by MIT Press in 1962. Anderson campaigned for Barry Goldwater for president in 1964 and advised both President Richard Nixon and President Ronald Reagan. Anderson played a pivotal role in advising Reagan on economic policy in both the 1976 and 1980 campaign. Once Reagan was in the White House, he served as an assistant to the president for policy development with an emphasis on domestic and economic policy. Later in the administration he served on the President's General Advisory Committee on Arms Control and Disarmament. Anderson worked off and on throughout his life at the Hoover Institution and published numerous books including *Revolution*, *Reagan, in His Own Hand*, and *Reagan's Secret War.*

Doug Bandow (b. 1957): Bandow is a Senior Fellow at the Cato Institute. He also has been affiliated with the Heritage Foundation and Competitive Enterprise Institute. He served as a Special Assistant to President Ronald Reagan. Bandow is a columnist for The American Conservative online, The American Spectator online, and Antiwar.com. He contributes regularly to The National Interest online, 19FortyFive.com, and other online publications. He also has been widely published in such periodicals as *Time*, *Newsweek*, and *Fortune*, as well as leading newspapers including the *New York Times*, *Wall Street Journal*, and *Washington Post.* He has written several books, including *Foreign Follies: America's New Global Empire*, *The Politics of Envy: Statism as Theology*, *The Politics of Plunder: Misgovernment in Washington*, and *Beyond Good Intentions: A Biblical View of Politics*. He received his B.S. in Economics from Florida State University in 1976 and his J.D. from Stanford University in

1979. He is a member of the California and Washington, D.C. bars.

Morton C. Blackwell (b. 1939): Blackwell has dedicated his life to the conservative movement. In his youth, he was the College and Young Republican state chairman in Louisiana. Blackwell was Barry Goldwater's youngest delegate at the 1964 Republican National Convention. Blackwell worked as executive director of the College Republican National Committee, off and on, from 1965 to 1970. Blackwell also worked for Richard Viguerie who helped pioneer direct mail. founded the Leadership Institute in 1979 and continues to serve as its president. Blackwell was also a delegate for Ronald Reagan at the 1968, 1976, and 1980 Republican National Convention. During the 1980 campaign he led the youth effort to elect Reagan. Blackwell served as a special assistant to Reagan from 1981 to 1984. In 1979, he founded the Leadership Institute and continues to serve as its president. LI prepares conservatives for success in politics, government, and the news media. Since its founding, the institute has trained almost 300,000 students.

Peter Brimelow (b. 1947): Brimelow was born in Lancashire, England and earned his bachelor's degree from the University of Sussex. Brimelow earned his Master of Business Administration from Stanford University. He worked as a financial journalist for his early career, serving as a writer and editor at the *Financial Post* and *Maclean's*. He served as an aide to Senator Orrin Hatch (UT) from 1978 to 1980 after which he went to work for *Barron's* and *Fortune.* From 1986 to 2002, Brimelow served as an editor at *Forbes*. He also served as an editor at *National Review* from 1993 to 1998. He published *Alien Nation: Common Sense About America's Immigration Disaster* in 1995. In 1999, he founded the website VDARE as an extension of the work he had done in his book. He continues to serve as its editor. The website opposes immigration and critics have labeled Brimelow as an advocate of white supremacy and white nationalism. Brimelow rejects these labels.

Steven Calabresi (b. 1958): Buckley, a World War II veteran, completed his B.A. in political science, history, and economics with honors from Yale University in 1950. He first achieved national notoriety with the publication of his 1951 book *God and Man at Yale*. In 1955, Buckley founded *National Review* magazine, which became a leading voice in post-World War II American conservatism. He was the author of more than fifty books, demonstrating his intellectual curiosity and range. From 1966 to 1999, he was the host of the Emmy Award-winning PBS debate program *Firing Line*, the longest running public-affairs show with a single host in television history.

Steven Calabresi (b. 1958): Calabresi earned both his bachelor's degree from Yale College and his JD from Yale Law School. After law school he served as a clerk for Judges Ralph K. Winter, Judge Robert Bork, and Judge Antonin Scalia of the United States Supreme Court. Calabresi served in both the Reagan and Bush White Houses. He advised Ed Meese while he was Attorney General and T. Kenneth Cribb who was Reagan's Domestic Policy Chief. In 1990, Calabresi joined Northwestern Law School as faculty. During his academic career he was a visiting professor at Yale Law School and Brown University. While at Yale, Calabresi and his friends founded the Yale chapter of the Federalist Society. Calabresi currently serves as the co-chairman of the Federalist Society. He permanently joined the faculty at Brown in 2010 where he continues to teach.

Midge Decter (1927-2022): Decter attended the University of Minnesota, the Jewish Theological Seminary of America, and New York University but did not graduate from any of them. She had a long career as a journalist and began as an assistant editor at *Midstream* before moving to *Commentary*. She later became the executive editor of *Harper's Magazine*. Decter eventually moved to publishing and served as an editor at Basic Books and Legacy Books. She frequently published in prominent journals and magazines and authored seven books.

Decter was one of the pioneers of the neoconservative movement in the 1970s and was the co-chair, with Donald Rumsfeld, of the Committee for the Free World. She had a long career in the conservative movement and served as a member of the board of trustees of The Heritage Foundation. Decter was a long-standing member of the Philadelphia Society and served as its president for a time. In 2008, she received the Truman-Reagan Medal of Freedom from the Victims of Communism Memorial Foundation.

Donald Devine (b. 1937): Devine earned his Ph.D. in political science from Syracuse University in 1967. He held a professorship at the University of Maryland from 1967 to 1980 when he left to serve in the Reagan administration. He later served as an advisor to Senator Bob Dole. He was the author of several acclaimed books on political science and the Reagan administration, including *The Political Culture of the United States* (1972).

Lee Edwards (b. 1932): Edwards received a doctorate in world politics from Catholic University as well as a doctor of humane letters degree from Grove City College. He did graduate work at the Sorbonne in Paris. He holds a bachelor of arts degree in English from Duke University. Edwards, former distinguished fellow in conservative thought at The Heritage Foundation, is a leading historian of American conservatism, who has published more than 25 books. His books include biographies of Ronald Reagan, Barry Goldwater, William F. Buckley, Jr. and Edwin Meese III as well as histories of The Heritage Foundation and the American conservative movement. His works have been translated into Chinese, Japanese, French, Hungarian, Polish, and Swedish. Edwards is co-founder of the Victims of Communism Memorial Foundation in Washington, D.C. Edwards was the founding director of the Institute of Political Journalism at Georgetown University and a fellow at the Institute of Politics at the John F. Kennedy School of Government at Harvard University. He is a past president of the Philadelphia Society and a media fellow at the Hoover Institution.

M. Stanton Evans (1934-2015): Evans received a bachelor's degree in English from Yale University and did graduate study in economics at New York University under the direction of Ludwig von Mises. He became an influential conservative journalist writing for *National Review*, *Human Events*, the *Indianapolis News*, and the *Los Angeles Times*. He also authored eight books on the conservative movement.

Tim W. Ferguson: Ferguson earned a bachelor's degree in economics from Stanford University. He has spent over forty years in journalism. From 1977 to 1983 he worked for various news organizations including the *Orange County Register*. He joined the *Wall Street Journal* in 1983 and remained there until he joined *Forbes* in 1995. Ferguson transferred to the Asian district of *Forbes* in 2002 where he held the top editorial position at leading Asia-Pacific business publication. Since 2019 he has served as the principal editor at *Etcetera*. He has written hundreds of articles and edited many more. Throughout it all he applies the economic way of thinking to his work.

Edwin J. Feulner Jr. (b. 1941): Feulner earned a bachelor's degree in English from Regis University and an MBA from the Wharton School of Business at the University of Pennsylvania. He was also a Richard M. Weaver Fellow at Georgetown University and the London School of Economics. In 1981, he received his PhD in political science from the University of Edinburgh. Feulner began his career as an analyst for the Center for Strategic Studies and later became a long-serving executive assistant to Congressman Phil Crane (R-IL). In 1973, he co-founded the Heritage Foundation and subsequently served as its president from 1977 to 2013. He briefly served as president again from 2017 to 2018. Feulner has served in leadership roles in the Mont Pelerin Society, the Intercollegiate Studies Institute, the Victims of Communism Memorial Foundation, the Council for National Policy, the Acton Institute, and the Philadelphia Society. In 1989 he received the Presidential Citizens Medal, the second-highest civilian award in the United States.

Thomas Fleming (1927-2017): Fleming served in the United States Navy prior to earning a bachelor's degree from Fordham University in 1950. For a decade he worked as a newspaperman and magazine editor before becoming a full time writer in 1960. His career spanned six decades and he published over forty nonfiction and fiction titles. Fleming is best known for his numerous books about the events and figures of the American Revolutionary era–including acclaimed biographies of Thomas Jefferson and Benjamin Franklin. He was a frequent guest on C-Span, PBS, A&E, and the History Channel.

Milton Friedman (1912-2006) : Friedman received his Ph.D. in economics from Columbia University. After serving during the Roosevelt administration, he took a professorship in the University of Chicago's School of Economics in 1946. He was the author of numerous important works in free market economics, including *Capitalism and Freedom* (1962) and *A Monetary History of the United States* (1963). In 1976, he was awarded the Nobel prize for his work in economics. He became an important economic adviser for Ronald Reagan and Margaret Thatcher and was a tireless defender and champion of free markets and individual liberty.

Paul Gottfried (b. 1941): Gottfried earned his bachelor's degree from Yeshiva University in New York and went on to earn a PhD from Yale University where his doctoral adviser was Herbert Marcuse. Gottfried is a paleoconservative political philosopher, historian, and writer. He even coined the term paleoconservative in 1986 along with Thomas Fleming. He worked as a political theorist for most of his academic career and served as the Chair of the History Department at Rockford College. Gottfried spent most of his career at Elizabethtown

College. He serves as editor-in-chief of *Chronicles* and is a senior scholar at the Mises Institute. Gottfried is also credited with coining the term alternative right, a term from which he has distanced himself.

David M. Levy (b. 1944): Levy is Professor of Economics at George Mason University. Levy's publications include four scholarly books, ninety journal articles, dozens of book reviews and chapters in academic books. The 2005 *Vanity of the Philosopher*, written with Sandra J. Peart, was awarded a Choice Academic Honors. The 1991 *Economic Ideas of Ordinary People* was republished twenty years after the first publication. His long association with James Buchanan and Gordon Tullock helped with the Peart-Levy view of analytical egalitarianism as a claim in model space. His service on the American Statistical Association's Professional Ethics Committee helped to develop the Levy-Peart model of sympathetic bias in estimation. Levy and Peart have co-directed the Summer Institute for the Preservation of the History of Economics for thirteen years. In 2012 Levy was made a Distinguished Fellow of the History of Economics Society.

Ed Meese (b. 1931) : Meese earned a bachelor's degree in political science from Yale University and a JD from UC Berkeley School of Law. He served in the U.S. Army on active duty for three years and retired from the U.S. Army reserves in 1984 as a colonel. Meese worked as a district attorney before beginning his lifelong work with Ronald Reagan. While Reagan was Governor of California, Meese served as his Chief of Staff until Reagan left office in 1974. Meese was also essential to Reagan's successful election campaign in 1980 and was key to the transition. Once Reagan took office, Meese served as Counselor to the President from 1981 to 1984–making him one/third of the Troika which included Chief of Staff James Baker and Deputy Chief of Staff Michael Deaver. Meese also served in Reagan's Cabinet and on his National Security Council. Meese became Attorney General in 1985 and held the position until late 1988. Meese joined the Heritage Foundation after leaving public office and has held the Ronald Reagan Chair in Public Policy there ever since. For over thirty years, Meese has remained actively involved in conservative circles serving on the board of numerous organizations. In 2019, he was presented the Presidential Medal of Freedom, the highest civilian honor in the United States.

Allan H. Meltzer (1928-2017): Meltzer received his bachelor's and MA degree from Duke University and completed his PhD in Economics at UCLA. In 1959 he became an associate professor at Carnegie Mellon University where he spent his academic career. Meltzer authored ten books and over 400 papers during his storied career. His most widely read books are *Why Capitalism* and his two-volume history of the Federal Reserve. Meltzer was critical of the Federal Reserve and from 1973 to 1999 served as the Chair of the Shadow Open Market Committee. He briefly served in the Reagan administration and was a visiting scholar at the American Enterprise Institute. Meltzer served as the Chairman of the International Financial Institution Advisory Commission in 2000, whose report recommended changes to the operations of the IMF and World Bank. Meltzer remained active in both scholarly and political debates about monetary policy until his death.

Stephen Moore (b. 1960) : Moore earned a bachelor's degree from the University of Illinois and a MA in Economics from George Mason University. He is an economist and author, serving as a Distinguished Fellow in Economics at the Heritage Foundation and a co-founder of The Committee to Unleash Prosperity. He is a frequent lecturer to audiences around the world on the U.S. economic and political outlook and is the author of six books including *Trumponomics*. From 1999-2004, Moore served as founder and president of the Club for Growth, an organization dedicated to helping elect free market candidates to Congress. In his tenure as president, the Club for Growth became one of the most influential and respected political organizations in the nation. From 2005-2014, Moore served as the senior economics writer for *The Wall Street Journal* editorial page and as a member of the *WSJ* editorial board. He remains a regular contributor to the publication. Moore served as a senior economic advisor to President Trump's 2016 campaign, drafting tax, budget, and energy policy plans.

Burton Yale Pines (1941-2019): Pines earned his PhD from the University of Wisconsin. He worked as a correspondent for *Time Magazine* in Hamburg, Bonn, Vietnam, and Chicago and also served as the editor of the World and Nation section. He became the Senior Vice President of the Heritage Foundation. During his career, Pines authored numerous books including *America's Greatest Blunder*, *Out of Focus*, and *Back To Basics*. When asked what made him most proud, he always responded, "Being a foot-soldier in the Reagan Revolution."

Benjamin Powell (b. 1978): Powell earned his bachelor's in economics and finance from the University of Massachusetts at Lowell, and his MA and PhD in Economics from George Mason University. Power is the author of over seventy-five scholarly articles and three books: *Out of Poverty*, *Wretched Refuse*, and *Socialism Sucks*. He has edited or co-edited five additional books including *The Economics of Immigration*. He currently serves as the Executive Director of the Free Market Institute at Texas Tech University and is a Professor of Economics in the Rawls College of Business. Powell is also a senior fellow at the Independent Institute and serves in various capacities for the Southern Economic Association, the Association of Private Enterprise Education, and the Mont Pelerin Society.

Ronald E. Robinson: Robinson earned his bachelor's from Canisius University and then a JD from The Catholic University of America. He served as executive director of Young Americans for Freedom (1977-79), president of the United States Youth Council (1983-85), president of the International Youth Year Commission (1983-84).

He was also an advisor to the U.S. Department of Education during the Reagan administration. Robinson is co-author of the book *Funding Fathers: The Unsung Heroes of the Conservative Movement*. He was the longtime president of the Young America's Foundation. Robinson served as a trustee of the Philadelphia Society and is currently a trustee of The Phillips Foundation, a director of Citizens United, the Citizens United Foundation, and the American Conservative Union, and he is the vice-president of the Free Speech Defense and Education Fund.

Edward Shapiro (b. 1938): Shapiro earned his bachelor's from Georgetown University and his PhD in history from Harvard University. His specialization is American history and American Jewish history. Shapiro spent most of his academic career at Seton Hall University. He is the author of seven books including *Clio from the Right: Essays of a Conservative Historian* and most recently *A Unique People in a Unique Land: Essays on American Jewish History*.

Shelby Steele (b. 1946): Steele received a bachelor's in political science from Coe College, a M.A. in sociology from Southern Illinois University Edwardsville, and a PhD in English from the University of Utah. Steele spent most of his academic career as an English professor at San Jose State University. He is an author, columnist, and documentary film maker who specializes in the study of race relations, multiculturalism, and affirmative action. Steele authored five books including *The Content of Our Character: A New Vision of Race in America*, which received the National Book Critics Circle Award. In 2004 he was awarded the National Medal of the Humanities. Today he continues his work as the Robert J. and Marion E. Oster Fellow at the Hoover Institute.

Stephen J. Tonsor (1923-2014): Tonsor was Professor Emeritus of History at the University of Michigan. He was the author of *Tradition and Reform in Education* and published essays and reviews in such publications as *Victorian Studies*, *Journal of Modern History*, *The*

Catholic Historical Review, and *The Review of Politics*. He received his B.A. from the University of Illinois in Champaign-Urbana in 1948 and received his PhD in history from the University of Illinois in 1955.

Michael Vlahos (b. 1951): Vlahos is an historian with expertise in strategy, culture, and war who comments on geopolitical controversies. He has taught at Johns Hopkins University and the Naval War College and headed the Center for the Study of Foreign Affairs at the United States State Department. He was a fellow at the Progress & Freedom Foundation and director of the Securities Studies Program at the Johns Hopkins School of Advanced International Studies. The author of several books, he holds his A.B. from Yale College and his Ph.D. from The Fletcher School of Law & Diplomacy at Tufts University.

Walter E. Williams (1936-2020): Williams was an economist and public intellectual who taught for forty years at George Mason University. He earned an undergraduate degree in economics from California State University, Los Angeles, and his master's and Ph.D. in economics from the University of California Los Angeles (UCLA). An advocate for the free market and limited government, he aligned himself with classical liberalism and became one of the most visible and vocal black intellectuals in the United States, gaining widespread fame through his syndicated columns and appearances on radio and television. He passed away on December 2, 2020.

Andrew Yuengert (b. 1960): Yuengert is a Professor of Economics and the Blanche Seaver Chair of Social Science at Pepperdine University. His research crosses the boundaries between economics, moral philosophy, and Catholic theology. His latest book is *Catholic Social Teaching in Practice: Exploring Practical Wisdom and the Virtues Tradition* (Cambridge, 2023). Previous books include *The Boundaries of Technique* (2004) and *Approximating Prudence* (2012). He holds a PhD in Economics from Yale University.

About the Philadelphia Society

The Philadelphia Society was founded in 1964 and for the past fifty-five years it has served as a venue for conservatives and libertarians to discuss the "foundations of a free and ordered society."

About AIER

The American Institute for Economic Research in Great Barrington, Massachusetts, was founded in 1933 as the first independent voice for sound economics in the United States. Today it publishes ongoing research, hosts educational programs, publishes books, sponsors interns and scholars, and is home to the world-renowned Bastiat Society and the highly respected Sound Money Project. The American Institute for Economic Research is a 501c3 public charity.

INDEX

Made in the USA
Middletown, DE
02 April 2024

52397540R00215